Also by Gayle Larson Schuck:

By the Banks of Cottonwood Creek, the first book in the Prairie Pastor Series

Secrets of the Dark Closet, a historical novel

What other authors are saying about these books:

- "A warm and satisfying read." Barbara Brabec
- "A sweet and encouraging story." Norma Gail
- "Looking forward to more from this author." Paulette Bullinger
- "A fairytale ending awaits you." Bismarck Tribune review by Vickie Reinhart
- "Compelling and appropriate for the Youth/Coming of Age genre" Linda Ann Lewis
- "A delightful read, one you'll want to share with others." Sonvy Sammons

Amber's Choice

Book Two of the Prairie Pastor Series

Gayle Larson Schuck

Blessings!
Gayle Larson Schuck

Amber's Choice
Copyright © 2019 Gayle Larson Schuck

This is a work of fiction. Names, characters, dialogs, events and places portrayed in this book are fictitious. Any similarity to real persons, living or dead, is coincidental and not intended by the author.

All scripture references are from the Ryrie New International Version Bible.

ISBN 978-0-578-53565-4

Schuck Communications

Printed in the United States.

Cover photo "Winds of Change" by Christy Brucks

Acknowledgements

Many thanks to:
The members of Dakota Writers, for five years of weekly encouragement and feedback;
Julie Henderson, for polishing the manuscript;
Korrine Lang, for exceptional proofreading skills;
Cinnamon Schuck, for that important last manuscript review;
Dr. Shelley Seifert, for your medical expertise;
Pastor Daryl and Betty Pennington, for sharing your memories of serving rural churches;
David's Bridal for providing catalogs of wedding gowns; and
Friends and family, your encouragement and prayers sustain me.

A special thanks to my husband, Larry, who sometimes wondered if I'd ever come out of my office, and who read the manuscript more than once; to Solomon and Benjamin Schuck for sharing my love of writing; and to Jonathan for enticing me away from the computer. And to Jesus Christ, your Word is indeed a lamp to my feet and a light to my path.

Dedicated to the memory of Sonvy Sammons, for leading Dakota Writers and inspiring this writer.

"There is no more lovely, friendly and charming relationship, communion or company, than a good marriage."
Martin Luther

"We are not trying to please people but God, who tests our hearts."
I Thessalonians 2:4

1986 Little Amber Rose

Amber Rose McLean sat playing beneath the tall cottonwood tree, her bright pink shorts and top a striking contrast to the feathery green prairie grass that waved in the wind. Overhead, the June sun reflected off a million shimmering leaves that spread shady relief over the eight-year-old girl and her toys. Its branches reached toward Cottonwood Creek, which flowed a hundred feet away.

Her mother, Jean, watched from behind the lace curtains that covered the window in the one-story farmhouse. Amber sat with her back erect and her legs folded under her. She held up a book for an audience of dolls and stuffed animals as she told them a story.

Jean considered searching for the camera to capture Amber with her curly golden hair tied back with a blue farmer's handkerchief. Sighing, she dropped the idea. Rummaging for the camera might wake up the little boys from their naps. She let the curtain drop back into place and went outside with a tumbler of Kool-Aid.

"Are you teaching school today?" she asked as she knelt next to Amber. The shade offered relief from the afternoon sun. Amber's Barbie doll sat to the left, her skirt flared around her, while Jean's old Saucy Walker leaned against an overturned bucket. Brownie bear and that monkey, George, sat in the back row. Jean noted that Rusty Ann, Amber's new Ice Cream Doll, sat closest to the teacher.

"Yes. I'm teaching Vacation Bible School," said Amber. "The girls are learning their memory verses, but those boys in the back are being naughty."

Jean left the drink with Amber, pleased that her daughter occasionally had time to play without her younger brothers plowing through her games. Back in the kitchen, the ironing board was piled high with line-dried clothes. She did not mind the work involved in caring for a family, however, she appreciated afternoons when Adam, three, and Daniel, one, took naps at the same time. Soon enough they would wake, their red hair damp from sleep and their compact little bodies charged with energy.

A few minutes later, the kitchen door squeaked open. "Momma!" Amber cried.

"Shhh," Jean cautioned, her finger to her lips, motioning toward the bedroom.

"Quick. Come outside with me," Amber said in a stage whisper. "We have a special visitor. Come and meet him."

Curious, Jean unplugged the iron and set it on the harvest gold stove. Who was this visitor? No one had driven into the yard in the last few minutes. She hoped it wasn't a skunk or other wild critter.

"Who's out there?" she asked.

"You'll see!" Amber said as she skipped out the door.

Jean followed her around the house. When they got to the north side, no one was there but their protective husky, Rover, who was thumping Brownie bear into the grass with his tail.

Amber looked around, her mouth turned down in disappointment. "He's gone!"

"Who's gone?" Jean asked. "Who was here?"

"A man dressed all in white."

"Woof! Woof!" Rover seemed excited about something, too.

"There was a man here in the yard?" Jean asked, alarmed. "Where did he come from?"

"From over there," Amber said, pointing toward the creek.

Jean couldn't imagine anyone arriving at the farm by walking along Cottonwood Creek. It cut through pastures and was some distance from the road. Besides, it was a sunny day. All the neighbors would be in the fields cutting hay.

A fearful notion entered Jean's mind. "Honey, did he touch you?"

"Yes," Amber answered brightly.

Jean tried to stay calm, however, it was upsetting to think a strange man had appeared and disappeared from their farmyard without her knowledge. Amber could have been harmed or kidnapped while she ironed shirts.

"Hello?" she called out, looking toward the creek. "Is someone there?" The only response was the rustle of the tree leaves.

Turning back to Amber, Jean demanded, "Tell me everything."

"Mama, don't worry. He was a nice man. He laughed when he saw Rusty Ann's little ice cream cone," she said as she scooped up her friend with the orange yarn hair.

"He put his hand right on the top of my head like this," Amber solemnly placed her palm flat on her head. "Mama, he..."

"He what?" Panic rushed through Jean's veins.

"He said that God has a special plan for my life," Amber said excitedly. "I said, 'Are you an angel?' He just smiled. Then I went in the house and when we came out he was gone."

She shrugged her shoulders and looked up at her mother with mossy green eyes. Sitting down, Jean pulled Amber onto her lap and quizzed her some more, but the little girl had nothing else to add. A few minutes later, Jean heard one of the boys crying. She hurried Amber into the house and didn't let her go outside again for the rest of the day.

Swept up in finishing the ironing, getting supper ready for Glen and the children, and washing dishes at the white enamel Youngstown sink, Jean forgot about the strange man. That evening as the sun lingered in the west, she finally sat down to relax. The children were in bed and Glen sat at the kitchen table reading the newspaper. A fan oscillated in front of an open living room window.

Jean often played piano in the evening, hoping the music would give her children sweet dreams. However, tonight, after only one song, she put the sheet music away and picked up her journal and began to write. "First cutting of hay underway. Meatballs for supper. Strange event of the day, Amber said a man in white visited her while she played in the yard. (I didn't see or hear a thing!) He put his hand on her head and said God has a special plan for her life. That girl either has a vivid imagination or a special calling on her life."

Impulsively, Jean tore the page from her notebook. Pulling the ancient McLean family Bible off a high shelf, she tucked the paper between its pages.

She peeked into the children's bedroom. Seeing Amber sleeping alone without her dolls, Jean realized that they had forgotten the tiny students outside. She strolled out the door and around the house toward the creek. Heat lightning flickered in the northern sky and thunder growled low like a dog protecting its bone. A cool gust of wind blew through the night, giving her goosebumps. She scooped up the dolls and stuffed animals and ran for the house as big raindrops began to fall.

Jean didn't notice that she left Rusty Ann behind. That night, as a storm rolled through Cottonwood Creek, the wind tumbled the little rag doll into the tall grass beyond the farmyard.

Chapter 1
Amber's Opportunity

In a perfect world, Amber Rose McLean would have left Bismarck at five o'clock the evening before Valentine's Day. In less than two hours, she would have been at Cottonwood Creek and in the arms of Kelly Jorgenson, basking in their newfound love.

However, this isn't a perfect world. As Amber hitched her purse and briefcase over her shoulder, ready to escape another marathon workday, a buzzer summoned her to the office of Benson Gates, the company president.

"You wanted to see me?" she asked as she rapped on the door of the corner office, her car keys in hand. Through the window behind his desk, she saw steam rising in the frigid winter air. The sun hung just at the top of the window, waiting to make its evening arc through the pale blue winter sky. Amber hoped to be seventy miles away in Cottonwood Creek when it set.

"Close the door and have a seat," Benson said from behind a stack of documents. He was fifty-five, with thinning hair and some middle-age spread. He retained a down-home charm that hid the business savvy that helped Gates Insurance Agency to prosper.

Amber pushed the door until it clicked shut, then perched on the edge of a leather chair. The toe of one black suede boot tapped silently on the carpeted floor.

As she waited for him to speak, Amber's thoughts strayed to Kelly. Their relationship had done a one-eighty since that fateful day when they'd met last summer. They'd gotten off to a bad start when he caught her in an unguarded moment at Cottonwood Church. After that, she avoided him like a nest of spiders.

Ironically, as the new pastor of the church, Kelly wowed the rest of the McLeans. Her father called him an earnest young fellow. Divinely appointed, her mother said. And in the highest compliment of all, her brothers agreed he wasn't bad for a preacher.

Months later, when her mother invited him for Christmas dinner, Amber groaned at the idea of meeting him again. Did he remember that day last June? Would he embarrass her by telling the family about it? Her face had turned pink with the possibility.

However, none of her worries came true. Instead, Kelly Jorgenson was sincere, entertaining, and good looking. Not once did he mention their first meeting or even give her a calculating look.

Instead, Amber was the awkward one. Seated next to him at the holiday table, she had dropped her fork and sounded like a ninny when she tried to speak. Even as a schoolgirl, she'd never felt as self-conscious around a boy as she did while sitting next to him.

Then, late in the afternoon, she decided to take a walk. While her brothers played with the video game Kelly brought them, the other adults visited or dozed in the living room. Only Kelly offered to join her.

Before the day was over, Amber felt attracted to Kelly like metal to a magnet. Since then, every moment they spent together was better than the last. She could barely make it through each workweek as she anticipated the seventy-mile trip back home to see him.

Now, it was only Wednesday, and her clothes had been chilling in her beloved Jeep all day, ready for a quick getaway. She and Kelly had a big date planned for tomorrow, their first Valentine's Day together. Since she seldom took any time off, her colleagues had raised eyebrows when she announced she'd be out of the office for the rest of the week. She didn't care what they thought. What better use for the vacation days she'd amassed?

Coming back into the moment, Amber realized Benson was speaking to her. Had been for a few moments.

"...a remarkable young woman. A rising star in the industry. You've earned your license, met other requirements, and added to the client list you inherited."

Amber fingered one of the golden ringlets that refused to stay behind her ear, wondering where this conversation was going.

"There are some new business developments that I need to brief you on before you leave." Benson patted the papers into a pile and placed them in a folder.

Amber sighed. This wasn't just a wrap-up meeting at the end of the day. Giving up her hope for a quick exit, she put her keys away and lowered her purse and briefcase to the floor. Oh, Kelly, she thought, I'm so sorry. I'm going to be late.

"As you are aware, Gates Insurance is a respected part of the insurance industry in North Dakota." He lifted the folder of materials and tapped it on his desk. "However, since the terrorist attack last September 11th, the insurance industry is being shaken. Our agency is doing okay, however, we can't continue to do what we've always done and expect things to work out."

"That's worked pretty well, so far," Amber said.

Ignoring her comment, Benson continued his spiel. "We have no strategic business plan, except our good name. Heck, our marketing plan is to hand out calendars at Christmas."

Amber smiled and nodded. Even as a kid, she knew that Gates Insurance gave away great calendars. They featured folksy illustrations by famous American artists.

"I've met with a Minneapolis firm, Mammon Global, that helps develop business plans for companies like ours."

Amber thought of the marketing classes she'd taken in college, and the training she'd received through the agency. "Isn't our business plan to take care of our clients?"

"Do you have to be so logical?" Benson grumbled. "Of course, serving our clients is our number one priority, but in the twenty-first century, we need to be strategic in what we do.

"Here's what I see," Benson leaned forward, and so did Amber. "People want more security now. For the agency to meet the challenges, we must have a solid business plan."

Amber liked that word "security." Although her faith in God had strengthened her through many difficult days, her family's finances and health had been unstable for years. She had learned how to do without new shoes, and shop for groceries with a small amount of cash and no credit card. Growing up, she had often declined school activities. She not only couldn't afford the fees or other expenses, she was needed at home because of her mother's failing health.

It wasn't until she had a good job with Gates Insurance and steady income of her own that she really felt safer. Certainly, security was uppermost in her clients' minds as well.

"I want you to be involved in our new strategic business planning from the beginning. I know you'll do a great job. And it'll be another promotion for you."

Amber studied the toes of her boots. Just the year before, Benson helped her take over the accounts of an agent who was retiring. She'd put in countless hours to train for the position and there was still much to learn. Taking on more responsibility didn't seem like a good idea, especially now that daydreams of Kelly often sidetracked her mind and heart.

"I'm flattered. Truly flattered. And thankful. Truly thankful for all you've done for me." Amber paused. "However, I'm not sure about this. How do you picture me being involved?"

"I want you to be the liaison with Mammon Global. Of course, you'd also need to keep your present position for now. You're so capable, juggling the two shouldn't be a problem."

Amber considered all the hours she already put in every week.

"What would I do as liaison?"

"I'll be in charge of the project. What we need is a person to, well, to do the actual work." Benson cleared his throat. "I'm not a fried chicken anymore. The project will need more energy than I have."

Amber tried not to roll her eyes. Benson was known for mangled metaphors.

"First, Mammon Global will provide training in the strategic planning process. Later they'll do a S.W.O.T. That's the acronym for saying we'll evaluate our strengths, weaknesses, opportunities and threats. Then, a plan will be developed. You'd receive a sizable raise to make it worth your while," Benson promised. "It'll look good in your Y2K."

Amber puzzled for a moment, then realized he was talking about her 401K savings plan.

"Can I have the weekend to think about it?" she asked. She liked to pray about things before making big decisions, and she wanted to talk to Kelly and her parents.

"I understand why you'd want to think about it," said Benson, "Except there isn't time. There's a seminar next week in Minneapolis that I hope you can attend."

They locked eyes. He was as determined as she was reluctant.

"You want me to go to Minneapolis next week?" she asked, weakly.

"Tuesday morning."

"So soon! What about the appointments I already have scheduled?"

"You'd either need to reschedule them or do them by phone in your spare time. I don't want to push you, but there won't be another seminar until June. Why don't you plan on going whether you accept the position or not? I really need you to attend and report back to me."

Amber's shoulders slumped. How could she refuse Benson? She briefly considered canceling her plans to go home for Valentine's Day. Isn't that what a good employee would do when offered a promotion?

Glancing past Benson's shoulder into the now black February night, she could imagine their whole sweetheart weekend evaporating like the sun slipping behind the horizon. The heel of her boot dug into the thick sand-colored carpet.

"Benson, about my trip back to Cottonwood Creek..."

"You should still go. Take a couple days off. The next several weeks might be very busy." He smiled and handed her the folder of information. "Take this and review it over the weekend."

Later, as she drove away, Amber felt confused. She wanted to advance in the company and strategic planning might be interesting. Plus, who wouldn't like a raise? Yet, no matter how appealing her career was, her heart always strayed back to Cottonwood Creek.

Chapter 2
A Small Box of Chocolates

Amber was happy that her overnight bag was packed and in the backseat of her Jeep. She wouldn't need to waste time going to her apartment to pick it up. After a quick stop for groceries and medications, she'd be northbound on Highway 83.

Still dressed in a blue business suit and suede boots, she clacked purposefully down the aisle of the largest grocery store in Bismarck, pushing a cart piled with food items. As she moved methodically through the store, her mind shifted away from business and back to personal matters.

"Five gallons of milk, five loaves of bread, five pounds of apples, five boxes of cereal. That should hold them," Amber murmured to herself. She rounded a corner and headed toward the checkout, tossing in a giant jar of peanut butter and a bag of candy bars.

Then she paused for a full minute to choose a small box of Valentine's candy for Kelly, picking out one with chocolate, peanuts, and marshmallows. Finding a card took longer. She wanted one that neither gushed about love nor made a joke about it, so she was happy to spy a sweet card featuring a favorite cartoon character. It seemed light and serious at the same time. A lot like Kelly, she thought.

At the checkout, the clerk, a woman in her late fifties named Ava, noticed Amber looking at her watch. "Are you running late, dear? I'll try to hurry. Do you want paper or plastic?"

"Plastic," Amber said, as she tucked her mass of blonde hair behind her ears and began to empty the cart.

"You must have a large family or a big event coming up," Ava pried as she scanned items. Amber smiled and shrugged. Bismarck still had a small-town atmosphere where strangers could strike up a conversation.

"I usually make this grocery run on Friday evenings," Amber explained. "I pick up supplies for my parents. My four brothers are still at home and they eat like a herd of buffaloes." "Know what you mean. Raised six kids myself. Putting the last ones through college. I see you bought some candy for your sweetie," Ava said, as she dropped the box covered with red hearts into a bag.

"Yes. We're spending Valentine's Day together." Amber pictured Kelly and suddenly the whirlwind at the office seemed less important. Just thinking about his blonde hair and blue eyes mesmerized her. Maybe it was a good thing that they only saw each other on weekends. Regardless, their relationship was heating up.

"Hmm, must be the real thing," Ava said as she examined the credit card and ran it over the scanner.

"Oh, I don't know," Amber, said, blushing. "I...he... we..." Amber felt her cheeks turning pink. She sounded like she'd flunked speech class.

"Looks like you've got it bad."

"Well, he is pretty special," Amber admitted. "We haven't been going out for long."

"Love at first sight is the best kind," Ava affirmed as she handed Amber her receipts. "You have a wonderful day with your young man."

Amber shivered as she pushed the grocery cart across the icy parking lot to her Jeep. She loaded the milk and fruit into a cooler that she kept in the back so perishables wouldn't melt. Or in this case, freeze.

Before getting on the road, she stopped to pick up a prescription for her mother. Diagnosed with multiple sclerosis ten years earlier, Jean McLean was growing more dependent on her family every day.

"Oh, Mom," Amber said to herself as she got back

into the vehicle. "If only I could pick up a magic potion that would take away your disease."

She hadn't left the parking lot, before her cellphone began emitting a Sousa march. She pulled over, put the Jeep in park, and answered.

"Amber, I'm glad I caught you." It was Benson. He knew that thirty miles out of town, she would be out of reach by cellphone.

"Hi, Benson. Everything was under control when I left," she quipped.

They both laughed. He often called her with business questions after office hours. Clients had crises, computers crashed, schedules disintegrated, but she always told him everything was under control. In truth, things were seldom in control at the office.

"Amber, there's something else I need to discuss with you."

"Okay. Go ahead." She took the Jeep out of park, turned onto Highway 83, and accelerated into the dark, her phone squeezed between her head and shoulder. The clock on the dashboard read 8:30 and she had seventy miles to drive.

She looked in the rearview mirror, catching sight of the tiny cross dangling there. "Lord, please be with me as I drive," she prayed silently, as she tried to pay attention to Benson.

Rising early the next morning, Amber wandered out to the kitchen in her fuzzy pink bathrobe. Her father, Glen, sat at the long oak table, his lanky body bent forward as he ate his eggs and toast. He has the classic look of a farmer, she thought, with his faded jeans and a blue-gray plaid flannel shirt. His hair still had the copper highlights she remembered from her childhood. However, his hairline had receded and the color was softer.

When Glen saw his daughter, he laid down his fork and folded his arms across his chest in a comfortable way that suggested he wanted to talk. A steaming cup of coffee sat near his right elbow.

"Got home late last night."

"Yes. New development at the office," Amber replied casually. She would tell him about the job offer later.

"Big date today?" he asked.

Amber smiled shyly. "You might say that."

"Been seeing quite a bit of Pastor Jorgenson," he said.

"Every weekend since Christmas." Amber opened the fridge door and looked in. She planned to take a cooler of food so she and Kelly wouldn't need to drive into town for lunch. She wasn't going to depend on leftovers from church potlucks that she often found in Kelly's fridge.

"I don't recall you ever going out with someone more than once or twice."

"Never met anyone like Kelly before," Amber responded. He was everything she wanted in a man. For some illogical reason, she suddenly knew she wanted very much to tell Kelly that.

"Sunshine, this seems to be getting serious," Glen said. Something like a smile crossed his face.

Amber slid into a chair. "I've never felt this way about anyone before." She wanted to say more, but wasn't about to tell her father how she was physically attracted to Kelly. She liked his good looks and how he carried his six-foot frame. However, there was so much more about him that she liked.

"He has a lot going for him, Dad. He's very responsible. He left everything. His family. Friends. Palm trees and sandy beaches. That takes a lot of courage. I know a few guys our age that still live with their parents.

"Plus, I see how much he's helping Mom and how much she likes him."

Glen nodded. "I like him, too. He's a good guy!"

Amber warmed to the conversation, eager to tell her father about her relationship with Kelly.

"What really drew us together is something we recognize in each other. We both had to mature pretty fast. His brother's death still hurts him. For me, it's the seriousness of Mom's MS. Plus, we both love the Lord."

She paused for a moment before asking, "Dad, do you believe in love at first sight?"

"When your mother and I met, I'd gone out with a few girls while I was in the Army, and I was ready for a North Dakota girl," Glen responded. "I knew right away she was the one."

Amber hoped he would say more. Just then three of her brothers burst up the stairs, ready for breakfast. The school bus would be rolling up the driveway soon and chaos prevailed. By the time the boys were out the door, the mood was broken.

Glen put on his outdoor clothes, and then turned to Amber. "I'll be praying for you and Kelly today," he said with a wink.

Amber frowned. That's a strange comment, she thought, as she packed the lunch. After helping her mother get ready for the day, she made the eight-mile trip to the parsonage. The route was familiar, because Kelly lived across the creek from her home church.

She walked to the back door, the only one visitors ever used. Like a typical farmhouse, the front door was on the far side of the house. There was no sidewalk leading to it.

Just when she reached the door, it opened. Kelly stood in his stocking feet with a big grin on his face.

Amber held out the candy and card. "Happy Valentine's Day!"

"It's going to be the best ever!" Kelly declared as he ushered her inside.

Chapter 3
Snow Angel

A few hours earlier, the winter sun had peeked over the horizon at Cottonwood Creek, looking like a wide red eye scanning the new day. The first beams of light shone on the church steeple rising serenely from the dormant prairie. The deepening gray silhouette cast on the white snow gave the illusion of an image developing in a dark room.

The only moving shadow in the quiet landscape was that of a lone man gliding along the frozen creek bed on skis. His breath came in frosty puffs as he pushed along. Kelly Jorgenson, the pastor of Cottonwood Church, looked forward to these jaunts, however, this Valentine's Day his foray into the cold was extra special.

In just a few hours, he planned to propose to his sweetheart, Amber Rose McLean, on the wooden footbridge between the church and the parsonage.

"Will you marry me?" Kelly said aloud, rehearsing his words. "No, that's too abrupt." When he moved to the prairies of North Dakota last summer, he'd been surprised at the distance between neighbors. He could make a lot of noise and only the birds and other wildlife heard him. Now, eight months after arriving, it seemed natural to speak aloud as he slid through the icy dawn. If only he could find the right words.

"Amber, I know we haven't dated very long, but I love you and want to marry you."

Too lame.

"Amber, you're the only girl for me and I hope you feel the same way."

He shook his head and muttered, "No, no, no."

"Amber will you be my valentine for the rest of our lives?"

He groaned. Way too cheesy. Somehow, asking this

important question was harder than giving a whole sermon. He finally turned around and pushed back toward home, his face and fingers feeling the bite of cold.

Happily, by the time Kelly arrived at the bridge, he had found the right words to use in his proposal. Plans firmed up, he turned, side stepped up the creek bank, and headed back to the parsonage to warm up.

Three hours later, Kelly and Amber strolled toward the footbridge, walking in the path his skis had made. The sun, now the shape and color of a sugar cookie, rose in its arc across the southern sky, warming their faces and hinting of the start of a new season.

Kelly still felt bashful in Amber's presence, yet he also felt as if he had known her forever. He stole a look at Amber's dancing green eyes and upturned nose. That summer day when they first met, she had disappeared before he could learn her name. He had spotted her once during a service, and then she disappeared again before he could talk to her.

For months, he asked around about her, but no one could identify the piano-playing Golden Girl who had visited the church. The seasons slipped by. It was on Christmas morning near this very spot on Cottonwood Creek that he'd finally surrendered his quest.

Later that day he was invited to have dinner with the McLeans. When he arrived, he learned that his Golden Girl was Amber Rose, the daughter of Jean and Glen McLean. Finally finding Amber was the best Christmas gift he'd ever received. Their romance took off like a firecracker in July.

Most of their dates began with Amber preoccupied with her work and family. Eventually, she would relax and recover the beautiful, serene spirit that had first intrigued him. They would linger, not wanting to end their times together.

Then, in January, as they watched the fire crackle and shared a bowl of popcorn, she finally poured out her heart to him.

"My life is so busy, Kelly, sometimes I feel like I'm losing my soul," she confessed. "I'm turning to plastic. Good old plastic Amber, she can do it all. Then when I'm with you, I begin to get 'me' back. Do you know what I mean?"

Kelly had nodded. The physical and spiritual attraction between them was intense. Now, he also felt an emotional bond forming. His heart melted at her words. He didn't fully understand what she meant, but he did know the answer to helping her: Marriage.

When he called his parents in California to tell them about his plans, his father advised him to slow down, that it was too soon to think about marriage. However, Kelly was twenty-four and he knew what he wanted. He was eager to share every moment of his life with Amber.

This morning, it was a wonder to Kelly that Amber walked beside him, her curly ringlets spilling from her stocking cap. As they neared the creek on this day dedicated to love, Amber didn't know he carried a red velvet box in his pocket or that his knees were turning to pudding at the thought of proposing.

"What a lovely place to spend Valentine's Day," she mused as she surveyed the Currier and Ives scene that included the creek, church, and a stand of trees. "Cottonwood Creek is my most favorite place in the world."

She let go of Kelly's arm and twirled around in the snow. "Have you ever made a snow angel?" she asked, throwing herself down on the ground and flapping her arms and legs.

"No," he stammered as he stared at the flailing angel. "No, I haven't. Snow is in short supply where I come from."

"Well, try it! It's hard to do right now, because the snow is so hard," Amber explained, still swinging her arms and legs. "Say, this snow is perfect for making snowballs." She rolled over, grabbed a handful and began forming it into a ball.

"You wouldn't do that!" Kelly began just as a snowball flew past his shoulder. "Why, you!" He scooped up some snow to throw at Amber, but she jumped up, screamed and ran out of range.

For the next thirty minutes, Kelly forgot his proposal as they played in the snow. Finally, out of breath, the couple leaned on the rail of the footbridge.

He looked into her eyes and a current like electricity flowed between them. He wanted to draw her into his arms and propose in that moment, however, he realized that they were covered with snow. Perhaps it was time to go into the house.

"Let's make some hot chocolate and build a fire," he said, taking her hand and pulling her toward the parsonage.

Chapter 4
Fireside Proposal

Kelly built the fire while Amber prepared hot chocolate. They settled on the aging blue couch watching as the small flames leapt through the kindling. His gray tabby, Mildred, jumped up and touched her nose to Amber's arm. Then she walked across her and snuggled down between them.

Kelly took a deep breath and began. "Do you remember the first time we met?"

Amber smiled and nodded. "I wasn't very happy. You invaded my sanctuary," she said.

Kelly frowned. He didn't want his plan to propose derailed again, but he wanted to explain his version of the story.

"That was a bad day. Mildred was a stray cat then. I'd let her in the house, and the next thing I knew, she'd delivered kittens. Then Kate Schulte chewed me out."

Amber stroked Mildred's gray fur and grinned. "The whole county fears Aunt Kate. Your visit with her must have been terrifying."

"It was. She still makes me feel like a naughty schoolboy," Kelly said. "Yet, the worst thing that day was getting into an argument with Linda Jackson. Who knew two nice people like Mavis and Maury could have such a, um, misguided daughter?"

Amber shook her head. "Linda was a couple grades ahead of me in school. She changed a lot after her friend died."

Kelly reached for her hand and guided the conversation back to his rehearsed topic.

"After all the trouble that day, when I walked into the church, it was like walking into heaven. You were singing and the light coming through the windows turned the room to gold," Kelly said dreamily.

"The peace in the room. It was what I hoped to find when I moved here. Then you left before I even learned your name."

Amber squeezed Kelly's hand sympathetically.

"After that, I tried to find you, like in the story of Cinderella where the prince tries to find her. So, was I happy when I spotted you in church that Sunday in September," Kelly said.

"You looked like you had all the women you could handle that day," Amber commented dryly. "Your friend, Brianna Davis, was attracting a lot of attention, and Linda Jackson was more than a little jealous. By the way, people still think you and Brianna are a hot item."

"They are so wrong," Kelly declared. "You are the only girl I'm interested in. I saw something in you that first day. I fell in love with you then and there. Amber, you're all I want. You're all I've ever needed."

Amber's eyes widened at Kelly's words. Then to her astonishment, he dropped to his knees and reached into the pocket of his jeans. With an eager, hopeful look, he opened the cover of a red velvet box. A solitaire surrounded by smaller diamonds glittered up at her.

"Oh," said Amber, realizing for the first time what was happening.

"Amber Rose McLean, I love you. Will you marry me?"

She looked into his expectant blue eyes for a moment.

"Oh Kelly," she exclaimed. Then she stood up. Going to the trio of windows on the south side of the living room, she stared at the scene outdoors, her back to him.

Kelly frowned. He had expected her to say "yes" right away. Had he misjudged their relationship? What if the bond he felt with her existed only in his mind? What if she said no?

Amber stood trying to absorb the proposal and all it meant. She had never been in love before, yet she was pretty sure the heart-racing, toe-tingling, head-bending bond she felt with Kelly was love.

She sighed. Her life had been an unwavering drive to complete school, care for her family and succeed at work. Boring, boring, boring. She'd missed most of the fun times other kids had in high school, like hanging out with friends or going to the prom. In college, she had studied, worked part-time, and sang in the college choir. No time for a social life. For the last two years, she'd done nothing but work in Bismarck and drive back to Cottonwood Creek to help her family on weekends. Good old reliable Amber, she thought.

And then Kelly came along. She'd found herself skipping out on her duties to do things such as taking off this long weekend. Going on dates instead of serving her family. Playing in the snow. She smiled. Kelly and I play well together, she thought.

Amber couldn't ignore the irony of being offered a promotion and a marriage proposal within twenty-four hours of each other. Marriage wouldn't deliver her from her demanding schedule. In fact, it would only complicate it. She didn't have time for marriage, not to mention the unique obligations of being a pastor's wife. It was a crazy idea. They had only been on seven dates. Seven. What was Kelly thinking?

She needed to say no. Then again, what would it be like to do something impulsive? Who am I? A businesswoman or a country girl?

Amber pushed her hair behind her ear. Perhaps a more vital question was who did she want to be? When she was at work, thoughts of Kelly faded, yet when she was with him, work seemed far, far away. And then there was her family. By working in Bismarck, she was able to help them financially, however, if she married Kelly and moved back here, perhaps she'd be more available to help her mother.

Which is the right way? Benson's pleading voice called to her. Kelly's proposal lay before her. Her parents' dilemma begged for her help. The conflict between love and logic warred in Amber's head like a military battle between two enemies.

Then she had a new thought. Do I need to choose between a career and a personal life? Don't all things work together for good for those who love God and are called according to his purpose? Hasn't God opened the doors for my career and brought Kelly into my life?

Kelly's words rushed into her mind like the cavalry coming to her rescue. He had said, "You're all I want. You're all I've ever needed." They were the words she'd been singing the day he came upon her in the church, words she often sang during her prayer time.

Today, his words had a double meaning. She knew he had surrendered his life to God, but he was also saying he loved her with the same self-abandonment. A deep yearning opened in her heart. She wanted to share her life with Kelly. Like a tide of rushing water, his words transported her into a world where she longed to live.

Amber could feel his eyes on her as she continued to stare out the window. How she wanted to please him. Taking a deep breath, she decided to leap before her logic took over again.

"Yes!" she said, turning to face Kelly. "Yes, I will marry you!"

Kelly had been growing more anxious by the moment. Now, he almost fainted with relief. They beamed at each other and laughed self-consciously. Kelly slipped the ring on her finger.

Magic filled the air. Bells rang. Birds sang. Rainbows

reflected across the ceiling. A marching band went by. The fire crackled its satisfaction. They embraced, captivated with the idea of marriage as their next chapter.

Chapter 5
A Visit From Kate Schulte

Lost in the moment, the newly engaged couple cuddled on the couch.

"Amber Rose. My Golden Girl. I love you," Kelly whispered over and over. The fire crackled and a radio played a country western song in the background. They were unaware of anything but each other.

"Kelly," Amber whispered as she clung to him. "You're everything I could ever desire in a man. I planned to tell you that today, not knowing you were going to propose. I love you, my sweet, serious, handsome prince. Every moment with you is better than the last."

Her words confirmed that they belonged together. His lips found hers for a slow kiss.

Outside, a car door slammed. Moments later, someone rapped loudly on the kitchen door.

"Yoo-hoo!" called a familiar voice.

Kelly and Amber pulled apart, looked at each other wide-eyed and said, "Aunt Kate!"

Springing to his feet, Kelly went to the kitchen to greet Kate Schulte, the eighty-six-year-old matriarch of Cross Church. It was the other church Kelly pastored, located in the village of Schulteville a few miles away.

Amber hung back, trying to cool her flushed face. Kate lumbered into the kitchen, tapping her cane on the floor. She wore a long black coat and a bright yellow scarf. A cloche sat jauntily on her fluffy white hair.

"Pastor Kelly, I'm sorry to interrupt if you have company. I thought we had a meeting today about the Good Friday service, but maybe I was wrong. Is that Amber's car outside?"

She peered into the living room, arching her eyebrows as she spied Amber.

"Well. In the middle of a workday," she blurted out. "I mean, I'm surprised to see you here at all, Amber. Especially in the middle of the week."

Kelly interrupted. "Aunt Kate, we have some breaking news."

He reached out to Amber as she walked toward him. Taking her left hand, he said, "I just asked this beautiful woman to marry me."

"And I said yes," Amber said, still blushing.

"Oh!" said Aunt Kate inspecting Kelly and then Amber. "This is a surprise! Well, I guess congratulations are in order, as long as it's not a hurry-up wedding."

Kelly choked hard at the implication of her words and started to cough.

Having known Kate all her life, Amber wasn't surprised by the woman's audacity. She pressed her lips together to suppress a smile, and then turned to Kelly.

"Are you okay?"

Kelly nodded as he stood at the kitchen sink downing a full glass of water.

"Let me see that lovely ring." Kate grabbed Amber's hand, twisting it to catch the light. Then she trilled, "Very nice. Very, very nice."

"It belonged to my grandmother." Why do I feel defensive about giving Amber a nice ring, Kelly wondered. His teeth were clenched.

"It belonged to your grandmother?" Amber exclaimed.

"I didn't have time to tell you that. It's a family heirloom." He smiled into Amber's eyes.

"Oh, well. That explains how you could afford a diamond that size," Kate muttered.

"I suppose your parents are happy about the news?"

This was directed at Amber.

"Not yet. We're on our way to the farm to tell Mom and Dad," Amber said. "He asked me just a few minutes ago. This is a Valentine's Day to remember."

Amber managed to smile sweetly. Inside, she fumed that they shouldn't have to explain anything to this busybody.

"I'm just an old lady with no reason to remember Valentine's Day," Kate said, her voice now dripping with self-pity. "However, I firmly believe it's good for a pastor to have a wife. Especially a young pastor."

She arched an eyebrow at Kelly. "Although, my dear brother, Ted, pastored for fifty years without feeling the need to marry."

He ran his fingers through his hair in frustration. Without a doubt, Kate enjoyed messing with him. Whether he married or stayed single, he doubted he could measure up to her standards.

"And it's lovely that you've taken an extra day off this week," Kate said pointedly.

"I didn't. I usually take Mondays off, but I spent the whole day preparing ideas for the Easter services. I wanted to ensure I was ready for our meeting tomorrow."

"Oh, tomorrow. Of course," Kate responded. "I obviously had the dates mixed up."

"Tomorrow," Kelly said evenly. "At ten o'clock, right here at the parsonage."

"Oh. Well. I'll see you tomorrow then." Kate took their hands and squeezed them. "I must go so you can drive over and tell your parents. Congratulations. Toodle-oo!"

Kelly escorted her to the door and the couple watched at the kitchen window. Kate lumbered to her large classic black car, slammed the door after she wedged herself in, and bumped out of the driveway.

"It's not like Aunt Kate to get dates mixed up," Kelly observed.

"No, it isn't," Amber said. "It is like her to 'happen' to drive by the church to see what the young pastor is doing."

"And it's just like her to make it her business to find out why my Jeep is parked here. You know what, Kelly? We better tell my parents before she announces our engagement to the whole county. Of course, she'd do it in the nicest way, but..."

"I'll get our coats," said Kelly.

Perhaps it was a blessing that we were interrupted, he thought while shrugging into his parka. There were many reasons to wait until marriage to become intimate. Kelly assumed Amber felt the same way, although they had never discussed it.

He paused at the door. "Amber, I love you so much, and I want us to start off right. With no regrets. I want our wedding night to be the first one we spend together...."

He stopped, not knowing how to directly say what he meant.

"Me too," she said, touching his cheek with her hand. Their frank discussion was making her own cheeks turn pink again.

"Please understand, I know it's old-fashioned. I want to wait until our wedding night and make it the most amazing night of our lives. Let's not ruin it."

Their faces were close now. Her hand found the lobe of his ear.

"It might be hard," she said, her green eyes smiling into his.

"Let's not wait too long to get married. I'm not good at resisting temptation."

Backing away, she squeezed his hand and then reached for her gloves.

"Let's go tell the world we're getting married!" Kelly said.

Chapter 6
Social Media, Country Style

When they arrived at the farm, Jean and Glen were sharing afternoon coffee. Amber noted that her father gave Kelly a silent nod of understanding.

As they sluffed off their gloves and jackets, he realized how familiar the McLean farmhouse had become. Because Jean was housebound, Kelly visited her every week. At first, he dropped by as part of his job. Now he looked forward to seeing her.

Kelly realized he had spent more time with Amber's mother than with his-bride-to be.

Kelly admired Jean. She still directed the household and supplied motherly counsel to her brood. He found it amusing that she often puzzled her energetic eleven-year-old twins by thwarting their silly or risky schemes.

Another person might have been lonely or depressed by the limitations Jean lived with. After all, she was only forty-six and dependent on others for her care. She had four sons living at home. Adam worked with his father or hired out to other area farmers and ranchers. Daniel, a senior in high school, was also fairly independent. However, the twins, Timothy and James, were only eleven, and most days she couldn't even bake a batch of cookies for them.

At first, Kelly assumed Jean spent her days alone, but after only a couple of visits, he noticed how God's presence encompassed her. Jean was a prayer warrior who lived in a unique power zone. The living room was her command center. The sun shone in the south window. Photos of her parents, siblings, and children filled one wall. A picture of Jesus, his head thrown back in laughter, took center place on another wall. Stacks of audio tapes covered the table near the green recliner where she spent most of her time.

She listened to praise and classical music, the Bible, and her favorite radio ministers.

Rather than feeling pity for Jean, Kelly felt awe.

A heart-shaped box of chocolate candy lay open on the kitchen table. Jean was parked at a right angle so she could more easily manage her cup. She smiled broadly when Kelly and Amber walked in.

"Mom, Dad, we have something to tell you!" Amber said. "Kelly asked me to marry him. And I said yes." She held out her left hand for inspection.

Jean opened her arms to Amber.

"Oh, Baby, come here," she said, tears filling her eyes.

Glen stood and grasped Kelly's hand and shook it hard with his farmer's steel grip.

"Congratulations. I know you'll be real good to my Sunshine."

"I appreciated our talk the other day," Kelly responded.

Then Jean held out her arms to Kelly. He leaned over the wheelchair and Jean kissed him on the cheek. "Welcome to our family."

They both admired the ring, while Kelly told how his grandfather had made payments for years so his bride could have a beautiful ring.

"A family heirloom," Jean commented.

Before more could be said, the school bus arrived. Tim and Jim jumped down the bus steps and burst through the kitchen door with the energy of sixth-grade boys. They dropped their books and papers on the floor and threw valentines in the air, scattering them across the kitchen.

"Girls!" shouted Tim, his unruly red hair standing straight up. "That creepy Margaret H. has the hots for me."

"Tim's got a girlfriend," Jim sang as he danced away from his brother.

"She gave me a mushy valentine. I'm going to get teased for the rest of my life." Tim grabbed his throat and made a choking sound.

"Timothy. James." Glen scolded, embarrassed by his sons' antics in front of the pastor and future son-in-law.

Amber got glasses from the cupboard and poured milk for each boy from a gallon jug. True to Amber's description to the store clerk, the boys gulped the milk like hungry calves.

"Candy!" Tim shouted as he spied the box on the table. "Can I have some?"

"No," Glen said, firmly. "You wouldn't like it. I bought it for my girlfriend."

"You bought Mom a box of candy?" Tim asked incredulously.

"You can have a few pieces," Jean said kindly.

"I'm not the only one with a girlfriend," Glen said as the twins munched away. "You didn't even say hello to Amber and Kelly."

"Hi, Preach," Tim said, halfheartedly. "Hi, Amber."

When Kelly and Amber first began dating, the twins had a lot of fun teasing her. However, now they appeared bored with taunting their sister about her love life. Kelly was patiently trying to build a relationship with them.

"Say, Amber, where did you get that fancy ring?" Jim asked.

"Kelly gave it to me."

"Why'd you do that, Preach?" Jim asked. Then he had a light bulb moment. "Are you gonna get hitched?" he asked in wonder.

"We are," said Kelly as he grasped Amber's upraised hand. "Looks like you're going to have a preacher for a brother-in-law. What do you think about that?"

The twins looked at each other, shock registering on their freckled faces.

"Oh boy," Tim groaned as he slapped his forehead. "I'll have to watch what I say and do from now on."

"No, you won't," Jim said, thrusting his elbow into his brother's side. "He already knows that only God can help you." A shoving match ensued, before the boys were sent downstairs to their room.

Amber began picking up the valentines off the floor just as the oldest brothers, Adam and Daniel, arrived. After showing off her ring again, the brothers offered shy congratulations, ducking their mops of red hair, their light blue eyes cast downward.

Kelly was ready to whisk Amber off to a nice dinner for two, when he saw her look around the kitchen. There was no meal preparation underway. She gave Kelly an apologetic look and shrugged. She couldn't bear to leave her family to an evening of tuna sandwiches while she went out for a nice meal. He nodded.

"Hey everybody, we want you to help us celebrate. Is anyone up for Salisbury steak?" she said brightly. Her parents both frowned and shook their heads, but the twins pounded back up the steps and responded with loud whoops and cries of, "Yes!"

Amber went to the chest freezer. She held up the unreliable lid with one hand, and dug out a large package of chopped steak with the other. Instead of leaving for their favorite restaurant, Kelly peeled potatoes, while she quick-thawed the steak and heated a cast iron pan.

After the meal was devoured, Jean nodded to Amber.

"We've already messed up your plans. Go and have some time together. The boys will clean up the kitchen."

A few minutes later, Kelly and Amber were back in his dusty blue pickup. Instead of going to the parsonage, they drove into Cottonwood City where they saw the lights on at Your Friendly Co-op. The ample-sized manager, Tiny Winger, had befriended Kelly when he first arrived. Since then he'd introduced the city preacher to standard rural entertainment, like fishing, hunting, bowling, and attending high school football and basketball games.

"Tiny must be working," Kelly said as he pulled into the convenience store, gas station, and auto repair shop. "Let's tell him the news."

As they walked into the store, Amber mused that it always smelled like a mix of tires, axle grease, and stale popcorn. Tiny sat hunched over the counter working on his computer.

"Hey, hey, I hear you're getting hitched," Tiny said, looking up.

"Oh-oh, the news is out," Amber groaned. "There's no way to keep a secret in this community."

Kelly groaned. "We haven't even called my parents or the church board members. How did you find out, Tiny?"

"It was on the news on channel eleven," Tiny said, his moon face beaming. "Just kidding. Maury Jackson was in. Wayne Selby told him."

Wayne and Marge Selby lived with Kate Schulte. They cared for Kate and her property in Schulteville. In turn, they had a comfortable home.

"Kate told Wayne," Amber concluded. "We better call your folks before it's on the national news."

Later, while Kelly dialed the phone, Amber scooped Mildred into her arms and rocked her like a baby. The gray kitty purred her appreciation. Then, Kelly turned on the speakerphone and Amber chatted with Steve and Nancy Jorgenson, her future in-laws, for the first time.

Afterwards, Amber tugged on her jacket. She felt positively limp with happiness and peace. The last twenty-four hours had been full of excitement, but now she was ready to put on her nighty and crawl between her flannel sheets.

She sighed and melted into Kelly's embrace one last time. "I don't know when I've been so happy, Pastor Jorgenson. You have a magical influence on me."

Chapter 7
The Youth Group

During the night a Chinook wind rose, waking Amber from a series of sweet dreams. She rolled onto her stomach and pulled the curtain aside.

The yard light cast a shadow into the north acre outside her room, painting the snow a soft gray. The clothesline swayed in the wind, while shadowy branches ducked and bounced like dancers doing a Virginia reel. She could imagine small animals scurrying in the shadows, their rustling movements covered by the cry of the wind.

Amber slid out of bed and pressed her face to the window, observing the sudden change in weather. The Chinook wind and warmer temperature were a harbinger of spring. Looking up, she noted a few stars flickering overhead as bright night clouds scuttled across the sky. Then she turned the ring on her left hand to catch the faint light.

"Do you know what this means?" she asked the night sky. "I'm getting married. Pledging my love to Kelly for eternity." The weight of the ring reminded her that it had been in Kelly's family for three generations. Wasn't it Psalm 78 that directs each generation to teach their children about God? In a way, the ring was a message from Kelly's grandparents about the sacredness of marriage.

That was no small thing, Amber thought. Marriage vows were often broken. Many couples didn't even bother to tie the knot. She had watched her parents work through financial issues, her mother's health, and raising a family. They had many for-better and for-worse moments, but their commitment never wavered. Amber longed for the same kind of bond.

Her reflection in the window showed a Mona Lisa smile that surprised her. Yet, why should anything ever surprise her again? Love had found her, and she'd never let go of it.

On Friday morning, Amber called Benson on her mother's princess phone.

"By golly, I'm glad you called," Benson greeted her. "I wish you were in the office today." His harried manner cast a cloud over Amber. She never wanted to let Benson down.

After a twenty-minute exchange, she hung up. Her mother had been listening to her side of the conversation.

"Mom," she cried. "I should have gone in to work today. There is so much happening and I'm starting a new project for Benson. He wants me to fly to the Twin Cities early Tuesday."

Jean's brows puckered. "You're going on a trip next week?"

Amber pursed her lips, the joy over her engagement gone for the moment.

"Mom, I really need your prayers for direction." Sitting on the footstool in front of her mother's chair, she told all about her last meeting with Benson.

"I am really interested in strategic planning. And it would be a bump in pay. Still, the timing couldn't be worse. My head says to take the job, but my heart wants to focus on our marriage."

She looked at her mother and lifted her hands in bewilderment. Jean reached for Amber and hugged her. When Amber was growing up, she could be won over with a quiet talk and warm smile. Jean often wished her boys were that easy.

Now, she declared, "Honey, you could be in the office seven days a week and it wouldn't be enough. For today, you need to focus on your engagement."

She continued, "If there's one thing I've learned from having MS, it's that outside of your health and those you love, nothing else matters. Spend some time with Kelly. And maybe some time with your mom?"

Amber bowed her head. It had been a long time since she and her mother talked heart-to-heart. On the weekends, she tended to act like a ball in a pinball machine, loading the washer, going for groceries, vacuuming the house. Now she studied her mother's face. She seemed thinner. There were new lines around her mouth and her clothes seemed loose.

"Are you okay?"

"I'm happy," Jean replied. "I have a wonderful daughter, who is marrying the nicest young man. I have a caring husband and healthy boys. And I have a God who says he will supply all of my needs."

"Oh Mom, you know what I mean. How do you feel?"

"I have a big checkup in a couple weeks. We'll see what the doctors say."

A wave of guilt passed over Amber. Suddenly Gates Insurance seemed far away. She belonged here today.

When Jean needed to rest, Amber went to the kitchen and mixed dough for a huge batch of caramel rolls. While the dough raised, she read through the packet of material from Benson and made some phone calls.

When the dough began to spill from the covered bowl, she plopped it onto the wooden breadboard and rolled it into a thin sheet. Once it was spread with butter and sprinkled with sugar and cinnamon, she deftly rolled up the sheets. The last step was slicing the fragrant cylinders and placing them on a mixture of brown sugar, butter and cream.

Once baked and cooled, she packed half of them to take to the Friday evening youth group meeting. She knew firsthand that teenagers were always hungry.

One of the surprises with Kelly's ministry was his popularity with the local teens. He hadn't planned to start a youth group, but after he and Tiny began meeting with a few of the boys for pizza and music, the gathering had grown.

That evening, she rode to the youth meeting with Daniel. When they reached the fellowship room, Amber surveyed the noisy crowd. She counted thirteen boys scarfing up pizza and pouring soda pop from two-liter bottles, while five girls huddled off to the side. Quite a crowd for the rural church on a Friday night, she observed.

Amber's caramel rolls were received with shouts and high-fives. While this response pleased her, it also brought out her inner bossy big sister.

"One apiece, guys, and if there are any left, you can maybe have a second one," she chirped. Out of the corner of her eye, she caught Daniel nudging a buddy as though to say, "See what I put up with?"

After she sat down, the girls scooted their chairs around her. One of them, Kelsey, introduced the others. Janna, Zoe, Anna, Charlotte. While she knew most of their families, they had been little girls when she moved away for college.

Kelsey was tall and willowy, the natural leader. Janna and Zoe were sisters. Janna had a big smile and a direct gaze, while Zoe's eyes continually strayed to the boys. She can't be over thirteen, Amber thought, and she's already boy crazy. Anna was pudgy, and the only girl to eat two caramel rolls. Charlotte sat staring at her hands.

"The boys rule," Janna confided. "Pastor Kelly is nice and all, but we're still outnumbered."

Amber asked them what grades they were in, their favorite subjects, and how long they'd been attending the youth group. Soon, they were talking like old friends.

Before long, Kelly quieted the group. He sat on a stool at the front of the room, the florescent ceiling light reflecting off his blonde hair. Being the day after Valentine's Day, his lesson was about love. He planned to announce their engagement at the end of the evening.

"1 John 4:19 is one of my favorite scriptures. 'We love because he first loved us.' Tell me, who are you most attracted to, someone who shows you love and acceptance, or someone who condemns you?

"Jesus draws us to himself by his love. He wants to be our best friend. He'll always be there for us. We don't need to fear him, because He accepts us as we are."

He paused and looked around the room, about to ask if they wanted a closer friendship with Jesus. At that moment, someone began humming "Here Comes the Bride."

Glancing around the room, he tried to find the guilty party.

"Pastor Kelly, if you're going to talk about love, maybe you should use you and Amber as an example," said a voice from the back of the crowd.

Kelly almost choked. A ripple of laughter went through the room.

"Hey, does that mean you love Amber because she loved you first?"

Hooting, hollering and clapping broke out.

Realizing he'd lost control of the group, Kelly threw his head back and laughed. The teachable moment had passed. He motioned for Amber to join him, and she found her way through the crowd, looking a little flustered.

Tiny whistled shrilly and the group began to settle down.

"So you've heard the rumors." Kelly stood with his arm lightly around Amber. "Let me tell you the real story." The room stilled instantly.

"When I saw Amber last summer, I fell in love with her right away."

One of the girls uttered a soft, "Oh-h-h."

"However, we've only been dating since Christmas."

"That isn't very long," someone commented. "We heard you're engaged."

"When God brings two people together, it doesn't take long to know you want to be together forever," Kelly said softly, his eyes on Amber.

"Too many people date around. They're careless with their hearts and bodies. Hearts are broken, bodies get used, and emotions damaged. That isn't God's plan. He wants us to wait for someone who will cherish us.

"Yesterday, I asked Amber to marry me, partly because we cherish each other, and way more than that. You can't always trust your feelings. This is something I want to talk with you about soon.

"I pray each of you will find someone who cherishes you. Until then, guard your hearts and bodies, and focus on a friend that sticks closer than a brother: Jesus."

Amber squeezed Kelly's hand. Across the room, the teens stood to their feet and began to clap. Later, many of the teens hung around to congratulate them. Amber was surprised when Charlotte approached her.

"I'm glad you came tonight," Charlotte said shyly. "Will you be back?" The other girls nodded in agreement.

Amber's heart was melted by the silent plea in the girls' eyes.

Chapter 8
Date Night

On Saturday evening, Amber felt as giddy as a schoolgirl as she drove to Kelly's home. After a day of cleaning house and doing laundry, she had made enough braised beef to feed half the county, or at least enough for all her family, and the two of them. She also brought along a romaine salad and fresh brownies.

They took their food into the living room to eat before the fire. Mildred chaperoned by sitting between them, again, as they talked and scraped their dishes clean. Amber was ready to tell Kelly about her job offer and upcoming trip, when Kelly said, "In our wedding vows, we should add that you'll do all the cooking."

Immediately distracted, Amber responded, "Sure. I don't mind cooking. But, we must also add that you will do the snow shoveling until death do us part. That's one a job I don't like."

"Oh, my Golden Girl, thou will never lift a shovel again," Kelly stated in mock seriousness, though shoveling was his least favorite form of exercise.

Throughout the evening, they carefully avoided embracing. The flame they felt for each other needed to be tamped down and guarded until their wedding day, especially since the whole youth group was paying attention to their romance.

There was so much to say, so many dreams to weave, so many emotions to reveal. It seemed as if only a few moments went by before Amber had to go back home. It was now or never. She needed to tell Kelly about her job offer, even though work seemed light years away.

"I have to tell you something important," she said, just as Kelly echoed the same words.

Dumbfounded, Amber said, "You go first."

Kelly's shoulders slumped. "I didn't want to bring this up this evening, however, you need to know about something that's been weighing on me."

"That's amazing. I've done the same thing." They smiled at the irony, reaching across Mildred to hold hands. "What's going on?"

"There's a board meeting at Cross Church tomorrow evening. The only agenda item is whether to close the church. I think they're going to do it."

"Oh, Kelly. I'm so sorry. I know how hard you've worked to revive Cross Church."

"I tried," he said, looking down. "I walked around town, and introduced myself to everyone. Had some great conversations and invited people to church. I went to a lot of neighboring farms, too."

He shrugged and sighed. "Some people have another church home and that's good. What bothers me are those who are just drifting spiritually or they have a lot of troubles. They don't understand that God might help them find a way.

"I worry about their kids, too. My family didn't go to church, so Kyle and I didn't have biblical truths to lean on as we grew up. Thank God, Kyle found the way, and later so did I."

"Cross Church is such a pretty church. When do you think it will close?" Amber commiserated.

"Sometime this spring. I hate that it's happening while I'm the pastor."

They sat in silence for a moment before Amber reminded Kelly that this wasn't about him, and that God was in control.

"All things work together for good for those who love the Lord and are called according to his purpose."

"I know, I know. I just need to have more faith."

At that moment, Mildred decided to turn the couch into a bathtub. She stretched, raised a leg and began washing with her rough tongue.

Amber giggled. "Mildred, you're not being very modest."

"Maybe she thinks it's time to change the conversation. Tell me your news."

"Possible changes at work," she said, and then reported her conversation with Benson.

Kelly wasn't enthused about the additional work or the trip.

"Are you sure that's what you want? What about our wedding? I hoped you'd be spending more time here and not be so focused on work."

"Like I told Mom, my head says take this job, while my heart longs to be back here."

They discussed the pros and cons of her new position, before Amber rose to leave. As she gathered up her containers, Kelly brought up another delicate subject.

"You're planning to be in church tomorrow, aren't you?" he asked, catching Amber off guard. She suspected he didn't want to bring up the fact that Amber regularly missed church. By now, she knew he had looked for her every Sunday between June and December, and she had shown up exactly once.

"I plan to be in church every Sunday. It's just that stuff always keeps me away," Amber explained. "Sometimes, Mom's having a bad morning and I don't want to leave her. Maybe I haven't cleaned the house yet or started the laundry, so I do that. Last weekend the furnace went out in the middle of the night. Did we scramble to get it fixed!"

"You don't mind attending church? You're just prevented from coming?"

"I love going to church. And I will be more mindful about being there from now on."

"Tomorrow I want to invite you to come up front during the service at Cottonwood for the official engagement announcement. Is that okay with you?"

"Will I have to say anything?"

"Not a word. Simply be willing to stand with me."

Amber gave great work presentations and she could play piano in front of an audience, but the idea of saying something in church gave her brain freeze.

"I was wondering, from now on will you sit in the front row to be close to me?"

"Oh, Sweetie, of course. I'd like that. Our family has always taken up the whole fourth row, west side. We certainly haven't been there much lately."

"Your family is going through a tough time."

Amber bit her lip. So much had changed in her family as her mother's health had declined. It was clear Kelly knew and understood that. He might have been critical of their dismal attendance record. Instead, his compassion had shown through.

Amber wrapped her arms around Kelly and looked up for a kiss. And that concluded any further discussion.

Chapter 9
Sunday Morning Coming Down

That night, Amber dreamed she sat in the front row at church, wearing a wedding gown. Her veil drifted from a sparkling tiara and spilled up the aisle, forming a carpet of white petals. Instead of a bouquet of flowers, she carried her briefcase. As she listened to Kelly's sermon, her cell phone rang. She tried to put the briefcase down, but it wouldn't leave her hand. The people behind her began to murmur with displeasure.

When a door slammed somewhere in the distance, she jumped. Like a deep-sea diver swimming up toward the light, she kicked away the frustrating dream. A cold draft wafted under her bedroom door as she heard feet stamping snow.

"Boys!" It was her father's voice. "Get dressed. Number 24 is in trouble."

Amber burst out of sleep, fully awake. Calving season was an intense labor of love for cattlemen. When the heifers were about to calve, her father herded them into the barn, which became a bovine maternity ward. He'd obviously been up during the night and found a distressed cow. The clock showed it was five-thirty.

"Adam and Daniel!"

Amber heard them answer. Then her father left, slamming the door and rattling the fancy china plate that hung on the kitchen wall. A few seconds later, the young men bounded up the steps from their basement bedroom. Again, the kitchen door slammed and the plate rattled.

It reminded her of an incident that happened when she was young. It was perhaps her first memory. At that time, they lived in a mobile home on the farm and she still slept in a crib. Her grandfather had stuck his head inside the door early one morning and called, "Glen, one of the cows is in trouble." Her father had rustled out of bed, putting his pants on over his long johns.

That's all she could remember. The next year, Grandma and Grandpa McLean died in a car accident. Her father unexpectedly found himself taking over the farm long before he was ready for that much responsibility.

Daddy must have been so young then, she realized. He was perhaps Kelly's age, with a wife and child. And suddenly his parents were gone.

Farming doesn't allow for much transition time. Animals need tending every day despite any human tragedy that might be taking place. All of the work and every decision about the livestock and crops were suddenly on her father's shoulders.

Glen's sister, Sandy, was still in high school when their parents died. Glen, Jean and Amber had moved into the farmhouse with her. Sandy stayed there while she finished high school. Now she was a nurse living in the Chicago area.

Amber recalled how close her mother and Sandy became. Together they ran up and down the ladders, painting and wallpapering the old farmhouse. They wore caps from the hardware store, and belted out songs along with the local AM radio station.

Amber got out of bed, put on her robe, and padded into her parents' bedroom.

"Good morning, Amber," her mother whispered from beneath a puffy quilt.

"Morning, Mom," Amber whispered back as she sat down on the side of the bed

"How was your date?"

"Wonderful. We had dinner in front of the fireplace and toasted marshmallows afterward. Put them on our brownies!" Amber beamed at the memory.

"I think Kelly is good for you," Jean said as she patted her daughter's hand.

"We're going to announce our engagement this morning."

Jean turned her head away, then whispered, "I wish I could be there for you."

"Me, too."

Jean could have attended church with some effort, but the cold weather worsened her symptoms. She had made peace with being housebound for the winter months, until now. Her daughter's engagement announcement stirred the desire for a life outside the walls of her home.

"If this cow delivers in time, I'm sure your dad will go."

Unspoken words filled the bedroom that was still papered in mauve and forest green. Amber could sense her mother's frustration with her body and disappointment that she couldn't be part of the excitement.

She took her hand. "Mom, can we say our morning prayers together?"

"I'd like that very much."

Afterwards, Amber locked herself in the house's only bathroom for a shower. Then, still in her bathrobe, she stirred up a batch of pancakes as bacon began to sizzle in the frying pan.

She and Jean ate breakfast, whereas the rest of the food warmed in the oven until the men came in. When her father hurried through the door, Amber saw the worry on his face.

"Looks like Number 18 is going to deliver today, too," he said on his way to the phone to call the local veterinarian for advice.

"It doesn't look like Dad, Adam or Daniel will be in church," Amber concluded after he left again, the door slamming, the china plate rattling a third time.

"Maybe the twins will join you."

Amber groaned. Her youngest brothers were still nestled in their beds. She went downstairs and woke them. Surprisingly, they were eager to come along.

"The new band at church is pretty cool," Jim explained.

"Well, you better move fast," she declared. "Get dressed. Sunday clothes. There are pancakes in the oven. Be ready to go out the door in twenty minutes."

I sound like a drill sergeant, Amber thought, but at least part of her family would be at church for the special announcement.

A few minutes later, looking in the mirror over the bureau in her room, she smoothed her royal blue dress, applied pink lip-gloss and a spritz of her favorite scent. She evaluated the woman who looked back at her. Today, when her engagement was formally announced, the congregation would look at her with new eyes. Instead of seeing the energetic girl with all the hair, they would evaluate whether she would make a good wife for their pastor.

Suddenly, she turned and knelt by her bed. "Oh Father, how can I ever measure up to being a pastor's wife? Don't they need to be more than perfect? Well, as you know, I'm flawed. Please make me worthy to be Kelly's wife. I pray he will always be glad to have me at his side."

She got up and straightened her dress. It was twenty minutes to ten. She wrestled the boys into the Jeep for the eight-mile drive. The service began at ten o'clock. They were barely going to make it.

Chapter 10
Joy Comes in the Morning

They arrived at the church a minute before the service started. When Tim and Jim saw her start for the front of the sanctuary, they balked. Not wanting to argue, Amber found seats in the back row, stepping over people to reach the last three spots.

She could see Kelly at the front, scanning the room for her. She raised a hand and waved, but he didn't see her. Then, the new teen band began playing the first song. As the congregation stood, a pair of big square shoulders blocked the view. Kelly for sure couldn't see her now.

Amber squeezed closer to Jim, trying to see around the man, however, the woman next to him wore a large hat. She moved to the right, stepping on Tim's foot.

"Ow!" he complained loudly.

I feel like a student trying to get the teacher's attention, Amber thought, as she resigned herself to remaining hidden for now. However, as she sang along, she plotted how to escape at greeting time.

"Listen," she said to the twins a few minutes later, as people began to shake hands. "Kelly asked me to sit in the front row and that's what I'm going to do."

"Pastor Kelly asked you to sit in the front row?" Tim asked incredulously. "Then why aren't you up there?"

Amber huffed. Why indeed. "Listen, do you want to come with me or will you be good boys if you're sitting by yourselves?"

"We'll stay here," said Jim. He sounded serious.

"We'll be good," promised Tim. She noted that his collar was lopsided and his hair stood up like a rooster's tail. His hands were behind his back, which probably meant his fingers were crossed.

"Remember, even if I'm not watching you, God is," she whispered in their ears.

The church filled with the chatter of friends and neighbors. Amber stumbled out of the row and squeezed up the aisle, dodging anyone who might delay her from reaching Kelly.

She could see the sun glinting off his blonde hair. As he talked with a small group of people, his eyes scanned the congregation. Then their eyes met.

She grinned at him and pushed forward. Stopping in mid-sentence, he took a step toward her. One of the teens Kelly had been talking with gave Amber a thumbs up.

When they reached each other, Amber held out her hand. Kelly grasped it and pulled her to him. "Where were you?"

"Back row. Behind the hat."

"Why didn't you come up front?"

"The twins are with me. Since two cows are calving, Dad couldn't make it."

Kelly leaned over and, in front of God and the whole congregation, kissed her forehead. Then, his hand at her waist, he guided her up the steps to the podium.

"May I have your attention?" he said into the microphone. Quiet fell over the congregation as they spied Amber at their pastor's side. Everyone shuffled to their seats.

Amber surveyed the congregation. The twins peeked out from behind the shoulders and the hat. With their red hair and freckles scattered across their noses, they looked like a double image of Alfalfa from the Little Rascals.

She also noted that only a few people were in the fourth row, where her family usually sat before her mother's illness. Are they saving that space for my family, she wondered. If only one day Mom, Dad, and the boys can fill up that row with redheads again.

"You may have heard a rumor that I proposed to Amber Rose McLean. Well, it's true. I proposed on Valentine's Day and this lovely woman has agreed to marry me."

Someone, it sounded like one of the twins, yelled, "Yahoo!" Applause rippled through the congregation, growing louder and louder. One of the guitarists did a riff. Touched beyond measure, Amber bit her lip to keep tears from trickling from her eyes.

They get it, Amber thought. They took a chance on this young man from California and now he's marrying a local girl. Joy comes in the morning!

When it quieted again, someone called out, "When are you getting married?"

"We haven't set the date yet," Kelly stated. He and Amber smiled at each other. "But we're not going to wait too long." More applause. A drumroll.

"You'll all be invited to the wedding!" he added.

Amber gasped. They obviously needed to talk about the details of a wedding. She would have chosen a small wedding, and assumed Kelly felt the same way.

Looking at the smiling faces, sensing the happiness flowing through the sanctuary, Amber realized there was no way around inviting the whole congregation. Kelly had won their hearts, as well as her own. If there was any doubt, she only had to look to the east side of the church. Two rows of teenagers clapped and cheered loudly, and the eager teen band waited to perform the offertory.

Her eyes landed on the girls she'd met at the youth meeting. Standing together, they beamed up at her. Kelsey wiggled her fingers and Amber returned the greeting.

As she stood there, blushing slightly, her hand in Kelly's, tension and pressure fell away like a radio being turned down. Her heart overflowed.

Amber was certain that she belonged at Cottonwood Creek. What could possibly be more wonderful than to be here with Kelly? She knew these people, their craggy faces, their family scandals and successes, which county roads to drive to find their mailboxes. She and Kelly both belonged with these people. She loved them, and there was no doubt the feeling was mutual.

Time seemed to pause. Golden rays of sunlight streamed into the sanctuary from the high east windows, shedding grace across the room. Beams of light danced across their heads.

Amber stood transfixed by the power of the moment. She had felt this presence many times when she played and worshiped here alone, but never with a roomful of people. Her eyebrow creased as she tried to recall a memory. Light filtering through the leaves of a cottonwood tree. A man who radiated love. The same joy that filled her that day was present now.

Kelly was squeezing Amber's hand. She looked around the room. The congregation was getting settled, moving purses and bulletins in order to take their seats. Kelly nodded for her to sit down, a slightly puzzled look on his face. She took a couple shaky steps and dropped into the front pew. What just happened? she wondered.

Chapter 11
Be Still My Soul

Amber tried to concentrate on Kelly's sermon. The aura of light remained. Her heart felt cradled in the holy presence. Kelly and the congregation seemed far away, as though she had entered another dimension.

It's like when I was little and Mom held me in her arms, Amber reminisced. It's as warm as those moments after I wake from a deep sleep and the bed feels soft and cozy. It's coming home after being gone a long time. That's it! I'm coming home.

Absorbed in her own thoughts, she was surprised when the congregation rose and began flipping through their hymnals. She had missed most of Kelly's sermon.

What am I going to say when he asks how I liked his sermon, Amber wondered. She jumped up and grabbed a hymnal. The board on the wall showed the hymn's page number. She didn't need to look at it. She knew this song by heart, even remembered the author was Katharina von Schlegel.

"Be still, my soul: the Lord is on thy side..." Amber found her voice and sang the first verse, the words touching her heart. "...Leave to thy God to order and provide; In every change, He faithful will remain."

However, it was the second verse that burned past her doubts and fears. "Be still, my soul: thy God doth undertake to guide the future as He has the past. Thy hope, thy confidence let nothing shake; All now mysterious shall be bright at last."

That's how I want to live, putting all my confidence in God, Amber thought.

Her voice soared.

Kelly glanced over at her. He'd heard her ange. voice before, but never like this. Her rich tone ascende with such clarity and perfect pitch that those around hei took note, and their voices fell away. Amber sang on as the third verse began, unaware that she was attracting attention.

Kelly looked across the congregation and saw emotions stirring in the stern, Midwestern faces. People who seldom showed any zeal, especially in church, now looked like dry plants bathed in gentle rain. A few wiped the corners of their eyes and a woman near the center aisle lifted her hands in praise.

When the hymn ended, the last words seemed to linger in the air like the tone of a bell after it has rung. A hush fell on the sanctuary. It felt as though they had slipped into an eternal realm.

Kelly let the peace linger for several moments. He didn't know what had happened with Amber, yet he could see how she had brought comfort and hope to those present. When they left this church building, they'd face individual trials of grief, illness, worry over children, and struggles with the farm economy. However, they'd also leave refreshed by the presence that now filled the church. For once, no one was in a hurry to leave.

"The Psalms have the word Selah at the end of some verses," Kelly commented. "Selah was a call to rest and reflect. I believe we've just experienced Selah. Please take time today to enter that quiet place again where you can think and pray.

"May the God of hope fill you with all joy and peace as you trust in him, so that you may overflow with hope by the power of the Holy Spirit. Go in peace to love and serve the Lord."

Taking Amber's arm, he escorted her to the vestibule. Amber floated along at his side, still locked in a secret

As the door banged shut after her twin brothers exited, Amber asked, "Kelly, what scripture did you base your sermon on this morning? It seemed to have an effect on the twins."

"I noticed that. It's strange how sometimes people think I'm directing a sermon at them. The scripture was Proverbs 14:2, about fearing the Lord and walking uprightly."

"Hmm, I'll have to write that down and hang it where the boys can see it!" Amber said with a smile.

Turning serious, she put her hand on the chest of his suit jacket. "Something happened here this morning. We need to talk."

His eyes searched hers and his arms encircled her waist. "God used you to encourage people today. I could see it in their faces. You have a special gift that they need, I need."

They stared into each other's eyes and she was again captivated by the bond they shared. Whatever she had experienced this morning belonged to Kelly as much as to her.

"Can you come for lunch?"

Kelly shook his head. "Not today. Cole called just before the service and said Sadie isn't feeling well. He's been taking her to Cross Church and then coming here to play in the band, but he stayed home with her. He's that worried."

Amber was familiar with Cole Jensen's story. Abandoned by his parents, Cole now lived with his great-grandmother.

"That's a lot of responsibility for a high school boy," she said.

"I agree. Anyway, I need to check on them." Kelly looked longingly at Amber, then grabbed her and pulled her around the corner. Out of sight, they shared a kiss.

"This is in case I don't see you before you leave for Bismarck," he explained.

"Oh, we must find time," Amber said, her hands looping around his neck.

"You could come with me to visit Sadie."

Amber shook her head. "I've got the boys along. And I need to figure out something for lunch. I can come over later."

"I may end up taking Sadie to get help, plus I need to finish preparing for the Cross Church board meeting."

Outside, a familiar car horn began to toot.

"The boys," she sighed. Giving him a forlorn smile and a quick kiss, she slipped away.

Chapter 12
A Doll Named Rusty Ann

Late Sunday afternoon, Amber slipped out of the farmhouse for some fresh air. Wearing her scruffy hiking boots, she wandered along the creek, reflecting on the events of the morning.

Her first unusual experience at Cottonwood Church happened when she was a senior in high school. Like this morning, it had been a spiritual rest stop. A Selah moment.

It had been a warm Saturday in May. The wind whipped whirlwinds of dust around, belying the fact that it was spring. The trunk of the car was filled with groceries. She would spend the rest of the day putting them away, removing a clothesline full of dried sheets, and making supper.

Swigging a can of warm soda, Amber had felt as dry and restless as the day. When Cottonwood Church came into view, she impulsively pulled into the yard. Wandering up the shady church steps, she rattled the front door. It opened easily.

Amber had never been alone in the building before. She was surprised by the hollow sound of her sandals on the wood floor, and the lonely sound of the wind pushing against the west side of the building. A rainbow of colors refracted from the stained-glass windows.

The piano bench felt cool beneath her legs when she sat on it. Striking a few chords, she listened as the sound echoed off the ceiling and walls. She began singing and playing a popular Christian song. Soon, however, her voice trailed off and her hands lay quietly on the keyboard. A sense of majesty swept the room.

Later, when she arrived home, the bucket of ice cream in the trunk had turned to chocolate soup, but she didn't care. Her mind was focused on eternal things. Shortly after that May visit, she was awarded a full-ride scholarship to a private college. She had always believed there was a link between that quiet interlude and the scholarship that arrived soon after.

During college breaks, Amber often stole away to the church en route from grocery shopping. When her family teased her about bringing home melted ice cream, she just smiled mysteriously in response. They didn't need to know about her secret time with God.

Then, last summer she'd been found out when the new pastor wandered in as she sat at the piano lost in praise and worship. Meeting Kelly there that day was a divine appointment if there ever was one.

Amber wandered away from the creek and toward the barn. Once inside, the scent of alfalfa and cattle filled her nose. One of the barn cats came up and rolled at her feet.

"Cally! How are you? Goodness, you had those kittens, didn't you?" Amber bent down to pet the calico cat before following her up the steps to the haymow. There, in a corner under the eaves, was a nest of tiny kittens.

Amber counted six little heads that looked like fuzzy golf balls. "You've outdone yourself, Cally!" she said. The mother cat seemed to smile at her, pleased with the attention.

As Amber was about to go back down the haymow steps, she spied something and cried out. The sun slanted through the round window at the top of the barn, shining on the two-by-four walls. A grimy face, almost hidden from view, gazed at her.

Amber reached out to touch the tattered doll. "You look like Rusty Ann," she whispered, remembering her Ice Cream doll that had been lost many years earlier. "You can't be."

She disentangled the doll from its hiding place and examined it. Although gray with dust, its dress faded and torn, the doll was the right size to be Rusty Ann. Even the yarn hair had a tint of red, like her doll's hair. Amber brushed at the bit of rag.

"You are Rusty Ann! How did you ever get up here?" Amber murmured, as she held her old friend close.

Later, driving through the dusk on her way back to Bismarck, she considered the astonishing events of the weekend. The tattered doll lay on the seat beside her, the engagement ring encircled her ring finger, and peace filled her heart. If she had been crowned princess of the world, she couldn't have been happier. Instead of pushing the gas pedal to the floorboard, she cruised along Highway 83 at the speed limit.

When her cellphone started ringing, she searched her purse with one hand to find it and flip it open.

"Hi, Kelly!"

"Your cell phone works. You must be close to Bismarck?"

"I'm about ten miles out. Just passing Circle C Ranch. How is Sadie? What happened at the board meeting?"

"I took Sadie to the emergency room at Turtle Lake. She was diagnosed with pneumonia and sent home with a bag of medications. Cole is with her, but he has school in the morning. The women from Cross Church are willing to help out."

"Poor Sadie. I hope she has a speedy recovery," Amber said. The elderly woman had enough to handle without a serious illness.

"How did the Cross Church board meeting go?"

"I didn't have any extra prep time since I was at the clinic for so long," Kelly said. He was grateful to talk with Amber, even if she was speeding away from him. "The Cross Church meeting will make history."

"They voted to close?"

Kelly didn't answer. Amber waited for him to continue. She was nearing the new Walmart store. She couldn't fathom why they had built it so far north of Bismarck.

"Kelly, please remember every year they vote on whether to keep Cross Church open. It's been a matter of time."

"The vote was unanimous. All three board members agreed to close the church." Kelly's voice trailed off.

"Heaven knows you've given it your best shot," she sympathized. "Don't feel guilty."

Kelly continued, sounding more upbeat. "The meeting was at Kate Schulte's house and she asked us to stay for dinner. You won't believe what she served."

"Try me," Amber said, a smile already spreading across her face.

"Well, we all knew about the vote and how it would go, so she had Marge roast a goose."

"Goose?" Amber asked, amazed. "That's different."

"Yes. It was symbolic, because the church's goose was cooked."

Amber chuckled.

"We had pickles and stewed prunes, because we were stewing about eliminating the church and in a pickle over it." They both laughed.

"That Kate. What did you have for dessert? Upside down cake?"

"Devil's food cake."

Amber groaned.

"Enough about board business. I want to know what was going on with you during the morning service."

Amber sighed. "Oh, Kelly. I sensed so much love from everyone and for everyone. I'm feeling drawn back to Cottonwood."

"That's wonderful. You are loved and wanted and

needed here. Especially by me. We're going to make a great team."

Amber smiled. "Kelly, this afternoon the strangest thing happened. I don't suppose you remember when we were kids and Ice Cream dolls were popular?"

"Afraid not. Kyle and I were into action figures."

"This afternoon, I went up to the haymow to check out a batch of kittens. Cally had six kittens! Anyway, there was my Ice Cream doll, Rusty Ann, tucked between some boards. I haven't seen her since I was seven or eight."

"That's nice about the kittens. And the doll," Kelly said, obviously wondering where the conversation was headed.

"All I remember about Rusty Ann's disappearance is that I left her outside. I cried when we couldn't find her after a thunderstorm. For some reason, the faith I had as a child is intertwined with Rusty Ann. I don't understand why."

"Maybe it'll come to you."

"Yes, and there's something else. While driving tonight, I've been thinking. Tomorrow I'm going to tell Benson I don't want that new position and I'm not flying to the Twin Cities on Tuesday."

Kelly was quiet for a moment.

Amber pulled into the parking lot of her apartment building and shut the Jeep off.

"Okay, I'm home. I need to go inside. Can we talk some more tomorrow night?"

"Of course. I love you so much."

"And I love you." After a long, sigh-filled goodbye, they hung up.

Before leaving the Jeep, Amber checked for messages. Benson had called a dozen times. In the last message he said, "Call me as soon as you get this." She flipped the phone shut and dropped it in her purse.

Chapter 13
A Reasonable Offer

Amber was at the office for a couple hours the next morning before anyone else arrived. She loved getting through paperwork before the phone began ringing. When she heard Kimberly at the reception desk, she put her computer to sleep and went to see her.

Today, it was impossible not to smile at the very thought of Kelly.

Kimberly looked up. "Whoa, you glow, girl! What happened? Did you win the lottery?"

Amber tilted her head to one side, looking smug. She leaned over the edge of the high front desk and slowly trailed her left hand in front of Kimberly's eyes.

"You could say I won the love lottery."

Kimberly sucked in her breath and grabbed Amber's hand.

"You're engaged. Wow, that's a beautiful diamond."

They chatted for a couple minutes before Kimberly handed over a stack of messages. "These will keep your mind off Kelly," she quipped. "Oh, and Benson wants to see you. pronto."

Amber went back to her office to review the information Benson had given her Wednesday evening. After talking with her mother and Kelly, she knew she was facing the proverbial fork in the road.

"Two roads diverged in a wood, and I—I took the one less traveled by, And that has made all the difference." She quoted Robert Frost from memory. These days, making traditional marriage a priority over career advancement was a road less traveled.

With that in mind, she squared her shoulders and rehearsed what she planned to say. "Benson, you've been a wonderful mentor and I hate to disappoint you, but I'm not interested in pursuing a career change."

"I hope you had a nice break?" he asked a bit sarcastically when she knocked. "I tried to call you to let you know your tickets to Minneapolis came by courier late Friday." He waved an envelope in the air.

Amber felt her cheeks pink up. I'm slipping away from here, slipping right into Kelly's arms, she thought. She eased into her usual chair and opened the envelope. Dismayed, she saw the tickets weren't returnable and that she would be in the Twin Cities for three days instead of just one. Hotel reservations were included, along with a transportation voucher.

"They covered everything," she murmured, before looking directly at him. "Benson, we need to discuss this strategic planning avenue."

"Of course. It's going to be the goose that lines your nest with silver," he said.

Amber stared at Benson for a moment before laughing.

"Benson, if you mean the fairy tale about the goose that laid the golden egg, it didn't end happily for the goose or its owners." Then she shifted back to their original topic.

"You asked about my weekend. Valentine's Day was especially wonderful," she said, holding out her left hand.

Benson's eyes focused on her ring. "What's that? Not an engagement ring! My, my, my," he said. "What is this guy's name again?"

"Kelly Jorgenson."

"Maybe I need to talk with him!"

"No need to have 'the talk.' Apparently, my father already did that," she said dryly.

"Let's see. He's the country preacher," Benson recalled. "So you're going to marry this fellow? Are you sure that's what you want?"

Amber nodded, her golden curls moving with her head.

"Well, then, congratulations. Have you set a date?"

"Not yet." She tried to imagine preparing for a wedding with all that was going on, especially now that the whole church would be invited. Even more reason she needed to keep her current job rather than venture into something new.

"I see. And how will marriage affect your career?"

"That's what we need to discuss. I want to stay in my present position and not have a role in the strategic planning. Maybe someone else can make this trip."

"I don't think you understand." Benson's words were clipped. "I'm depending on you to attend the seminar this week and help me with this new venture."

"I see my life going in a different direction," she said, frankly.

"Amber, most people never get an opportunity like this. I expect you and your country preacher would benefit if your income increases significantly. Also, think about those braces your brothers need and how much you could help your family," he appealed.

Amber gulped. He'd cleverly hit her insecurity buttons. She wanted to marry Kelly and live happily ever after, yet, it would be happier if they weren't worried about money. Besides, she needed to help her family.

"Ever since the September 11 terrorist attack, people are increasingly fearful of what may happen next." Benson leaned across the desk. "My instincts say we haven't seen an end to the chaos. Security is going to be everything in America in the coming days."

Gloom and fear seemed to enter the room. Amber could almost reach out and touch it.

"The insurance industry is being rocked by changes. We can play an important role to help clients feel secure, but we must not leave the future to chance." He thumped his fist on the desk to emphasize his point. "We must think and act strategically. Mammon Global will help us be on the cutting edge."

Amber didn't know what to say.

"I hope you'll be part of developing this plan." His voice had taken on a humble tone. "You're the right person to look at our distribution channels, direction and goals. Career-wise, you'll be set up for the future."

Amber sighed, wondering if he had even heard that she wanted to continue working with her growing list of clients. As if reading her mind, he said, "Listen, you're talking about making a blanket refusal without knowing what this is all about."

Sweat trickled around the collar of her white blouse. Maybe she hadn't reasoned things out. Maybe, it wasn't realistic to marry Kelly and keep her current job.

Benson smiled at her kindly, trying to win her to his way of thinking.

"Let's compromise. Go to this seminar, learn what you can, and then decide."

She hesitated a moment. "Well, I guess it's reasonable to check things out."

"Yes." He nodded emphatically. "It is reasonable."

After the meeting, Amber sat at her desk, her mind replaying their conversation. Perhaps Benson was right. Keeping current in the business and considering new options made sense. Then, with dismay, she remembered the dream where she was carrying her briefcase and cellphone at her wedding.

That's not the way I want my life to be, Lord, she prayed. There had to be a way to balance work, family, a new marriage, and ministry.

Chapter 14
Kelly's Plans Scatter

That afternoon, as Kelly sat working at the computer surrounded by papers and reference books, the shrill sound of the phone startled him. He pushed away from the desk with a jerk, only to have a pile of papers splash across the floor.

Mildred had been draped over his feet snoozing, but now she jumped in alarm, hit the leg of the desk, and then scurried away through his papers, scattering them even more. He walked into the kitchen to answer the harvest gold phone that hung on the wall.

He needed a phone on his desk, he thought crossly. The parsonage had been built in the 1920s when most families had only one phone. While there was one on the second floor, it would be expensive to rewire the house for any additional phones. If only his cell phone worked out here. A rumor continued to circulate that a cell tower was being built nearby. So far, it hadn't happened.

"Good afternoon. This is Pastor Kelly."

"Hi, Kelly." It was his Golden Girl. Kelly relaxed, happiness washing over him.

"Kelly, do you have time to talk?"

"I always have time for you."

Amber enjoyed his flirting. Lowering her voice, she said, "I must have called for a reason, but my logic just flew away like a feather on the wind. That's what happens when I talk with you."

Her words and emotions floated between them like a moisture-laden cloud, warming Kelly's heart. He forgot his frustrations, including the mess of papers on the floor. Proverbs is right, he thought. Gracious words are sweet to the soul.

He smiled. "Oh, Amber Rose—"

"Kelly, I have an update. Remember how I planned to tell Benson I didn't want to make a job change now?"

"Did you tell him this morning?"

"Yes. It didn't go as I hoped. He already had the airline tickets. Nonrefundable. He insisted that going to the seminar was the reasonable thing to do. I leave in the morning."

"But you already decided to not to go to the seminar or accept this new work."

"I don't want to make a career move, yet he is right about one thing. I decided before knowing what it's about."

Kelly sighed. "What about your regular job? Your clients?"

"I don't know."

Kelly should have been happy about Amber's career break, however, he had an uneasy feeling. Finally, he asked the obvious question.

"Amber, I wonder if you take on more work, how will that affect us? We haven't even set a wedding date."

"Oh, Sweetheart, I know," Amber said sympathetically. Kelly could hear pages flip as Amber went through her desk calendar. "Would June 15 work for you?"

Kelly shifted uneasily. He didn't like making decisions about their future by phone. It made him feel uneasy. Plus, what if she took the new job? Maybe they should wait to set a date.

"June fifteenth is the first anniversary of when we met," she said. "Isn't that romantic?"

Kelly nodded numbly, the receiver tight against his ear. Although the word "romantic" normally made his toes tingle, right now, he could not feel a thing.

Over the phone line, he heard the distinct ding as an email arrived on Amber's computer. She received dozens of emails every day. When he'd stopped by her office after their second date, the phone had rung five times in the few minutes he'd been there, while two people waited in the outer office to meet with her.

"You're plenty busy now," he stated. "If you accept this work, won't it get worse? How does this fit with your call to ministry?"

Doesn't he understand, she wondered.

"Kelly, Benson is counting on me. I'll go to the seminar and see what it's all about. I expect to turn down the job, and having more information will help make the decision easier."

Kelly sighed.

"It'll work out. You'll see," she added resolutely.

A strange sound caused Kelly to turn around. Mildred was rummaging in his papers.

"Mildred! Get away from there!"

The cat shrank away from him, and then trotted to the safety of the living room. He had never raised his voice to her, even though she'd caused a basketful of trouble since she strayed into his life

"What is Mildred doing?" Amber inquired.

"Being a cat," Kelly responded. He felt like he did when his shoes were too tight.

"Look, let me know what happens when you get back home tomorrow, okay?"

"I will. But I actually won't be back until late Thursday."

Kelly's shoulders slumped.

"I'll call you tomorrow evening," Amber said. "And Kelly? I want to spend every minute with you. Except, we have to face reality."

"What reality is that?" Kelly asked.

"We can't live on love, Sweetie."

Kelly ran his fingers through his hair again. It would be difficult to have Amber continue in her current position, although he figured they could work things out. However, taking on another work project right when they were getting married? He didn't like the idea. He didn't like it at all.

"Listen, we need some time together. How about if I drive into Bismarck tonight? We can have dinner at that restaurant where we went on our first date."

"I'm sorry, Kelly. Tonight I'll probably work late, and I still need to pack for the trip. I must be at the airport at five in the morning."

"Amber, we've got to do some serious talking and praying."

"Yes, we do," she sighed. "When I get back, we'll sit down and talk about everything. And I'll call tomorrow night."

After he hung up, Kelly got down on his knees and began gathering his scattered papers. His relationship with Amber suddenly seemed complicated.

Mildred studied him from the living room, her tail flicking back and forth. Then she stood, stretched and walked haughtily past him to her food dish

"Big help you are," he said to her retreating backside.

Chapter 15
A Call From Brianna

As usual, Amber arrived home late from work. After eating a bowl of cereal, she emptied her weekender suitcase and began to repack. When her cellphone rang, she hoped it wasn't Benson again. It wasn't.

Without introduction, a voice said, "I just talked with Kelly and found out we're going to be sisters-in-law. I'm so excited! Congratulations and welcome to the family."

Amber paused and held the phone away from her ear. It identified a California area code and Brianna Davis as the caller.

Amber frowned. In her head, she knew there was no romantic spark between Brianna and Kelly. Their bond was based on mutual trauma and grief over Kelly's twin brother. They had both been with Kyle when he was killed two weeks before their high school graduation while at a beach party. The shooter was a kid who had been drinking. Kyle had died in Brianna's arms.

Still, she didn't entirely trust Brianna. Amber's first experience with her last December had been bizarre, and now she was weirdly pretending to be part of the Jorgenson family.

"Hi, Brianna," Amber said cautiously.

"Hi, Amber. Listen, I probably sound as though I'm crazy. Let me start over. I've been hanging out with the Jorgenson family for so long, it's as if they've become my family. I'm happy for Kelly. He adores you and you've got a winner of a guy." A sob escaped.

"Um, Bri? Are you okay?"

She sniffed several times before finding her voice.

"I'll be fine. It's just another way I see time moving on without Kyle. Back in high school, I figured Kyle and I would be married long before Kelly found someone."

Guilty relief filled Amber's heart. Maybe it was time to surrender her worries that Brianna was in love with Kelly.

"I know two things for sure. One, Kelly isn't Kyle. Two, my feelings toward him are all brotherly, not 'loverly.'"

Amber chuckled, sympathy fill her heart.

"Bri, I hardly know you, although if you feel like part of the Jorgenson family, then I'm happy to claim you as a sister-in-law. I've always wanted a sister."

"That's the nicest thing you could say. Do you remember asking me to be your roommate if I ever decided to move to North Dakota?"

That wasn't how Amber remembered it. She'd invited Brianna to be her roommate because she was in the Denver airport on her way to North Dakota with a plan to move in with Kelly. In order to prevent the scandal that would have occurred, Amber invited her to live with her in Bismarck.

Still, always tenderhearted, Amber's invitation had been sincere. She would have welcomed Brianna because she was Kelly's friend and needed help.

"I remember," Amber said. "Are you still thinking of giving up your life in San Francisco?" Brianna's career as an interior designer was flourishing.

"I guess not," Brianna said, sounding dejected. "When I visited last year, at first I didn't appreciate the wide-open spaces. I'm used to life in the city. Still, I learned to like living there in the land of cows and corn. I put a sunflower in every design I do now!"

"That's surprising."

"It's so peaceful there."

"It is?" The words escaped her lips before Amber could stop them. There wasn't much peace in her own life. The pressure only lifted when she spent time praying. And when she was with Kelly. How she needed Kelly.

"Amber?"

"I'm here. I was thinking about the meaning of peace. Living in a quiet place doesn't guarantee life will be peaceful."

"Something like you can live in a crowded city and still be lonely," said Brianna. "That's how I feel."

"Oh, Bri."

"Even after Kyle died, I had my parents and Kelly. Now that I live in San Francisco, I don't know many people."

Amber curled up on the couch, listening.

"Jontel is my best friend here, but he has another life and it doesn't include me. Did you know my parents put their house up for sale and moved overseas?"

"I'm sorry you're having a hard time," Amber said. Then she had an idea. "We haven't begun planning our wedding. When we do, can I bounce ideas off you? Like sisters?"

"I'd love that." Brianna's voice sounded more cheerful. "Well, it's time to lock up the office for the day. Call me when you begin making wedding plans."

Afterward, reflections roamed through Amber's brain. Brianna was lonely and wanted a friend. The girls in the youth group needed encouragement and a listening ear. As a pastor's wife, she would need to be available to serve together with him. This was in addition to her career and her parents' and brothers' needs.

Yet, even now she often rushed through her weeks with barely enough spiritual fuel to see herself through. How could she pour hope, peace, love, or joy into someone else's life when her own tank hovered near empty?

Then she remembered a verse from Romans that she had memorized as a child.

"May the God of hope fill you with all joy and peace as you trust in him, so that you may overflow with hope by the power of the Holy Spirit," she said aloud. "Oh, Father in heaven, I can't possibly do this without your power. Please fill me up."

Chapter 16
The Interview

A mber parked her Jeep at the Bismarck Airport before dawn on Tuesday morning and dragged her suitcase toward the terminal. The parking lot was a bumpy mass of ice that had frozen and thawed a dozen times in the last few months.

Flying into the Twin Cities this morning and returning by late evening would have been simple. Staying three nights required more preparation. She'd asked Kimberly for advice. The administrative assistant looked up from the filing cabinet where she deftly sorted a set of folders with very long, blue fingernails.

"I was planning to wear my navy suit and to be back here in time to sleep in my own bed," Amber moaned, holding up her tickets. "Any advice about what to pack?"

Kimberly turned, revealing her large hoop earrings. "Better take something to wear in the evening. Mammon Global may want to wine and dine you."

Amber wrinkled her nose. "I don't even have evening clothes. Before Kelly, I had no social life. When we do something together, I usually wear a sweater and jeans."

"I know. It's not your cup of tea, but you need to roll with it. You must have a dressy top and pants somewhere in your closet."

Amber sighed. "Yeah, I guess."

Kimberly sat down and propped her chin on her hand. "You don't have to guzzle martinis or stay out until two in the morning, you know. Order some sparkling water, and when you're ready to leave, simply say you need to make some phone calls."

"And that would be the truth," Amber said, grateful for her friend's social savvy. "I'll give a full report when I get back."

"It's a deal. I'll bring carrot sticks and meet you in the break room on Friday afternoon."

They laughed. Neither of them ever succeeded at dieting. A trip to the break room usually meant one of them had brought donuts or cupcakes.

Amber took a cab from the airport to the Mammon Global office, which was located along the I-494 corridor. On the way, she enjoyed viewing the office buildings and shopping areas, however, the housing developments hidden behind concrete barriers made her feel claustrophobic.

While getting out of the cab, she stared up at the glass and steel building. Impressive. If this was Mammon Global's regional office, what did the headquarters in Belgium look like?

Once inside, she was unexpectedly ushered to the office of Slate Nadoff, the manager in charge of education and training. Amber wondered why she hadn't been pointed toward a meeting room. She had attended seminars before and never once had they begun with a meeting with the person in charge.

A receptionist opened the double doors for her. Amber entered a spacious room with a tiled floor and sleek chrome and black furniture. Slate Nadoff sat in the center of the room at the largest desk she'd ever seen. Amber couldn't help staring at him. He was easily the most handsome man she had ever met. Outside of Kelly, of course, but Kelly was cute-handsome.

This guy was GQ-cover handsome. He had a strong chin and smoky eyes. A curl spilled over his tanned forehead, and, judging by the sheen of the fabric, his suit was expensive. She judged him to be about thirty-five. She felt out of her element wearing a suit she'd purchased at a discount store.

"Ms. McLean, may I call you Amber?" He walked around his desk and offered his hand. She was surprised to see that his fingernails were professionally manicured, and quickly curled her hands so he wouldn't see her nails. She'd given them a quick coat of polish late last night.

"Sure," she said, sounding decidedly North Dakotan.

"You must call me Slate." Still holding her hand, he smiled into her eyes. Finally, he released her hand and gestured toward a suede chair across from his desk.

Amber sat down primly and crossed her legs at the ankle. She felt like a country mouse visiting the city. Of course, I am a country mouse, she thought, amused to find herself in this position. She certainly wasn't qualified to represent Gates Insurance at this seminar. Why hadn't Benson attended?

"Coffee?"

"No, thank you." Her airport breakfast had included enough caffeine to launch a rocket.

"Then, let me explain the agenda before we walk over to the meeting room." Sitting in his high-backed chair, he looked like Caesar. I bet he doesn't do his own typing, Amber thought.

"Mammon Global was profoundly affected by the terrorist attacks last September 11." He looked into her eyes. Again, Amber found it impossible to look away. He definitely had magnetism.

"Our board of directors believes that security will continue to be top priority in the future There is a domino effect at work. The terror of September 11th has spread. The stock market is shaky. Many jobs have been lost." He spoke calmly, his facial expression grave.

"Insurance companies hold the key to helping people in this five-state region to feel secure again. We plan to assist companies in developing strategic business plans."

Amber knew all of this. She nodded and remained silent. He continued to study her so carefully that she wondered if she looked okay. Had she smeared lip-gloss onto her face? Spilled coffee on her blouse? More likely, her hair had frizzed up again. She patted her head.

"Pardon me. I don't mean to make you feel uncomfortable," he said suddenly. "I requested a meeting with you, because I am looking for a liaison to work with clients in the region. Your skill set and education match what we are seeking."

"Me? How do you know that?"

He smiled broadly. "I have seen your resume. Perhaps we can talk about the position later, after you learn more about Mammon Global? I will personally give you a tour of our offices."

"Okay," she said, flattered but uncertain. How had he gotten a copy of her resume?

"The position will be opening this spring. It'll be a great opportunity for whomever is selected. Being on the ground floor of this new venture has many benefits," Slate said, his eyes meeting hers again. "Your starting salary would mean a substantial increase."

For a moment, a different life flashed through Amber's mind. She saw herself dressed in a finely tailored outfit, while stepping out of a red Jaguar in front of her trendy loft apartment. Under other circumstances, she might be tempted to work for Mammon Global.

"You've given me something to think about," she stammered politely.

"We can discuss this later," he said, his perfect white teeth highlighted by his tan. Imagine, Amber thought, having a tan in February. He probably has a vacation home in Mexico.

"By the way, on the first evening of the seminar, we take everyone out for dinner. I hope you will join us tonight."

Amber nodded. She knew exactly how Alice felt when she slipped through the rabbit hole into another world.

Chapter 17
A Day at Mammon Global

Amber spent the next several hours taking copious notes at the seminar. The twelfth-floor meeting room had a magnificent view. Five agencies were represented. She was the only person from North Dakota. Lunch was served in a rooftop restaurant with a glass ceiling. She was surprised that the sky was as blue in Minnesota as it was at Cottonwood Creek.

During the afternoon break, Slate singled her out. As they strolled through the halls, Amber admired the modern architecture and beautiful artwork on the walls.

"Here is our last stop," he said as he opened a door. "This office is reserved for the person who takes the liaison position."

The roomy office had new furnishings and a lovely view. Amber couldn't help comparing it to her office in Bismarck, which had a small window looking out on the railroad tracks. When a train rumbled by, she had to raise her voice to be heard on the phone. Her desk looked like something issued by the government thirty years ago, and the black metal cabinets lining the walls bulged with files.

Amber arrived at her hotel late in the afternoon and saw it had a five-star rating. Her room was a king suite, that included a soft bathrobe, huge fluffy towels, and a basket of snacks. The contrast between the well-appointed room and her Spartan apartment caused her to tell herself, "Don't get used to this!"

After unpacking her suitcase and shaking out her evening clothes, she took out her Rusty Ann doll out and hugged her. Time spins by so quickly, she reflected.

"Thank you for traveling with me," she told the doll. "I can use a friend to talk to. Do you realize it's only been five days since Kelly proposed?" She hadn't spent much time enjoying her new status as an engaged woman before being thrown headlong into this work situation.

Opening her flip phone, she dialed the parsonage and got the answering machine. When she called the church, the phone rang and rang. Giving up, she began to get ready for the evening. Slate was picking her up for dinner in half an hour.

After slipping into a long green sweater that complemented her eyes and hair, Amber looked into the mirror and moaned.

"Oh, Amber, this sweater really exposes your curves. You need to cut back on the muffins," she told her image. Then she slipped on her black flats, sucked in her stomach, and rushed out the door.

Slate stood waiting near the hotel concierge. He arched his eyebrow approvingly as she walked up. When he opened the door of his white Lamborghini, she slipped into the heated leather seat like Cinderella getting into the carriage.

At the restaurant, the congenial group met in a lounge as they waited for their table. Jazz played in the background and glassware and bottles gleamed against a dark mahogany bar. The unfamiliar odor of alcohol permeated the dimly lit room. When Amber ordered a pricey bottle of water, Slate made her feel at ease when he called it "haute couture."

Amber noted that she was the only woman in their party who hadn't worn black. Still, she enjoyed visiting with the others and appreciated Slate's attentiveness.

After three rounds of drinks, the noisy party moved to the dining room. A long candlelit table dressed in white linen was set for them in the corner of the elegant room.

Amber was seated across from a couple from Iowa. The insurance company that Ted and Felicia Rogers owned sounded similar to Gates Insurance Agency. It made Amber appreciate Benson's trust in her to represent their agency, although she wondered again why he hadn't come himself.

Picking up the large menu, she realized lunch was a distant memory and she was starved. Her eyebrows crinkled. She wasn't sure how to pronounce some of the menu items, and the prices weren't listed. She smiled as she remembered her first date with Kelly, when she had introduced him to buffalo burgers at a rural diner. This was certainly a different world.

"A penny for your thoughts."

She was startled by Slate's voice near her ear. His breath smelled like apple cider gone bad.

"I'm wondering what to order. What do you suggest?"

"Oh, I have suggestions," Slate breathed. His arm slid across the back of her chair.

I don't think he's talking about the menu, she thought as she leaned away.

He continued as though he hadn't noticed.

"I always suggest the baked sole. However, if you're struggling to decide, have the flounder. If you feel as though you're swimming upstream, order the salmon." His voice was intimate, as if he was telling her something private.

"Oh, aren't you witty?" she said, trying to ignore his overbearing manner, "I think I'll have the walleye. Did you know that it's the Minnesota state fish?"

The salad course began, and the group worked through plates of mesclun salad and crusty artisan rolls. Amber found the walleye much to her liking.

As she ate, Amber's mind began to drift. This setting was so sophisticated compared to life at Cottonwood

Creek. Had anyone here ever heard a meadowlark sing from a fence post? Watched baby calves frolic across a pasture? Sat in a church in the presence of the Lord, as she had just last Sunday?

She looked up to find Felicia Rogers smiling at her.

"Guess I was dreaming," Amber confessed. "This is much different than my life in North Dakota."

"For us, too," Felicia said. "We go out with clients and host a Christmas brunch at the office, but otherwise we're more family oriented. We go camping in the summer and cross-country skiing in the winter."

"Tell me about your family."

"We have two teenage daughters. They're with us, swimming at the hotel right now. There's a school break so we're making it a family vacation." Felicia's pride in her daughters was obvious.

"How about you? I see a flashy ring on your finger."

Amber beamed. "We just became engaged on Valentine's Day."

Felicia's eyes darted to Slate, who was busy ordering another drink.

Does she think I'm engaged to Slate? Amber wondered. Alarmed, she realized when he offered her a ride to the restaurant, she hadn't read anything into it. Yet, throughout the evening he'd become progressively more attentive. Now, Felicia had misread their relationship.

"I'm engaged to Kelly Jorgenson. He's the pastor of my home church at Cottonwood Creek. That's about seventy miles north of Bismarck."

Slate turned and smiled fondly at her. Head propped on his hand, he said, "You know, marriage is going out of style. It's boring and unromantic." His smoky eyes locked with hers.

"Marriage isn't out of style where I come from," she softly countered.

"It should be." Slate leaned closer, his eyes straying to her sweater. "Amber, you're way too hot to be hooked up with some country Bible-thumper."

Now, Amber's eyes were smoking, too.

"I beg your pardon?"

At the other end of the table, a veteran jokester had those around him hooting with laughter. However, those nearby were glued to the conversation between Slate and Amber.

"My dear, you're smart and gorgeous," His face was just inches from hers. "And I find your innocence very attractive," Slate said, gravely, though his words slurred. His arm wrapped around her shoulders as he attempted to hug her.

"For your information, what you call Bible-thumping, I call faith in God. I also believe in good manners. You should look into both," she said, tugging at the front of her sweater.

"You're even more interesting when you get excited," he said with a burp.

At that, Felicia stood up.

"We need to get back to the hotel. Would you like to ride with us?"

Amber nodded, grateful for a way out.

"Oh, please stay while we share a dessert wine and a last toast," Slate said, taking her left hand and crushing her engagement ring into her finger. "I'll see that you arrive safely back at your hotel."

Amber gave him a withering look and pulled her hand from his.

"Tomorrow, then," he said, as she stood up. He held his glass up to her, seeming clueless to how offensive he had become.

While Ted hurried to get their car, Felicia linked arms with Amber and they strolled out.

"He's had way too much to drink," Felicia whispered. "You handled him very gracefully."

Once safely in the car, Amber blurted out, "He's the biggest creep I've ever met. I don't think I can go back to the seminar tomorrow."

"I don't blame you," Felicia soothed. "Slate was awful tonight, but I'd hate to see you miss the seminar because of his behavior."

"The presenters are good," Amber admitted. "I just don't want to see Slate Nadoff."

"That's understandable, although the problem is his, not yours. Why don't you wait and see how tomorrow goes? Ted and I will be there for you."

"I noticed that he talked with you quite a bit today," Ted chimed in from behind the steering wheel. "You know you're considered to be a rising star in the industry."

"Why would you say that?" Amber asked, stunned.

"We see the numbers. You're doing great. Nadoff probably thinks you won't stay in a small market like North Dakota. I wouldn't be surprised if he makes you a job offer."

He did make me a job offer, she thought. Now, I know there would be strings attached.

They pulled into the hotel parking lot and Ted let the car idle as he talked.

"If anyone treated my wife or daughters like that, I'd be tempted to take him out ice fishing in the middle of the lake and use him for bait. I can do that for you, too, Amber."

"Ted!" Felicia cried, but his surprising comment broke the misery of the moment. Both women began laughing. "With Amber's Bible-thumping comment and your fishy idea, you two should form a comedy team."

"We could call ourselves Insured Laughs and be the featured comedy team at insurance conventions," Ted quipped.

Felicia shook her head in disbelief.

"Listen, I think you should document and report how Slate treated you."

"Oh, I could never tell anyone what he said and did. Not even Benson or Kelly. Please promise me you won't say anything?"

"Listen, honey, why don't you get some rest? We'll be praying for you. Let's meet for breakfast before we go over to the seminar."

"It's a deal," Amber said. "Thank you so much."

Chapter 18

Love Talk

Once back in her hotel room, Amber made a beeline for the shower. She stood under the cleansing flow, until she could no longer feel Slate Nadoff's arm around her or smell his breath.

She was grateful Felicia and Ted had stepped in to provide a way of escape from his advances. Their wisdom and humor had helped steady her.

Later, comfortable in her sweats and parked on her bed, she knew it was time to call Kelly. What would she tell him? About the conference? The job offer? Slate? If Ted Rogers wanted to make fish bait out of Slate, what would Kelly do if he knew Slate was hitting on her? No, it was better not to say anything.

Amber picked up Rusty Ann and stroked her hair. She had done her best to clean up the doll, who still had the bedraggled look of something that had spent over a decade in a barn.

"Rusty Ann, let me tell you, that barn isn't the worst place you could spend time. The rest of the world may be showy on the outside, but it stinks on the inside. They can treat you special one minute and act like they own you the next."

Holding the doll in the crook of her arm, she punched Kelly's number into the phone. He answered immediately.

"Hi."

"Amber Rose!" Kelly sounded so happy to hear from her.

"Have I ever told you how much I love you?"

"Why, I'm not sure. How much do you love me?"

"The sky and the moon and every high-rise in this city couldn't contain all of my love for you," Amber whispered.

"I like it when you talk that way. I love you back all

of that and more," he said, wondering why there were desperate notes in her voice. "Tell me about your day, Sweetheart."

"Mammon Global is impressive. I made a couple of friends from Iowa. The food at the restaurant was wonderful and expensive. My hotel room is deluxe. Deluxe. King-sized bed and every amenity you can imagine. Too bad I don't have anyone to share it with."

Immediately she wished she wouldn't have said that because an image of Slate Nadoff popped into her head. It made her wonder if everyone attending the seminar had rooms this nice or if she was receiving "special" treatment.

She sighed. "I mean, if I can't share it with you, I don't want anything fancy. I'd rather eat a buffalo burger with you than have that priceless walleye any day. All of these things are like a clanging bell without your love. Kelly, I really mean that."

"You're rambling. Is everything okay?"

Amber wiped tears from her face. "Yes, everything is fine. Just being away from you makes me realize what a cool guy you are and how lucky I am that we found each other. I can't wait until we are married and can be together more."

"Maybe you better start at the beginning and tell me about your day."

Amber took a deep breath as she chose what to tell him. Then she launched into a detailed story about the plane trip, the Mammon Global building, and how the seminar could help small agencies. As she talked, she finally relaxed.

Finally, she told him about her earlier conversation with Slate. "Here's something surprising. Slate Nadoff, who is in charge of this whole strategic planning enterprise, said they're going to have a job opening. He thinks I'd be well suited for it. I found it ironic, since I didn't even want to attend the seminar."

"Are you serious? A job in the Twin Cities? How did that come up?"

"I don't know," she said vaguely. "He offered to show me around during a break. Part of the tour included a peek into the office reserved for the new person, and he said the job will open in the spring. Great pay."

"Say, is this guy good looking?"

Amber remembered with revulsion how she thought Slate was handsome in the beginning. How superficial, she thought.

"Some people would consider him handsome."

"And you?"

"I only have eyes for a certain pastor with blonde hair, blue eyes, and the initials KJ."

"I'm flattered, and I only have eyes for you, too, sweet Amber," Kelly replied. "However, I have to ask. Would you want to move to the cities to work for Mammon?"

"I would never work for that company!" Amber shuddered at the thought of working with Slate. "No way."

Again, Kelly's radar went up. "I thought Mammon Global was a good company?"

Amber realized she'd said too much. "What I mean is, I wouldn't want to live here under any circumstance. My family and my life are at Cottonwood Creek. Can you imagine a thousand-mile round trip on the weekends?"

"Your quality of life would take a dive," Kelly helpfully pointed out.

"No more walks along Cottonwood Creek," she rejoined.

"No more romantic evenings by the fire."

"No more discovering barn kittens."

"No more brownies," he said sadly.

She smiled. "So there, that settles it. No job with Mammon Global."

Chapter 19
Little Flower of Lent

Early the next morning, Kelly pondered the phone call from Amber. Something was going on with her. Although he sponged up her loving words, he recognized a shade of desperation in her voice. An over-zealousness. He hoped to find out what was going on when she arrived home and they could talk face-to-face.

"Amber Rose, Amber Rose," Kelly murmured as he hiked the well-worn path from the parsonage to Cottonwood Church. He noted that even the golden sunrise hued in pink seemed to speak her name. No wonder people write poetry when they're in love, he thought.

He was delivering materials for the evening's Lenten service, but paused on the footbridge that linked the parsonage and the church. Nature had surprised everyone with a mild February. The sun had been at work all week, shrinking snowbanks and creating rivulets of water. Water now pooled on top of the frozen creek bed on which he'd recently skied. Winter was losing its grip.

Then, Kelly spied a bit of color peeking out from under the snow out in the churchyard. Curious, he made his way over to it and knelt in the dirt-speckled snow to take a closer look.

He had begun his first winter in North Dakota with a bring-it-on attitude. That was before the first winter storm stranded him overnight in a café with Linda Jackson, whom he rescued along the icy highway.

From then on, he checked the weather more often. Still, he enjoyed the first month or so of winter. He really did. He'd even naively gone ice fishing with Tiny Winger. He was still embarrassed that he'd panicked when Tiny boldly maneuvered his pickup onto the frozen lake.

Kelly had clung to the pickup's door handle, sure they'd plunge to their icy deaths. He gingerly got out and learned how to use an ice auger and drop a fishing line down. He had doubted that anything could live under several feet of ice, but they'd caught enough fish to fry up a good supper and put a couple packages in the freezer.

In January, the thermometer dropped well below zero and stayed there. A couple feet of snow covered his yard, with a mountain range forming along the driveway where he pitched the white stuff after each storm. The churchyard was another matter. It required a full-size tractor to keep the parking area clean.

He began to wonder how long the cold could last. The seasoned local people weren't encouraging. They enjoyed telling horror stories about the winter of 1966 or 1977 or 1997. His parents didn't help, either. They loved to chat about how well the orange trees in their backyard were doing in sunny Southern California.

Kelly surfed the Internet looking for scientific reports that a new ice age had begun. He vowed he would never complain about mowing next summer's tall green grass.

Now, admiring the little flower poking through the snow, he exclaimed, "Look at this!" If only Amber were there to share the sight of spring's first flower. His heart swelled as he considered the tenacity it took to push out of the frozen earth.

"Little flower, I think you might be the subject of a sermon on perseverance."

Perhaps the best part of being a new Christian was seeing the world with fresh eyes. He hadn't attended church as he grew up. Until he became a believer, Easter had meant a bunny delivered baskets of candy, and his family went out for a nice brunch at a local restaurant.

However, as he discovered more about the meaning and power of the resurrection of Christ, the Easter season became his favorite. A classmate had even teased him about celebrating Easter with the enthusiasm many people reserved for the Super Bowl.

Now, having lived through several months of winter on the cold dark prairie, he began to grasp how nature demonstrated the victory of Jesus's resurrection over death. Winter might have been long and bleak, but it didn't make spring any less certain. We humans can feel bleakness in our souls, yet that doesn't make God or his transforming power any less real, Kelly thought.

When he arrived at the church, he stamped the snow off his boots and proceeded to lay out materials he'd prepared for the Lenten service. As he checked the classrooms and the sanctuary, many ideas for celebrating Easter filled his mind. He could only implement a few of them this year.

The hallowedness of the sanctuary offered an inviting retreat from the rest of the world. He dropped into one of the seats to think and pray. First, he confided his hopes, fears, and concerns about Amber, releasing her into God's capable hands.

Next, he sadly considered the end of Cross Church. He'd been hired to serve the little Schulteville church, as well as the Cottonwood parish. While Cottonwood flourished, all of his efforts to boost Cross Church had failed. He'd been the pastor less than a year, and now the church was shutting its doors for good.

"Lord, why did this have to happen on my watch?" The board had seemed grave when they met on Sunday, however, after they made the decision, relief filled the room. They were ready to move on. Only he had viewed it as a personal failure.

Kelly was familiar with the story of Cross Church. Kate Schulte and her brother, Ted, had worked many years to keep the church open, even as the congregation shrank like the rest of the rural population. He knew many prairie churches were closing. He knew that these days people could easily drive a few extra miles to another church. He understood all of this, but it didn't make the knife slice through his heart any cleaner.

Lent, Kelly thought, is the season of grief and reflection. It was fitting that the last service at Cross Church would take place on Good Friday. Perhaps no other day in history had seemed as devoid of hope. A day when a man hailed as the Messiah was tried before dawn, then forced to drag his cross through crowds of jeering people. His final humility came as he died on a cross between two thieves. Little Cross Church would also pass away on Good Friday.

Later, walking back across the wide churchyard toward the footbridge, he recalled seeing abandoned churches, pigeons flying in and out of their steeples. He'd seen churches turned into museums and bars. He prayed that the building that housed Cross Church would continue to have a God-given purpose. At this point, it looked as unlikely as...he stopped in his tracks.

Scanning the yard, he tried to find the little purple flower. Instead, he found a dozen poking their heads through the snow. A good ending for Cross Church looked as unlikely as a delicate flower pushing through the snow. Or Amber accepting his proposal. Or Jesus being alive after the crucifixion.

Maybe buildings, like humans, could have second chances, he thought. A spark of hope filled his soul. As he strode across the footbridge, Kelly's steps grew lighter.

Chapter 20

Roller Coasters
and Role Models

Amber awoke early the next morning to spend time in prayer. When she finished, she felt the strength of her blessings: Kelly, family, friends, a good job, education, opportunity. God had been so good to her. She felt encouraged to take a step of faith and let go of the anger and frustration from the evening before.

"I choose to forgive Slate Nadoff," she resolved. If she let her feelings rule, she'd never forgive him. By choosing to say the words aloud, she was giving God permission to work in her heart.

At the hotel breakfast buffet, she picked out some fruit, yogurt, and pastry. Savoring a bite of apple fritter, she decided the hotel's bakery helped it earn a five-star rating.

"You're looking radiant this morning," Felicia said when she and Ted arrived a few minutes later.

"It's the fritter. You should try one." As soon as the couple went to get their food, Amber felt guilty. The fritter was good, but hardly the reason she was in a good mood.

After they brought their breakfast trays to the table, they bowed in silent prayer. Amber was smiling when they looked up.

"I must confess, I'm not in a good mood just because the fritter was delicious. It's because God is putting peace in my heart."

"I'm relieved to hear that," Felicia said, patting her hand. "We were worried about you."

"I don't want to minimize how Slate acted last night, yet I don't want to make too much of it either."

"That's a smart idea. I'm curious to see how Slate acts in the meetings today. Don't forget, we'll be with you and we know how he acted last night."

When they invited Amber to join their family for a trip to the Mall of America that evening, she responded, "You don't have to ask me twice!" It would give her time with her new friends and a chance to check out the mall. Neither did it hurt to have plans in case Slate approached her. She didn't need to worry about him, though. He was seldom in the sessions.

"I bet he has a hangover and a few regrets," Felicia observed.

Late in the afternoon, they met in front of the hotel. Ted introduced Amber to Molly and Holly, their teenage daughters.

"Such pretty names," Amber commented as she slipped into the car next to the girls.

"I like my name a lot better than the one Dad picked out for me," Molly said.

From the driver's seat, Ted protested. "Hey, there's nothing wrong with the name Jolly. Jolly Rogers has a nice ring to it."

"Dad! Jolly Rogers was a flag on a pirate ship. Is that a nice name for your daughter?"

"Can't figure why everyone objects to that name," Ted mumbled as he shook his head.

"Naming Molly 'Jolly' would be folly." Holly quipped. Then she turned to Amber and informed her, "Molly is a Gaelic form of Mary, who was the mother of Jesus, so that's pretty cool. Holly is an evergreen plant that we use at Christmas because it reminds us of eternal life."

Amber smiled. Holly was a walking fact file. She sat between them on the way to the mall. By the time they arrived, the girls had convinced her to ride the roller coaster with them.

Once they were at the mall, the girls hung on to Amber, until Felicia convinced them to find a special store they'd seen advertised. Ted headed for a bookstore.

Amber and Felicia strolled around gawking at the store displays. However, both women were more interested in getting to know each other than in shopping.

"You have a way with teens," Felicia said. "I couldn't believe how the girls opened up to you so quickly."

Amber frowned. They were almost the same words used to describe what had happened with Kelly's youth group a few days earlier.

Felicia studied Amber's serious look and wondered what was troubling her. "You don't have to go on the roller coaster," she ventured.

Amber smiled and shook her head. "I don't mind joining them. It's just that I'm not around teenage girls much, and it surprises me that we get along so well. Holly and Molly remind me of the girls in the youth group back home. The world is just opening up to them."

"That's what concerns me," Felicia said with a chuckle. "We hope we've given the girls the tools to make wise choices. And we're thankful when they find good role models, like you, to inspire them."

"I feel that way about my four younger brothers. They really like Kelly. A lot of the teens at Cottonwood Creek admire him. It's not something the church considered when they hired him as the pastor right out of college."

"It's interesting how God opens doors. Sounds like you and Kelly have a special call."

A call, Amber thought. Something else I hear over and over.

Eventually, they gathered at the food court, and then made their way to Camp Snoopy.

Amber rode the roller coaster with Molly and Holly. She found the upward climb boring, but within a few minutes they were pivoting at the top of the Ripsaw.

"Yieeeee!" she screamed as they bumped over the track and ground around the corners. The ride was thrilling, frightening, sometimes rough, and the water feature terrified her.

That's life, she thought as she stepped off feeling shaky, yet smiling broadly. Some people think life is a test. It's really a roller coaster ride, she decided. It wasn't about having the grit to do it all, or being able to control the future. It was about being in the place God has for you and trusting Him to bring you through life's hazards.

The girls walked on either side of her as they wandered through the theme park and stopped to make some purchases at the Lego store. Along with the girls, Amber was also drawn to Felicia, a strong woman who confidently navigated her roles as a wife, mother, faithful Christian, and CEO of Rogers Insurance.

It made Amber all the more eager to begin her married life with Kelly. If Felicia could handle all of her roles, Amber decided, she could as well.

Chapter 21
Muffins in the Morning

Slate kept his distance for the remainder of the seminar.

"He knows he made a fool of himself," Felicia told Amber the final day of the conference.

"Or he doesn't remember what he did," Amber countered, as they sat together at lunch.

Either way, she was relieved, and too busy to think about his drunken advances. During every break, she returned phone calls from clients or from Benson. Other attendees were on their BlackBerry phones. Eyeing them, she realized it wouldn't hurt to invest in the new technology so she could also check emails.

Her plane landed in Bismarck late Thursday afternoon.

Thursday, she thought. That means Kelly proposed a whole week ago. Somehow, it seemed like another lifetime instead of a few days.

After stopping at a supermarket to buy treats for the office, Amber staggered through the office doors. She was loaded down with her briefcase, purse, seminar materials, and a large box of fudgesicles that the whole office could share.

"So much for the carrot sticks," Kimberly mumbled as she grabbed a chocolate treat for herself. "How was the seminar? Did you get to wear your evening outfit?"

A shadow crossed Amber's face. "I did. And I took your advice. I ordered designer water and left early. You were a big help." Someday she might tell Kimberly about the embarrassing ordeal. Maybe they'd have a good laugh. However, the incident still stung and she wasn't ready to talk about it.

Amber met with Benson for an hour before tackling her emails. It was almost seven o' clock when Kelly called.

"Amber Rose, you made it back to Bismarck."

"I did. I'm halfway through the emails that were waiting for me. I'm only reading the ones marked urgent. The rest can wait until tomorrow."

"I hoped to meet you in Bismarck for dinner tonight, though I'm running late. Have you eaten? I could be there in an hour."

"Sounds wonderful, but how are the roads? It's snowing here."

"Yeah, the roads are a little dicey. That might slow me down, but it won't stop me."

Amber pulled up the weather radar on her computer. "There's a snow squall coming through the state. Maybe we better wait until tomorrow night."

"Can't do it tomorrow. I'm chaperoning a bus going to the basketball playoffs. Do you want to join us? The bus leaves at five."

"Not going to happen. I have clients coming in late tomorrow afternoon. I won't leave for Cottonwood Creek until in the evening."

"Well then, see you Saturday night?"

"Counting the seconds until then. I love you. Tell the youth group girls I miss them."

Saturday morning, Kelly had just come downstairs when a vehicle ground to a stop near the house. Mildred rose and trotted to the kitchen to investigate.

Soon someone swished through the back door and pounded up the steps into the house. As Amber popped into the kitchen, Mildred meowed and danced at her feet like a dog. Amber scooped her up, rubbing her head to the tune of cat purrs.

"Amber! Honey, am I glad to see you!" Kelly said in complete surprise. As he rushed toward her, Mildred scrambled to escape being crushed in the coming embrace.

With her voice muffled against his chest, she told him, "I couldn't wait until tonight. All week I needed this hug. Plus, we have so much to talk about."

Kelly kissed her, his true love, his Golden Girl.

"You smell like a muffin," he said, still holding her close.

"I couldn't sleep, so I got up early and made blueberry muffins," she answered. "And managed to save a couple from my brothers." She dangled a paper bag in one hand.

He brought out a jug of milk. They settled into the breakfast nook and shared a prayer. Amber savored the peace of Kelly's warm kitchen and the way he tenderly held her hand as he thanked God for her safe trip and for the food.

"This week I felt we were being pulled apart, and yet here you are," Kelly said, looking up. "I'm so glad you came over this morning."

Amber lifted a muffin, broke it in two, and gave half to Kelly. He poured the milk into two glasses advertising Your Friendly Co-op. The air between them felt charged.

"I don't understand how something as ordinary as sharing a muffin can feel so intimate when we're together," Amber confessed.

For a moment, she was sure he would lean forward and kiss her. Instead, he settled in his seat and said, "I've been worried about you. What's going on?"

Amber's hands encircled the glass in front of her.

"Hard to believe all of this started a little over a week ago. That's when Benson asked me to report to his office. I considered slipping out of the office without seeing him, but I didn't."

Mildred jumped up onto the bench next to Amber, rubbed against her, and lay down.

"He was excited about a new strategic business planning process and wanted me to be a part of it. Kelly, I didn't know at the time why he didn't go to the seminar himself."

"Then, you proposed the next day." She waved her hand in the air. "Everyone oohs and ahhs over my ring." Kelly reached for her hand, kissed it, and held it securely in his.

"Last weekend was wonderful when we just focused on us. However, this weekend, we need to talk about work."

Kelly nodded. "When we talked, you planned to tell Benson you didn't want to go on the trip or have anything to do with the new project."

"And I meant it!"

"I was shocked when you called Monday and said you were flying out the next morning."

Amber sighed. "He already had the airline tickets and he convinced me I shouldn't make up my mind without attending the seminar. Once there, I noticed that everyone else was the CEO or owned their agency. Also, at least two people represented each agency. I was the lone employee at the seminar.

"Although I was flattered by the trust he placed in me, I was baffled by why he sent me instead of going himself. Then, yesterday I found out."

Kelly tilted his head, waiting to hear the reason.

"He's been waiting for the results from medical tests. He has an aggressive form of cancer. It must be treated immediately."

"Wow! I'm sorry to hear that."

"He hopes to be in the office part-time, but he's already farmed out many of his duties to the other agents and employees. He gave me the strategic planning portfolio."

"And you didn't know about his medical problems until yesterday?"

"I had no idea." It made her feel sad to think of what Benson faced.

"I need some coffee," Amber said, distracting herself before she became emotional. Setting Mildred's relaxed body aside, she scooted out of the breakfast nook.

"What will you be doing with the strategic planning?"

"A lot of work," she sighed. "First there will be meetings with staff. Later, a consultant from Mammon will come in to spend a few days with us. I hope Benson is up for that part of it. After that, they'll develop a strategic business plan tailored for Gates Insurance. Then we must decide whether or not to implement it."

"Sounds like a long process."

"It'll take months."

Kelly groaned. "If you're involved in that, how are you going to handle your accounts?"

"I've been thinking about that. You know, many of them live between Bismarck and Cottonwood Creek. They're like family and I don't want to let them down." She sighed.

"So, I'll work longer hours. There won't be any lunch breaks or loitering at Kimberly's desk."

"So, you think you can plan our wedding and juggle all of this?" he asked.

"What choice do I have?" she asked.

Kelly didn't have an answer. All he knew was that they both wanted to be married and that weddings didn't plan themselves.

Chapter 22

The Holy Thursday
Pizza Party

Kelly looked over the congregation at Cottonwood Church where a standing-room-only crowd had gathered on Holy Thursday evening.

For a new pastor, putting together the program for the whole Easter season had seemed as complicated as prepping for a space launch. Midweek services for children through adults, thematic Sunday services, and now Holy Thursday, Good Friday and Easter Sunday.

In addition, holding the last service at Cross Church on Good Friday cast a shadow over the whole season. He moved toward the closing like a man sentenced to death.

Kelly had peeked out the back door of Cottonwood Church earlier to see that dusk had settled over the late March evening. A mass of stars began to appear. Observing the barren fields, he wondered what the night looked like as Jesus and his disciples gathered in the Upper Room for one last meal together two thousand years ago.

He was elated that the youth group was helping with this special service. Two teens stood on either side of the sanctuary doors with signs that read, "Enter Silently And Be Seated." As people approached, they saw the signs and dropped their conversations. Now a hushed congregation waited.

The idea for the service had come to him in full bloom just the week before. He had spent several evenings setting up the church and working with the youth to make it happen as he envisioned. Large pillar candles perched on the windowsills, casting flickering shadows across the sanctuary. Giant palm fronds filled jars at the front of the church, creating a backdrop for the scene that was about to take place. He'd dimmed the overhead lights, hoping to evoke the mood of the Last Supper. One hundred twenty people could fit in the sanctuary, the same number of followers who waited in the Upper Room after the resurrection.

When Kelly nodded to the youth choir, they began to sing a haunting version of the Lord's Prayer. Then Kelly read from Mark 14, the shortest version of the Last Supper story. When he reached the verse about the disciples coming into the city to prepare for the Passover, he paused.

The sanctuary doors opened and in walked several youths dressed in robes. They carried a twelve-foot table, which they set up at the front of the church. Others laid a white cloth over the table and set chairs around it. Four youths brought in pitchers of grape juice and baskets of unleavened bread baked by two of the girls in the group. Finally, a boy dressed in white took the center seat at the table as others sat around him.

Kelly continued reading Jesus' words about the one who would betray him. The one dressed in white took a piece of bread and dipped it in a bowl. He handed it to the one playing Judas, who quickly got up and left.

Kelly read on. "While they were eating, Jesus took bread, gave thanks and broke it, and gave it to his disciples, saying, 'Take it; this is my body.'" Kelly paused while they took the baskets and began distributing bread among the congregation.

When they were seated again, Kelly read, "Then he took the cup, gave thanks and offered it to them, and they all drank from it." Again, the youth arose. They took the four pitchers, poured juice into tiny cups, and handed them out. The only sound was their movement through the crowd.

When everyone finished the bread and juice, Kelly finished the passage with verse 26. "When they had sung a hymn, they went out to the Mount of Olives."

Behind him, the compelling voice of Cole Jensen rose. "Were you there when they crucified my Lord? Were you there when they crucified my Lord? Oh, oh! Sometimes it causes me to tremble, tremble, tremble..." Softer voices hummed along. The congregation sat in quiet reflection.

After several moments, individuals began to stir, looking for belongings, helping children put on jackets. Two disciples held up signs that read, "Please Exit Silently." Slowly, the congregation filtered out. Kelly could hear the church doors open, car doors bang shut, and engines turn over.

He wondered what it felt like in the Upper Room after Jesus and the disciples left. This sanctuary still had an aura, as though Jesus himself had presided at the table. Kelly was humbled and grateful to God. None of his plans would amount to much without the power of His presence.

So much of the Last Supper was about relationships. Luke's account said that Jesus eagerly desired to eat the Passover meal with his disciples. During this intimate meal, he'd carefully and bluntly prepared them for what was to come.

Jesus clearly knew his disciples' weaknesses, yet clearly loved them.

As Kelly watched, some of the youth gathered the communion cups and put the chairs away, while others talked quietly. He realized how much he cared for these kids. In a way, the youth had become his own disciples. He desperately hoped he could safely shepherd them through their teen years.

"You guys did a fearsome job tonight," Kelly said, using their word for excellence. "I'm so proud of you." It was all he could manage to say without getting emotional. Together, they blew out the candles, hauled the table to the basement, and drank leftover grape juice.

After the last car left the parking area, Kelly trudged to the bridge. The ice had thawed and now the water from the winter snows ran high and fast. In the moonlight, it looked like a piece of rippling blue velvet.

Being the pastor of a country church had its lonely moments, yet Kelly usually didn't mind. He enjoyed peaceful, contemplative moments. However, now he felt painfully alone. For some reason, he missed his twin brother, Kyle, more than he had in a long time.

"Hey, Kyle. Are you watching?" Kelly's voice cracked. "I sure wish you were still here on earth so we could talk. I'd give anything for even an hour with you."

Lost in his musings, Kelly didn't notice Amber approaching.

"I thought you might be here," she said. "Kelly, the service was beautiful, just beautiful. You made it extra special. And the youth were spectacular."

"Amber." He'd never been more grateful to see her loving face. When she put her arms around him, his thoughts of Kyle began to fade.

"I didn't see you in the church."

"I arrived late and saw how packed it was, so I squeezed into the back. After the service, I went over to the parsonage. When the lights went out at the church, I decided to walk out and meet you part way."

"I'm so glad you're here," he said, swaying back and forth with her. "I need you. Do you know how much I need you?"

They were silent a moment.

"Were you thinking about Kyle?"

"How did you know?" Kelly peered at her through the darkness.

"The atmosphere around you seemed heavy. I don't know how else to put it."

"Sometimes it's as if he is right here. I miss him every day, but for some reason tonight it's worse. Some of the kids in the youth group are about the age Kyle was when he died. I feel alone without him."

"It's okay. I'm here for you," Amber said close to his ear. "I'm here now."

As they strolled back to the parsonage, Kelly's mood brightened.

"I found some flowers growing out in the yard the other day. They were coming right through the snow."

"Were they lavender?"

"Yes. What are they?"

"Crocuses. They're shy little flowers. Hard to find, because they like the native prairie grass and so much of it has been cultivated."

"They're hardy, too. I couldn't believe something so fragile could bloom in the snow."

At the parsonage, Kelly built a fire, while Amber made hot chocolate and popcorn. They snuggled on the couch, engulfed in their feelings for each other.

"We're two old souls who are so lucky to have found each other," Amber said. "I need you so much."

She took their cups and set them on the coffee table. They were face-to-face, her arms around his neck, his arms encircling her waist.

Kelly almost forgot to breathe, aware only of her warm softness in his arms. He kissed her in a way he hadn't dared to before, in a way that showed how much he wanted her.

Lights flashed. Horns honked. Laughter rang through the air. Kelly and Amber pulled away from each other.

"That was quite a kiss," Amber said.

"No, that's the youth group!" Kelly answered.

They quickly composed themselves as a dozen young people burst through the door, bearing boxes of pizza and two-liter bottles of soda.

"We thought it was time we bought the pizza," said Cole, who stopped short as he assessed the fire, the cups and the couple.

"We aren't interrupting anything are we?"

"Yes," said Amber while nodding vigorously. "I mean, no! We're ready for pizza."

"You bet we are," Kelly agreed. "Come on in. Throw your coats in the laundry room."

After the teens trooped into the dining room, Kelly noted that Amber had turned a new shade of pink and he felt a little off center himself.

"Once we're married," he whispered. "We've got to keep that door locked."

Amber smiled.

The Holy Thursday pizza party lasted well into the night.

Chapter 23
Good Friday

Kelly was in high gear when he picked Amber up on Good Friday morning. He wore his black suit, which had required a vigorous brushing to remove the telltale gray cat hair. After debating about which necktie to wear, he gave into his customary blue silk, which matched his eyes, according to his mother.

Amber bounced out of the house as fresh as the new day in a crisp black suit with a soft green shirt that matched her eyes. She carried a raincoat and her black patent purse. Easing herself into the pickup, she tugged modestly at her narrow skirt and gave him a dazzling smile.

"What a beautiful day. Unusually warm for this time of year," she exclaimed as she looked around at the cloudless blue sky. The ditches brimmed with spring runoff water, and the hay-colored grass was streaked with the lime green of new growth.

He wanted to take her in his arms, but when he saw the twins grinning through the kitchen window, he instead put the pickup in reverse and backed around in the muddy yard before pulling onto the road.

"Amber Rose, you are beautiful," he declared. Never mind the stray cat hair on his suit or that his shoes needed polish, the whole world filled with happiness when he was with her.

"I'm so glad we can be together for the entire day."

"I'm happy the office is closed for Good Friday," Amber replied. "I can't do anything more on the strategic plan until after the consultant arrives, and all of my accounts are somewhat under control."

They were quiet for a few moments before Amber said, "Doing this day together makes it feel like we're really a couple, doesn't it?"

They chatted contentedly until they turned off the narrow paved road onto Schulteville's graveled main street. They cruised past the deserted bulk oil plant that Wayne Selby had run. The paint was peeling off of several buildings, while the metal buildings were rusting. Most were boarded up. The town still had a post office and a bar with a gaudy blinking beer sign in the window. The gas station was closed, however, locals could pump their own gas if they had a special code. A vending machine tucked under the eaves provided cold soda for fifty cents.

Signage on the community center indicated it had also been a grocery store and a video shop. Today it would reopen for the biggest event the town had seen in years; the closing of its only church.

Modest frame houses filled most of the townsite. Detached garages sat facing alleyways, connected to their houses by wire clotheslines. Outhouses remained in a few backyards, surrounded by barren stocks of hollyhocks and lilac bushes gone wild. On the outskirts of town, a few brick ranch houses built in the 1970s, provided homes for those who wanted to move into "town" from the farm.

The elevator, once on the far edge of Schulteville, had expanded and now dwarfed the rest of the town. This was farm country, after all. Back in the early 1900s, harvests of wheat, corn, and oats were brought to town in wagons pulled by horses or tractors. Today, farmers used semi-trucks to transport soybeans, canola, durum, or sunflowers to the elevator or nearby processing plants.

In contrast to the rest of the town, Kate Schulte's Queen Anne stood out like a yellow rose in a garden full of wilted blooms. Easily the largest home, the three-story house featured a turret in one corner and a wide veranda in front.

Kelly and Amber pulled up at Cross Church, which was located across the street from the Queen Anne. The church was a miniature of Cottonwood Church. The white building had a lovely steeple, though the town had dwindled in population before a bell could be purchased.

Today Kelly would conduct the last service, a duty he had resisted.

Amber noted he seemed more at peace about the situation.

"You seem to have come to terms with closing the church."

"You might say that," Kelly answered. "Good Friday is a bittersweet day. Bitter because the Messiah was unjustly murdered. Sweet because Good Friday wasn't the end."

He smiled mysteriously and made no further comment.

In the early planning for the day, Kelly had expected the last service to be a quiet affair, like close family gathered around a deathbed. Then he began to hear rumors.

A lot of local friends and neighbors intended to pay their respects. In addition, generations of people had grown up attending Cross Church. Many of them planned to return to Schulteville for Easter.

To honor the church's long history, he decided to hold a funeral service, complete with beloved hymns, a eulogy, and prayers of thanksgiving and commitment. He even had a special casket made to hold mementos of the church's history. Of course, a luncheon would follow. Anyone who wanted to visit the cemetery could wander out back.

Kate Schulte, the iron-willed matriarch of Schulteville and Cross Church, had dabbed her eyes when she heard of his plans for honoring the church and the work of

God. Her reaction was astonishing, and he hoped it was a sign that he was finally in her good graces.

Kelly had figured out how to squeeze more people into the forty-seat sanctuary by adding chairs at the ends of the rows and across the back. Special guests and the makeshift choir could wedge onto the stage.

Many local residents had volunteered to help prepare for the day. The luncheon, a logistical nightmare, was an example of what resourceful people could do by working together. Kelly knew a meal needed to follow the ceremony, but Cross Church wasn't able to provide a traditional funeral meal of salads, hot dishes, bars, and coffee for perhaps a hundred people. Of the eight regular attenders, one was a teenager and seven were between ages seventy-six and eighty-six. However, the capable Cottonwood Church women stepped in and offered to supply the lunch.

The church didn't have enough space to host a meal, so several local men unlocked the abandoned Community Center and cleaned it out with mops and brooms. They hauled in tables and chairs and set them around the room. The Cottonwood youth group decorated the space with banners and old photos supplied by Kate. People could stroll around the room and visit with others as they found photos of themselves, their parents or grandparents.

Shortly after Kelly and Amber arrived, an army of women showed up with food for a crowd. Cheerfully, they made do with a few overhead lights, exactly three electric outlets, and no running water. Kelly, a bachelor with only rudimentary kitchen skills, considered them to be miracle workers.

As the eleven o'clock hour neared, Kelly and Amber stood on the church steps greeting people as they arrived. Kelly was grateful for mild weather. It was so warm, that he propped the church doors open.

The building soon filled up. Latecomers didn't seem to mind standing outside, squinting in the sunshine and listening to the service inside.

Finally, the couple slipped to the stage. Kelly took a deep breath. The Lord was about to turn their mourning into joy.

Chapter 24
Farewell to Cross Church

Kelly stood solemnly at the front of the church seeing what he'd longed for since he first became pastor. The sanctuary was packed. Too bad it was the final service.

At the front, Marge Selby pushed the wheezing organ through the last bars of a familiar hymn. As the organ coughed out the last notes, Kelly stepped forward to welcome everyone and offer a word of prayer.

In the moments of silence that followed, Wayne Selby and Ed Thildahl walked in carrying a small-scale casket and set it in front of the stage. Someone in the congregation began crying softly. Kelly asked the congregation to open the dark green hymnals, and then nodded at Amber. Her clear voice rose to lead the congregation through four verses of "What a Friend We Have in Jesus."

After the long traditional "Amen" at the end of the song, Kelly stepped forward to give the eulogy.

"Cross Church was erected in 1914. It was meant to honor God and thank Him for the many blessings bestowed on the residents of Schulteville and the surrounding countryside.

"Here is the story of how it came about, as told to me by Kate Schulte." Kelly turned and extended his arm toward Kate, who sat on the stage next to Amber. Applause broke out. Flustered, Kate smiled and then waved her handkerchief at the congregation.

"As many of you know, Kate's brother, Ted, served as pastor here for sixty years. He passed away last year." Emotions clogged Kelly's throat at the memory of the older man, who had briefly been his friend.

He went on with determination. "Theodore and Martha Schulte moved here shortly after 1900. They bought land, lived in a two-room house, and worked hard. They prospered and life went well for them. However, Martha longed for children.

"In 1913, Theodore built a fine three-story Queen Anne house to comfort Martha. It sits right across the street today. The most elegant house in Schulteville then and now."

Behind him, Kate beamed smugly.

"Theodore felt guilty after it was built. He had a new home, but the town had no church building. The congregation still met in the schoolhouse. One day he went home and told Martha that he wanted to donate land to build a church.

"Martha had recently decided to let go of her grief over not having children. After all, hadn't God given them bountiful crops, good health, and each other? How could they ever repay the good Lord for all of these blessings? A simple thank you didn't seem big enough, so she happily approved Theodore's plan.

"That same week they deeded several town lots to the church. In the next year, Theodore donated lumber and his share of sweat equity to the building project. Cross Church was dedicated in 1914.

"About that time, a miracle happened for Theodore and Martha. Their baby boy, Ted, was born. Two years later, Kate arrived. The children grew up here. After college, they both returned to Schulteville, Ted with degrees in business and theology, and Kate as a teacher.

"Ted was a successful businessman. However, his true vocation was pastoring Cross Church. Kate became the superintendent of the local schools. They continued to live in the Queen Anne house and took care of their parents as they aged."

"Cross Church has withstood the scorching heat of summer and the breathtaking cold of winter. It has served the people of this community for eighty-eight years."

Kelly paused. Lost in the story, he'd spoken much longer than he intended. However, the faces in the congregation showed that they were with him. He turned to Amber. She nodded at him to continue.

"This is only one small church on the prairie, and yet, it has had an impact across the globe for almost ninety years. Hundreds, maybe thousands, of children have learned about Jesus here. Countless adults have found peace, courage and renewed faith at this altar. How many prayers whispered in this room have resulted in restored bodies or lives?

"Since moving here, I've heard countless stories about the children who grew up attending Cross Church. Some went on to serve as ambassadors, doctors, missionaries, scientists and teachers."

Kelly leaned toward the congregation, his sermon notes forgotten.

"Some of you are here today. Wherever you've gone, I believe you've taken with you the values learned here. The values of truth and integrity. Hope for the future. And that there is One we can turn to. For all these things, we thank God."

Kelly paused a moment. There were few dry eyes in the house.

"It's my pleasure to announce that though this building will no longer hold a church, it will continue with a new life."

A murmur of surprise rippled through the crowd.

"Wayne and Marge Selby have purchased the building for the staggering sum of one dollar. The Selbys have taken care of this building for years. Keeping fuel oil in the tank, paying the bills, making sure the church is sparkling clean each week.

"Transferring the title to them seems fitting. In the next few weeks, Cross Church Carpentry will open here. You see, Wayne has developed a business building church pulpits and other furnishings. He ships them all over the United States."

Kelly stepped down and ran his hand along the casket. "Wayne built this tiny casket in front of me. Items from Cross Church will be kept in it to remind us of God's faithfulness.

"Wayne has needed a better place to work. We think Jesus would approve turning the church into a carpentry shop."

Kelly started to say more, but stopped, shocked, when the congregation stood and began to applaud. After a few moments, he raised his hands, asking for silence. The congregation sat down again.

"Every time you drive by and see that Cross Church has a new life, remember that Good Friday wasn't the end for this building, just as it wasn't the end for Christ Jesus. Whatever you are facing, it isn't the end. It's only the beginning. Jeremiah 29:11 states, 'I know the plans I have for you, plans to prosper you and not to harm you, plans to give you hope and a future.'

"If God cares for a building made of wood and shingles, how much more does he care for you?"

Marge got the organ going and the choir began to sing, "It is No Secret What God Can Do." Kelly had never presided at such an emotion-packed service. His final blessing and dismissal seemed positively triumphant.

Chapter 25
After the
Good Friday Service

After the service, Kelly and Amber remained at the front of the church next to the tiny oak casket as people filed out the door. The last few members of the church came forward. They included the Selbys, Thildahls, Kate Schulte, Sadie Jensen, and a few others.

Amber noted that Sadie was as lean in body and spirit as Kate was ample. However, Sadie had just survived a bout with pneumonia and was taking care of a teenage boy, while the Selbys took care of Kate.

Photos, the original charter, and samples of Sunday bulletins through the decades rested inside the satin lining. Now they added a hymnal and the chalice they had used for communion services for many years.

Kate dropped in a white handkerchief edged in blue. Sadie leaned over and examined it.

"That's my hanky," she said, looking up at Kate.

"It belongs in the casket, since you've lost a hanky in church at least a hundred times," Kate explained.

Sadie's mouth dropped open. "Well, it seems like you've had a tissue or two fall out of your own sleeve. Maybe you should drop one of those in," she retorted.

Kate snorted. Everyone else shifted uneasily.

Kelly glanced at Amber and saw she could hardly contain her mirth. Kelly had noticed some tension between the women, both on the far side of eighty, but, he had never seen them tangle. He tried to diffuse the situation by taking the small white square out of the casket, but when he handed it to Sadie, she dropped it back in.

"Actually, it's a nice way to remember me. Thank you, Kate," Sadie said, seeing the best way to come out ahead was to give in. The women smiled at each other with guarded affection.

His admiration of Sadie grew in that moment. Living on a small pension, she had managed to raise her great-grandson almost single-handedly. Now a senior in high school, Cole was steady, smart, and talented. Kelly expected him to have a bright future, despite his troubled childhood.

The scene was interrupted when someone came to the church door and said Kate was needed at the hall. Former students were asking for her. The small group watched Kate leave, her head high, leaning on her cane with every step, her bright yellow purse in the other hand.

Those who remained gathered up the rest of the hymnals and followed her to the Community Hall. Everyone was invited to take a songbook home as a keepsake.

Guests piled their plates with salads and ham buns, before settling in to visit with old friends. Others wandered around the hall to view the photos and memorabilia.

By midafternoon, the hall was empty again. People had scattered. The paper plates and cups were tossed in garbage bags, tables and chairs were hauled away, and the floor swept clean. Finally, someone turned off the lights and locked the door.

Kelly and Amber sat on the church steps in the late afternoon. The hot, sunny day had taken on a chilly, humid feel. Overhead, clouds seemed to go in different directions.

Amber sat with a grin on her face, her arms wrapped around her knees.

"You are incredible, Pastor Kelly Jorgenson. What a day it's been."

"It went better than I hoped," Kelly admitted.

"Better than you hoped? Are you kidding? You nailed it. I can't believe how inspired that sermon was today. You helped people remember all the good things, the God things, that happened here for over eighty years. You made us see how even this remote church has a huge impact. I bet every person felt inspired to 'go into all the world.'"

"You exaggerate," Kelly said modestly. "It was exciting to have the ambassador to Belize and an MIT professor here. And some legislators."

"It was quite a crowd. But, seriously, Kelly, you are an inspired man of God." Amber wrapped her arms around him. "I am so blessed to have you in my life."

Ed Thildahl drove up about that time and Amber let go of Kelly.

"Did you deliver the ladies to their homes?" Kelly asked him, grateful for Ed's willingness to drive people to and from church. Ed and Wayne Selby would be providing taxi service to Cottonwood Church from now on for several people.

"Just in time, too," Ed said, gesturing toward the glowering clouds in the west. "Rain coming in." A chilly wind was kicking up.

"Yoo-hoo! Yoo-hoo!" Kate called from the yellow house across the street.

Kelly, Amber, and Ed looked up in time to see Kate slip on a step and fall on her bottom. They rushed over to help her.

"I'm fine, I'm fine," she muttered. "See?" she asked as she moved each of her limbs. "I wanted to invite Pastor Kelly and Amber for a dinner of non-funeral food. You, too, Ed, if you and Marion want to come."

She was still sitting on the step, her long black skirt askew, her cane on the sidewalk. The men helped her to her feet.

"Thank you for the offer, but Marion is already at home and I don't think she'll want to go out again," Ed responded.

Kelly looked at Amber, his eyebrows raised.

"I better get back to my family," Amber said. "I want to dye Easter eggs and do some baking for Easter."

"Nonsense," Kate responded. "Your family can wait. This is a big day for Kelly and Cross Church. Marge is making her delicious honey chicken."

The young couple looked at each other. Maybe we should stay and make sure Kate isn't injured, Amber thought. Kelly shrugged.

After holding back-to-back services on Holy Thursday and Good Friday, Kelly felt relaxed. The Easter service should be easy by comparison. Plus, he had all day tomorrow to make final preparations. Maybe it was time to kick back.

The couple stared at each other and then Amber smiled at Kate. "Okay, we'll stay. It's kind of you to invite us."

Inside the house, they eased Kate into her favorite wingback chair. Kelly studied her. He couldn't tell if she had been hurt or not. He'd learned that Kate could stir up a little drama when it suited her purpose.

Marge brought a carafe of coffee for Kelly, Kate, and Wayne, while Amber went to the kitchen to help with dinner.

Kelly was surprised when an hour had passed as they discussed all that happened. That's when he noticed big drops of rain pelting the street. Next came popping sounds as sleet began to fall. Kelly stirred uneasily. He wished he'd taken Amber home. By now, he'd be at the parsonage, with a fire lit and Mildred curled at his feet.

When the party moved into the dining room, Kelly noticed that Kate was getting along rather well for having fallen down the steps.

He glanced around. It seemed like they'd entered another era. The room was decorated in faded yellow wallpaper, which looked like brushed gold in the low light of a chandelier. A silver coffee service sat on the built-in hutch, which was packed with dishes. The gold velvet drapes were pulled over the window, secluding the room from the outside world.

Intimate, but intimidating Kelly thought. The long table could easily seat a dozen people. It was set with a linen tablecloth and napkins, and china so fine you could almost see through it. The stems on the glasses were thin as a straw. He hoped he wouldn't tip, drop or break anything.

He looked at Amber through the silver candelabra and pulled at his tie, wishing he could take it off. She smiled reassuringly.

Before they began to eat, he led grace, thanking God for the day, those gathered around the table and, of course, for the food.

Soon after they began to eat, Kate tapped a silver spoon against her water glass.

"I want to propose a toast," she announced. She lifted a glass of sweet cider and said, "To a dear old friend whose memorial service was held today. May it lead a resurrected life."

Kelly, Amber, Marge, and Wayne lifted their glasses in memory of Cross Church and the beginning of Cross Church Carpentry. The lively conversation resumed, and Kelly forgot about the rain outside, until a gust of wind shook the house and the lights flickered.

"We better find some flashlights and more candles in case the power goes out," Marge said with a nod to her husband.

"You think the electricity might go off?" Kelly inquired. The lights flickered again.

Amber went to the window and drew back the drapes.

"It was a dark and stormy night," she announced in a theatrical voice. "The wind beat against the house...and the streets turned to ice!" She looked at Kelly. "Maybe, we better head for home."

Chapter 26
Settling in for the Storm

Everyone, except Kate, rushed to the window and looked out.

"This isn't good," Wayne said. "We better drive around town and see how bad the roads are before you and Amber try going home. It must be fifteen miles over to the farm?"

"Eighteen." Amber was wringing her hands. "Do you mind if I call my parents?"

"Go ahead," said Kate, who remained at the table. Kelly thought she looked strangely pleased with the weather, rather than concerned.

Amber talked to her father for a few minutes and then turned to the rest of the group.

"Adam slid in the ditch, but was able to get out. He's safe at home now. It's icy and Dad said it will begin snowing soon. We need to go right away or we might not make it home."

"Is that what your father said?" Kate asked wisely.

"Well, actually, he said to stay put and don't try to travel," Amber bowed her head and folded her arms. "I think we should try to go home. This is supposed to last through Sunday."

"Sunday!" Kelly burst out. "What about the Easter service? This can't be happening."

"Oh, my dear man," said Kate, cheerfully. "Spring blizzards are common."

Kelly sighed. Because the weather had been nice, he'd already removed the winter gear from his pickup. Now he was dressed in a suit and Amber wore a short skirt and high heels. Their lightweight jackets were in the pickup parked across the street. In addition, Kelly wasn't eager to see if his winter driving skills had improved.

Still, when Amber gathered her purse and thanked Kate for the hospitality, he moved toward the door with her.

"Amber, why don't you stay put for a few minutes?" Wayne suggested. "Kelly and I will take the pickup down to the stop sign and see how things are. If it's bad in town, the highway will be downright dangerous."

Kelly remembered the ditches were full of water. If you slid off the road between Schulteville and the turnoff to the church, you'd land in icy water. Still, he and Amber both wanted to get home.

Wayne handed him a spare cap and coat and they stepped outside. Even the porch was slick. They went down the steps gingerly. Once out in the open, rain splashed Kelly's face as though buckets of ice water were being thrown at him. By the time they got across the street to the pickup, his black leather shoes were filled with water.

Kelly put the truck in gear and stepped on the gas. They slid sideways.

"Put it in first gear and see if you can get any traction," Wayne advised.

Kelly did as he was told, and they slowly moved forward. He drove a block east on the main street, but when they reached a four-way stop, the pickup slid right through the intersection.

"Let's turn around," Wayne said. "You kids better stay with us. It's a long way to the parsonage and even farther to the McLean farm. Not worth the risk."

Kelly gunned the pickup like he'd seen teenagers do on Friday evenings after football games. In a second the pickup had spun around to face west.

They pulled up in front of the yellow house and Kelly grabbed the few personal items he and Amber had left in the pickup. The light from the parlor window welcomed them back.

The men were both glad to be out of the storm. Kelly glanced across the room to where Amber stood watching him expectantly. He shook his head.

"Glare ice under the slush," Wayne said. "Aunt Kate, do you think we can take in a couple strangers for the weekend?"

"That depends," Kate said. "If it's Amber and Kelly, then by all means. We'll put Kelly on the third floor in the turret! Amber, you can sleep down here."

Amber went to the phone again to call her parents with the news.

"They're relieved," she reported after she hung up. "Dad is worried. He said he'll probably spend the night in the calving shed because a couple of the cows might come in."

Kelly looked at her blankly. "He's going to wait in the shed in case the cows come home?" he asked.

Everyone hooted at his city-boy ignorance.

"Oh, Honey, when you say a cow might come in, it means she might have a calf. When they're near giving birth, he keeps them in the corral or the barn. He's learned to be wary of spring storms because they are hard on baby livestock."

"I can imagine. It would be tough to be born outside in a storm like this," Kelly shuddered. "We'll have to add farm animals to our list of prayers."

The phone rang and Marge announced the call was for Pastor Kelly.

"Who even knows I'm here?" he asked incredulously. The prairie grapevine never failed to amaze him. A few minutes later, he hung up and turned to the others.

"That was Maury Jackson. He said we need to consider canceling church on Sunday. He thinks the storm might not be over until then."

"He's probably right," Wayne said. "Plan for the worst and hope for the best."

"I hope the electricity doesn't go off," Marge said.

"I hope my brothers are all at home," said Amber.

"I hope I left enough food for Mildred," Kelly said.

"And I hope you will all settle down and make the best of this," Kate said.

For the first time, Kelly realized that they had been milling around or standing at the window much of the evening.

"If it's all right, I'd like to check out my room," Kelly said, suddenly feeling very tired.

"I'll find a toothbrush for you and make up the bed," Marge volunteered.

Before retiring for the night, Kelly managed to pull Amber into the kitchen for a hug and a goodnight kiss.

"I'm glad you're sleeping in the turret and not me," Amber said, laying her head on his shoulder. "I've been up there, and it creeps me out."

"Hmm," Kelly whispered. "If we were married, we could both sleep up there and I'd protect you."

"I bet you would, Pastor Jorgenson," Amber said, smiling up at him.

Chapter 27
Easter Saturday

Kelly woke on Easter Saturday aware he wasn't in his own bed, but not grasping that he'd spent the night at Kate Schulte's. Then another wind gust rattled the windowpanes in the turret.

He peered through the lace curtains behind the bed, and saw the world had been painted white during the night. It all came back to him then. The last service at Cross Church overflowing with nostalgia and hope, Kate's invitation to dinner, his first realization that he and Amber were storm-bound in Schulteville.

Thoughts of Amber being downstairs forced him from under the warm covers. He could hear kitchen clatter and muted voices as he dressed. He rubbed the stubble on his chin. There'd be no shaving today.

Downstairs, worry about the storm had given way to the festive atmosphere sometimes adopted during storms. The kitchen smelled of coffee and cinnamon toast. A radio blared weather updates and cancellations. Kelly was embarrassed that he was the last one in the household to wake up. The others were already discussing what board games to play.

"Has anyone been outside?" he asked.

"Yep. Fell flat on my back right outside the back door," said Wayne as he rubbed his lower back. "Icy as all get out under a layer of snow."

"Kelly, the weather service is advising no travel through today," Amber said, as she pulled out the chair next to her at the kitchen table and patted it.

He plunked down. "Does this mean we need to cancel the Easter service?"

"I'd say if the forecast hasn't improved by noon, you might as well cancel," Wayne said. "Even if the snow ends today, we'll be contending with ice and the farmers will be digging out." "I'm just thankful that we have electricity," Kate added. "That's a miracle, considering all the ice that must be hanging on the power lines."

For a moment, Kelly remembered growing up in Southern California where the sweet scent of orange blossoms filled the air. He and Kyle had ridden their bikes to the beach all year round. They seldom listened to a weather report.

As though reading his mind, Amber looked at him curiously.

"One of the benefits of bad weather is that often you are shut in and get to spend time with people instead of constantly being on the go," she offered.

She looked relaxed, Kelly thought. More rested than he'd seen her in a long time. It made him wonder when she'd last had a full night's sleep.

At noon, Kelly called the church board members. In turn, they called members of the congregation and media outlets. An hour later, after he'd heard the Easter service cancellation on the radio, Kelly felt a weight lift from his shoulders. No service, no last-minute details, no checking on the choir. He was free.

Kelly wanted to pull Amber close. Instead, he kept his hands in his pockets. Marge and Wayne went to their quarters at the back of the house and Amber settled down to look at photo albums with Kate. Kelly went back to the turret for some time alone.

A steep stairway led to the third floor. About twelve feet in diameter, the round room had long, narrow windows on three sides. The walls were painted forest green and a rag rug covered the wood floor. The only furniture was a brass bed that leaned against a window frame, a small nightstand, and an antique walnut five-drawer chest of drawers.

He decided to pray.

"Lord, you stilled the storm on the Sea of Galilee. Please make this storm go away."

His words seemed to blow away with the wind outside. How often did people beg the Lord to take away the problems they faced, while His plan was to take them through?

"Not my will, but yours be done," Kelly surrendered. "Teach me your ways, oh Lord."

An hour later, he heard footsteps and Amber appeared. "Aunt Kate wants to visit with you and me this evening. We're formally invited to join her for dessert in the parlor."

Kelly ran his fingers through his hair. He could imagine himself trying to thread his fat fingers through the handle of a tiny cup while balancing a bone china dish on his lap.

"You must feel bad about canceling the Easter service," Amber said, sitting down beside him on the edge of the bed.

"I keep thinking of the lilies on the altar table. They're probably drying up like my plans for tomorrow," Kelly said. "And Mildred. Do you think she's eating the curtains by now?"

Amber laughed. "It's always harder to diet when it's not your idea," she said. "She'll be fine."

"You must wish you could be home with your family."

Amber nodded, her curls waving with her head.

"I dye Easter eggs and bake bread on Easter Saturday. And I need to spend more time with Mom."

"I never get over how quickly our lives can change," Kelly said reflectively.

"Such as when one week Mom was running down the driveway teaching Daniel how to ride his bike and the next week she was in the hospital?" Amber said.

Kelly nodded. "And one moment I was sitting on a log on the beach next to Kyle and Bri. And the next moment he was slumped over. Killed by a drunk with a gun."

Amber looped her arm through Kelly's arm.

"Our lives change and our good intentions fail," Kelly contemplated. "It requires faith and courage to go on."

"I remember reading something by Catherine Marshall. 'He will turn troubles into highways,'" Amber said.

"'He makes all things work together for those who love Him and are called according to His purpose.'" Kelly quoted a verse from Romans 8.

"I love those Bible promises. Because of the storm, that promise is coming true right now. We can spend the weekend together instead of each of us being focused on our other duties."

"Yes." Kelly smiled. "Let's be content with the situation and see what happens."

Just then, Marge called up the stairs, asking if they wanted to help dye Easter eggs.

"Kelly, would you mind going down alone?" Amber asked. "I'd like to have some time alone to think and pray."

Kelly went to the kitchen and participated in the age-old custom of dying Easter eggs. Then they played Yahtzee and Chinese checkers with Marge and Wayne. A couple hours later, he went to check on Amber.

She was propped up in the brass bed, a quilt snuggled around her.

"I can't remember the last time I was this idle," she said when he appeared in the doorway.

"I like you idle," Kelly said as he sat on the bed and reached for her hand. "You're always cute, but when you're relaxed like you are now, you have a special glow. How does it feel to not be working or driving or planning to work or drive?"

"Like I'm in someone else's body," Amber said. A look of wonder filled her face. "I'm beginning to feel like 'me' again."

Chapter 28
Kate's Offer

That evening, Kelly and Amber sat across from Kate, balancing plates of gooey bread pudding with caramel sauce and whipped cream on their laps.

"Children," she began. "Tell me, what are your wedding plans?"

Surprised by her question, Kelly and Amber looked at each other.

"We've set the date for June 15," said Amber.

"It'll be at Cottonwood Church," Kelly added.

"That's what I expected," Kate said in a clipped way that reminded Kelly that she had been a school superintendent. "Only two months to go and you have virtually no plans made."

"Oh, we have everything under control," Amber said, just as Kelly's plate of dessert slid off his knee and landed upside down on the floor. Caramel sauce and whipped cream oozed down his black suit pants and rested on the Persian rug.

Kate's chin went up.

"Have everything under control? You certainly do not! Now go get a rag and clean up that mess. Afterwards, we will talk about it some more."

Feeling like a child again, Kelly knelt and began scraping up the mess with his fork. At least the plate didn't break, he thought, as it slipped out of his fingers and broke in two. Amber hurried to find a kitchen rag and come to his aid.

Once Kelly's dessert was reduced to wet spots, they sat down again. Afraid to cause another upset, he scarcely moved. Kate didn't offer him another piece of dessert.

"Now, here is what I propose," she said. "I'm going to plan your wedding. The invitations, the decorations, the clothing. And I will pay for it all."

She looked mighty pleased with herself, while Kelly and Amber sat in shocked silence.

"Oh, no. We couldn't let you do that," Kelly said when he'd recovered a bit.

"Absolutely not!" Even as Amber said the words, she realized they hadn't done much planning since they set the date.

"I won't take no for an answer," Kate stated. "Amber, you don't have time to plan this wedding and the good Lord knows your poor mother can't help much.

"And you," she directed this comment at Kelly, "What do you know about wedding planning?"

Kelly ran his fingers through his hair.

"I didn't get to plan a wedding of my own," Kate warbled with a hint of self-pity. "Kelly, I've adored Amber since she was a little button nose. I want to help with your wedding."

Kelly and Amber looked at each other. Kelly raised his eyebrows in question.

Accepting Kate's help would be humbling, and probably complicated. Still, there seemed to be no polite way to refuse the offer.

He sensed her sincerity and eagerness to take on this project. Perhaps she needed a mission now that Cross Church was closed.

Amber searched Kelly's face for his response. When he nodded, she went to Kate and threw her arms around her. "Aunt Kate, thank you so much."

Kate brushed her away. "'Tis something I'll enjoy doing."

"Just one thing," Amber said. "We want to keep it simple."

"Nonsense," Kate snorted as Amber backed away. "You have a whole church full of young people that think marriage is going out of style. You've got to show them how to do it right. It must be the wedding of the year."

Amber slumped into her chair, realizing they just had lost control of their own wedding. Kelly bit his lip.

"We're going to do an elegant country wedding that everyone will want to copy," Kate said, clapping her hands together. "I can see it all now. Just leave the details to me."

They spent the rest of the evening working on the guest list and answering Kate's questions about their likes and dislikes. By the time they went to bed, the wedding was roughed out on paper and they each had a to-do list.

On Easter morning, Kelly woke before dawn to total silence. The wind had died down. He got up and looked out the turret windows onto the scene below. The snow had stopped, and the world looked surreal in the faint light of a waning moon.

After pulling on his clothes, Kelly slipped out the back door. He was braced for bitter cold, yet found the air to be as soft as a flannel blanket. The violet horizon in the east caught his attention.

What was it like that first Easter morning when two women visited the tomb of Jesus before dawn and found it empty? Kelly wondered. He breathed in the fresh air, aware that he hadn't been outside since Friday evening.

"Lord," he prayed. "I believe it was a morning like this in more ways than one. A lot of people had hopes and dreams that were smashed when you died. They were still recovering from the fact of your death."

Kelly smiled to himself as he imagined the surprise and confusion caused by the empty tomb. Yes, he thought. That's the story of Easter. When your last best hope has dissolved and you've given up, the Lord himself makes the impossible happen.

He turned when he heard the door open. Amber appeared, wrapped in a fuzzy bathrobe on loan from Marge.

"He has risen!" Kelly said in a traditional greeting.

"He has risen indeed!" Amber responded. "Our first Easter together. Do you think they will all be this unusual?"

Kelly wrapped his arms around her. "Every one of them will be incredible, because we will be together."

By the time Marge laid out an Easter breakfast of scrambled eggs, sausage, and caramel rolls, the sun shone brightly.

Afterward, Kelly and Amber said their goodbyes. As they crept along the road toward the parsonage, they were careful to stay away from the ditches filled with icy water and snow.

Mildred greeted them enthusiastically. They stopped long enough to refresh her food and water, and then Kelly took Amber to the farm. While he helped Glen and the boys clear snow from the yard and corral, Amber prepared a late afternoon Easter dinner of baked ham and candied sweet potatoes. Dessert consisted of shared Easter candy.

Late in the afternoon, Kelly and Amber got into their separate vehicles. It was so warm, that the last of the ice and slush on the roads was already melting. When he turned into the driveway of the parsonage, she tooted her horn and waved as she zipped by on her way to Bismarck.

That evening, Kelly called his parents to wish them happy Easter and to describe the Easter storm. The two-day lull in activity would become an enchanted memory for him, a moment set apart on life's journey.

Chapter 29
Kelly's Birthday Dinner

A candlelight dinner for two. Kelly couldn't think of a better way to celebrate his twenty-fifth birthday and the beginning of a new year. He looked around Peacock Alley, located in a historic Bismarck building. The subtle, tasteful décor was impressive. Word had it that the food was equally pleasing.

Amber sat across from him. The chandeliers cast a glow that highlighted her hair and creamy silk top. This was definitely the place to go for a romantic evening.

"Happy birthday, Kelly," Amber said, her eyes shining with love. "Our first of many birthday celebrations."

He'd been receiving birthday greetings all day. The mailman had knocked on the door and then walked into the house with a stack of cards, along with a package from his parents.

Three women from the church delivered cakes. A chocolate fudge, a carrot cake with cream cheese frosting, and a popcorn cake. He'd wedged the first two in the freezer. He could take them to the McLean's home for Sunday dinners and save Amber from making desserts for a couple weeks. He brought along the popcorn cake to share with Amber later at her apartment.

"So far, it's been a wonderful day, and this is the best part of all," he said, taking her hand. "I've missed you."

He hadn't seen Amber since the Easter snowstorm, over a week ago, because of scheduling conflicts. She looked tired around the eyes, yet her wide smile said she was enjoying the evening as much as he.

"We have a lot of catching up to do. Believe it or not, Bri called me last night."

"She did? I didn't even get a card from her, let alone a phone call," Kelly commented.

"You will. She planned to put your package in the mail today," Amber said, a mischievous look in her eyes. "Guess what we discussed." Amber paused for effect, while Kelly gulped. Were these two women ganging up on him?

"I asked Bri to be my bridesmaid."

"You what?" Kelly uttered a little too loudly. People around them paused to see who was causing a disturbance, then went back to their meals. "Since when have you and Brianna Davis been such good friends?" he inquired.

"Well, we were talking about the wedding and one thing led to another. It seemed like the most natural thing in the world to ask her. She is so unhappy and I was trying to encourage her. It just slipped out. And you have been friends for a long time..." Amber's voice trailed off.

Kelly suddenly felt ill. Aunt Kate and Brianna planning his wedding? He ran his fingers through his hair. "Well, if that doesn't..."

"She got so excited," Amber interrupted. "I think she was doing jumping jacks. It was fun to talk with her about plans. I don't have a sister or cousin to stand up with me."

"How about if we elope?" he asked.

Of course, Kelly was happy about the budding friendship between Amber and Brianna, but the turn of events felt weird. Brianna had been in his life for almost a decade, first as his brother's girlfriend and later as his good friend. After he moved to North Dakota, they had drifted apart. Now, she was back in his life, like a boomerang.

"Kelly, I know this is a surprise and I probably should have talked to you first." Amber paused for a moment. "I can't put my finger on why I felt compelled to ask her. Besides, I can use her help."

After their food arrived, they ate in quiet companionship. Finally, Kelly said, "I haven't decided who to ask to be my best man, either. It should have been Kyle."

Amber nodded sympathetically.

"Do you have any classmates you'd want to ask?" she inquired.

Kelly shook his head.

"Cousins?"

"None I'm close to."

"Anyone here?"

"I have lots of friends here. Tiny. The Jackson brothers. Dave Johnson over at First Lutheran. Father Joe. None of them seem to fit." Kelly put down his fork. "Would it be okay to ask my dad to be my best man?"

"Yes, of course," Amber said without hesitation.

"That's what I want to do. I want him to stand up for me."

"Then ask him! I'm sure he'll be honored."

Later, the couple sat on the couch in Amber's apartment munching on the popcorn cake. Kelly had never tasted one before and he found the chocolate, nuts, and caramel addictive.

"I'm moving this cake up to the top of the list. It's now my favorite," he said as he pushed the plate to the far edge of the coffee table. "This has been a wonderful birthday, Amber."

"We'll make it your birthday tradition. Dinner out followed by popcorn cake."

"We have one more 'first' before our wedding."

"What's that?"

"Your birthday. May 20. It will also be the first one we celebrate together."

Amber held his hand tightly. "Actually, we have another event before the wedding. Daniel is graduating from high school at the end of May. I want to do something nice for him."

Kelly froze at the word "graduation."

For the most part, he had moved past Kyle's death, but occasionally something triggered a flashback that took him right back to the beach where Kyle had been killed two weeks before their high school graduation.

Amber went on, oblivious to his misery. "Out here, graduation celebrations are as big as weddings. Our neighbors up the road? A couple years ago when their daughter graduated, they remodeled their house and updated the landscaping. They invited every friend and relative. And then, after all the fuss they held the party in their garage."

Kelly struggled to breathe, to hear Amber's voice. He couldn't bring himself to tell her how painful the topic was to him.

It had taken every bit of his courage to walk across the stage the night of his graduation and receive both his and Kyle's diplomas. His parents and Brianna had also been in the auditorium. Brianna had walked across the stage a couple dozen graduates before him. Later, they agreed it was one of the hardest things they'd ever had to do.

By the time he reached center stage, the audience was frozen in silence, so that his footsteps echoed across the auditorium. He had been handed both his and Kyle's diplomas. Back at his seat, when he'd put Kyle's diploma on the empty chair next to his, it fell to the floor and rolled away. He'd grabbed for it, as though by retrieving the diploma he could save Kyle. When he raised up again, diploma in hand, the surrounding students stared at him, panic and pity written on their faces.

Because of that experience, Kelly understood how isolated you could feel in a crowd. It was one of the experiences that had bonded him with Brianna.

He'd avoided graduation ceremonies since. Like a burn that crusts over while the healing continues beneath the surface, his sorrow had been healing ever since, yet the pain surfaced at moments like this.

Finally, Kelly asked, "How can I help?"

His voice sounded strange. Amber looked closely at him and realized she had accidentally entered a sensitive subject area. Kelly had explained Kyle's death to her in detail, but hadn't talked about what happened at the graduation ceremony two weeks later. Now, the pain of it was etched on his face.

"Oh, Kelly. We don't have to do this. Daniel will understand completely if we don't have a party. In fact, maybe he'd rather not do anything."

"No, I want to help Daniel celebrate," he responded. "It's been seven years. Time to replace painful memories with newer, happier ones."

"If you think so," Amber said slowly. "We can do this together." She smiled and put her arms around him. "By together, I mean you, me, and Jesus. He is well acquainted with grief. He'll know how to help us through this."

They held each other tight, tighter than ever before, as if courage and healing and love could grow by clinging to each other. And Kelly knew, there in the soft lamp light, that just as no brother could take Kyle's place, there would never be another woman for him. Amber fulfilled his greatest longing for a soul mate.

Chapter 30
A Graduation Blessing

The night before Amber's birthday, Kelly surprised her by driving to Bismarck and taking her out to dinner. Later he presented her with a gold cross necklace, and they finished the evening with chocolate mint ice cream. The birthday provided a peaceful interlude amidst work, wedding planning, and graduation plans.

Kelly had an oh-oh moment as graduation day approached. It happened when the youth group was in the middle of a jam session. Three guitars, drums, keyboard, and a saxophone filled the church basement with sound that rattled the framed Sunday school certificates decorating a wall.

Kelly had forgotten that Cole Jensen was also graduating. He was sorry to see either Daniel or Cole leave the youth group. Daniel had brought many of his friends into the group. As the drummer, he punned that he was "instrumental" in the music they made on Friday nights and occasionally during Sunday church services.

Cole was the first teen Kelly had approached last fall to be part of the youth group. The young man provided quiet, steady leadership for the other kids. In spite of his tumultuous childhood, Cole excelled in school and seemed wise beyond his years. He was an old soul, like Amber and himself, so that Kelly felt privileged to be part of his life.

"Hey Cole, how are the scholarship apps coming?" he asked when the band took a break.

"Heard from another school this week," the young man said. "I have to decide between three scholarships." This didn't surprise Kelly. Cole was a top student.

"Which one will you choose?"

"Not sure yet," Cole said with a sigh.

"Are you having a graduation party?" Kelly asked.

Cole shook his head and looked the other way.

"I told Grandma not to worry about it. There'll be plenty of other parties that day. We'll go to those."

Kelly understood instantly. Sadie had slowed down quite a bit in the past year, done in by arthritis and pneumonia. He suspected that now Cole took care of his great-grandmother instead of the other way around. There certainly wasn't any extra money for parties.

Kelly excused himself and went to the church kitchen to use the phone.

"Hi, Glen. Has Amber made it home yet?" Kelly asked. Every week the girls in the youth group asked if she'd be there, but so far her work schedule had been too demanding. She usually didn't get back from Bismarck until at least nine on Friday evenings.

"She's here, Son. Let me put her on," Glen said as he handed off the receiver.

After quick greetings, Kelly explained that the youth group was in session and he'd had an idea.

"Do you think Daniel would mind combining his graduation party with one for Cole?"

"Doubt if he'd mind. What's going on?"

"Cole isn't going to have a party, otherwise," Kelly explained. "I don't think Sadie is up for planning or paying for one."

"You're right. Let me talk to Daniel when he gets home."

"Thank you! I hoped you would agree."

"Why Pastor Jorgenson, don't I always agree with you?" Amber asked demurely. "One thing, though, instead of having it at the farm, can we hold a combined party at the church?"

"I don't see why not. Talk it over with your folks and Daniel. Then I'll make sure the board is comfortable with it before I talk to Cole and Sadie."

After he hung up, Kelly rubbed his hands together, excited about being able to help Cole.

Late Saturday afternoon, Kelly and Daniel turned up the lane leading to the Jensen place. Located on a few acres and hidden by a woodland of elm and cottonwood trees, the tiny house had a Scandinavian look with red paint and elaborate window frames and eaves.

"This looks like something out of a fairy tale," commented Daniel, who had only been to the house once, when the youth group had painted the kitchen and living room.

"Yeah, The Three Bears and Little Red Riding Hood." Kelly wondered how Sadie would manage alone out in the country when Cole left for college in a few months.

"Why, Pastor Kelly! Whatever brings you our way?" Sadie asked, when they knocked on the door. "And Daniel! What a surprise. Come in." She opened the wooden screen door for them.

"Cole just got home from his job at Tiny's," she said, before turning and calling out, "Cole, come in here. We have company."

Soon they were all seated around the Formica-topped kitchen table, that was old enough to be trendy again.

"We're here on a mission," Kelly said as he gestured to Daniel to make his case.

"Amber and Kelly dreamed up this idea to have our graduation parties together," Daniel said, with a shrug. "I'm cool with it."

"What a lovely idea," Sadie said.

"I'm not planning on having a party," Cole stated.

"We want to do this," Kelly said for reinforcement.

"We'd hold it at the church right after the graduation ceremony. Amber already has plans underway, with the food and decorating. All you'd need to do is invite whomever you want. She's planning a taco bar and we'll have a cake for each of you. What flavor do you like, Cole?"

Cole, with his dark hair and eyes, looked at Sadie, who sat still like a little bird with its feathers fluffed up. She took a hanky out of her pocket and dabbed her eyes.

"It would mean so much to me if you could have a party," Sadie said wistfully. "Pastor, did you know Cole has been named valedictorian?"

"No, but I'm not surprised. Congratulations."

"I wanted to do something. How could I put a party together with these crippled hands and feet?" She held up her misshapen hands and tried in vain to move her knotted fingers.

Cole shrugged like Daniel had done a few moments ago.

"Okay. A party." Then he smiled.

A genuine smile, Kelly thought. Cole so seldom smiled at all.

"Then it's a deal?" Kelly asked.

"Do you think I could have a chocolate cake?" Cole asked.

A few weeks later, Kelly leaned on the footbridge, listening to the night birds call one another in the stillness of the fading light. The evening was in perfect contrast with the hectic activity at the church a few hours earlier. Dozens of people had laughed and talked as they celebrated the graduation of two of the church's young men.

There'd been a chocolate cake with chocolate frosting, and a picture on the top of Cole singing into a microphone. Daniel's vanilla cake showed a picture of him next to his red pickup.

Kelly mused about how different Daniel and Cole were. Daniel was a lanky redheaded country boy, who almost always wore jeans and cowboy boots. He had a reputation as a good worker among area farmers. In the youth group, his bass voice boomed as loudly as the drums he hammered. Auto mechanics was his favorite class, so it wasn't surprising when he purchased an old pickup and turned it into a hot rod. You could hear it rumble a mile away. In the fall, he planned to attend trade school.

Cole had dark hair and eyes. He played keyboard and guitar, but it was his clear tenor voice that was a showstopper. Although quiet, he was a positive influence on the kids in the youth group. It wasn't what he said, but what he stood for. Most of the kids knew he'd been abandoned by his parents. Sadie had taken in a sad, scrawny twelve-year-old, and he'd transformed into a kind, handsome, and intelligent high school valedictorian.

Tiny had hired Cole to work in his convenience store and helped him in other ways. For instance, after watching Cole chug along in his great-grandmother's 1980s K-car, Tiny had found a reliable Toyota Camry for sale. Tiny bought it and let Cole make payments to him.

At the end of the graduation party, Cole let go of his closely guarded feelings and hugged Kelly and Amber tightly. The memory brought a satisfied sigh from deep inside Kelly. The pride that shown in Sadie's eyes as she sat watching the festivities would also remain with him.

Then in the stillness of the night, Kelly smiled when he thought of how he'd cheered along with everyone else for Cole, Daniel, and the others at the graduation ceremony. He had made it through the event without so much as a stab of pain in his heart over Kyle.

He had focused on helping the two young men. In turn, the Lord had given Kelly the gift of forgetfulness. By losing himself in helping others, he'd gained a victory in overcoming grief.

"Wow. Praise you, Lord! Thank you for helping me get through this. Thank you for Cole and Daniel. Bless them as they go into the next phase of their lives."

Kelly couldn't begin to express all that filled his heart. As the first stars of the night filled the sky, he could only lift his hands to the Creator of it all.

Chapter 31

The Groom's Morning

Delivering a van full of flowers was the last thing Kelly Jorgenson expected to do the morning of his wedding day. As a pastor, he often found himself with "other duties as assigned," but this took the cake.

Just a year ago, he had arrived at Cottonwood Creek to a warm welcome. He'd moved to this remote community hoping to find peace for his soul, and instead found his life's mission in serving the good people here. And he fell in love with a girl with golden hair and an angelic face. A girl who was soft and sweet, strong and smart. The girl of his dreams.

Thinking about Amber Rose McLean took his breath away. A smile played at his lips as he realized the irony of the day. He was living the dream of marrying his beloved Golden Girl, however, this dream was wrapped in a ridiculous to-do list issued by a bossy eighty-six-year-old woman. Thinking of how Kate Schulte took over planning his wedding to Amber Rose made him run his hand through his hair.

He was often surprised that plans, dreams, answered prayers and even falling in love seldom looked like he pictured. Today was a good example of that. His marriage to Amber Rose was a spectacular dream about to come true, a genuine gift from God. In a perfect scenario, he'd have looked out the parsonage window to see a wedding planning company pull up to the church to set up the creekside wedding. Instead, he was driving a borrowed van, delivering the flowers himself.

Kelly admired the self-reliant people out here on the prairie. No one, not Amber, her parents, or Kate had considered hiring a wedding planner. Not that they could even find a service like that in the phone book. Enter Kate, who knew everyone in a hundred-mile radius. Cane in one hand, phone in the other, she had been in full throttle wedding planning mode since Easter.

The flowers weren't from a florist, either. There wasn't one in Cottonwood City. Kate simply called someone who had a shelterbelt full of lilacs and arranged for the lavender blooms to be picked up. She also found a bountiful supply of white peonies, which she pronounced "pee-own-ees." After that, she commandeered Kelly to get the flowers to the church on time.

He brushed an ant off his arm, unaware that ants were attracted to peonies.

The wedding cake had a similar story. A woman in town baked cakes for graduations, showers, and weddings. She had baked a multi-layered cake for this day. Kelly was thankful that, as far as he knew, he didn't have to transport the cake for his own wedding.

"You have the ring?" his father, Steve Jorgenson, asked for the third time from the passenger seat of the van.

"It's at the parsonage," Kelly responded again. "I'll put it in my pocket when I get dressed."

"It's a nice clear day." This comment came from his mentor, Wallace McDougal, who sat in the backseat. Wallace had been alarmed by a thunder-cracking, lightning-studded storm the day before. By midafternoon, the sky had turned dark as night and the electricity had gone off temporarily. The California native had a special concern about the weather because he was performing the outdoor ceremony the next day.

"The storm cleared the air," Kelly said with some authority. He'd seen a few storms in the past year. A summer tornado. A December snowstorm. And most recently, a two-day Easter blizzard. Each time, the following day had been beautiful.

"That rainbow late yesterday was a sign of good things to come," he said to reassure himself as much as his companions.

Then he changed the subject. He was still perturbed that Kate sent him out like an errand boy on the morning of his wedding. Shouldn't he be doing something else, something groom-like? He wondered what grooms usually did before the ceremony.

"Do either of you remember what you did on the morning you got married?"

"Do I ever," said Pastor McDougal. "We were in Scotland, because our families came from there. My wife's dream was to have a Scottish Highland wedding. We put on our wedding attire and away we went to this place with a view of the mountains and the sea.

"That was the best of it. Here's the rest of the story. All the way through the ceremony, you could hear sheep bleating on the other side of a stone fence. Baa! Baa! Moreover, the wind blew a steady thirty miles per hour. The clergyman's frock billowed like a black balloon. So did Margaret's wedding gown. The wind almost blew her over. Her bouquet went tumbling across the field."

"A wonderful story," Kelly said. "But what did you do the morning of your wedding day?"

"I have no idea," the kindly pastor answered, a bit bewildered.

"And you, Dad?"

"As you know, we were married at a Spanish mission," Steve said. "Everything about the day was perfect. The weather, the setting, the bridal party. There was only one problem. Because I was so nervous, I forgot to bring the wedding ring. My brother drove back to our hotel several miles away to find it. Meanwhile, the ceremony got underway. I was sweating, trying to figure out plan B. He rushed in and gave me the ring a moment before I was supposed to put it on Nancy's finger. Saved the day, he did."

"Another great story," Kelly said, finally understanding his father's concern over the ring. "But what did you do on the morning of your wedding?"

"I have no clue," Steve answered, a puzzled look on his face. They all burst out laughing.

As they talked, Kelly began to see that driving a flower delivery van could be a joy rather than a duty. They drove to the church and unloaded the baskets of lilacs and vases of peonies, carefully setting them on the west side of the building out of the sun.

They arrived back at the parsonage in time to shower and dress. More than once, Kelly patted the pocket where he kept Amber's ring, ensuring that history wouldn't repeat itself.

Before long, Kelly's mother and Brianna strolled in after a trip with Amber to Maggie's Magic Makeover beauty shop.

Kelly thought about the events of the last six months. On the evening of his first date with Amber, Brianna had called to say she was coming from California to stay with him. Alarmed at Brianna showing up as he was beginning to date Amber, he was up all night thinking and praying.

He'd hung on a thin rope between the past and the future that night. Brianna represented the past and the comforting friendship he needed as he dealt with his grief over Kyle's death. Still, Kelly and Brianna's friendship had never blossomed into romance.

Kelly had risked his future with Amber by telling her who Brianna was and that she planned to come and live with him. Amber had taken the news well, and together they figured out how to deal with the dilemma.

Now Brianna was Amber's bridesmaid. Six months ago, he would never have guessed that outcome. Amber later said his story about Brianna wanting to come live with him was so ridiculous and unlikely that she believed him. Not only that, it had helped her see what a naïve sweetheart he was. Her words.

Years later, Kelly's memories of the morning of his wedding would remain clear. He'd spent the morning with the two most important men in his life. His father, Steve, was the reason he had been born at all, of course. And a few years earlier, he had experienced a rebirth through the ministry of Pastor McDougal. Now, these two men had traveled over fifteen hundred miles to stand with him on the most significant day of his life.

The camaraderie as they rode the back roads of North Dakota lifted his anxiety. Their help in loading and unloading the van gave him room to focus on the importance of the day, rather than the fact that he served as Aunt Kate's delivery boy.

No one snapped a photo of the three men as they drove the prairie roads to deliver flowers. Still, Kelly knew he would always remember this moment in time. The van windows rolled down, meadowlarks trilling on fence posts, the scent of clover rippling across the rain-washed prairie, his father by his side and his mentor gazing out the side window.

The peace and joy of this morning overshadowed the details that brought his dreams and prayers to reality. A man lived for moments such as this, Kelly thought, unaware that these memories would help anchor him in the coming months. He hadn't considered that just as reality seldom resembles our dreams, there are ruts on the road to happily ever after.

Chapter 32
The Bride's Morning

With the wedding only a few hours away, Amber absently fingered the soft fabric of her gown as she reminisced.

Impulsively asking Brianna to be in her wedding had cost her a lot. First of all, she'd forfeited her pride. Brianna and Kelly had known each other a long time and had weathered a tragedy that knit them together. Inviting Brianna into their new life might have created another set of problems, but her compassion overruled any concerns.

Jealousy had also circled their relationship from the very first, looking for a way to get in. Amber had ample opportunity to envy Brianna, who oozed glamour. Tall and attractive, with big-city sophistication, she possessed all the qualities that made Amber feel plain. Now, she was glad she had taken the risk, because Brianna was turning into a trusted friend.

What was it about Kelly that made her take risks she would have never considered before? Saying yes to marriage without a firm plan in place. Asking Brianna to be her bridesmaid.

Still, Amber had no regrets. Later, when she did think things through, she knew taking the high road and asking Brianna was a great idea. Kelly and Brianna's lives were already tangled together by tragedy. It only made sense for Kelly's bride and his friend to become friends.

After working on the wedding details with Brianna the past few weeks, Amber had learned to see past the bold, beautiful image Brianna portrayed to the world. She had glimpsed Brianna's hidden soft side, the one devastated by Kyle's death. The one who felt totally alone.

As vulnerable as she felt asking Brianna to be her maid of honor, all her fears disappeared in the following weeks as the two women kept in touch by phone and email. The threat of being overshadowed by Kelly's good friend turned into an opportunity to forge a friendship.

As the date drew near, it was Brianna who filled in all the details not covered by Aunt Kate. For instance, it was Brianna who asked if Amber had bought a ring for the groom and whether she had purchased any new clothing for the honeymoon. Amber, as usual, was stretched too thin to think much beyond the mountain of work she tackled each day at Gates Insurance in Bismarck and in helping her family on weekends.

What would she have done without Brianna and Aunt Kate? Elope, she decided, as she swished out to the kitchen in her pink robe. She and Kelly could have run away together.

She turned the oven on and pulled an egg casserole from the fridge. She'd made it after the wedding rehearsal the night before, determined to fortify her family for the day. Then she started the coffee pot and set a stack of plates on the table. Two bags of bakery rolls, cleverly hidden in the dryer to keep them out of her brothers' reach, were placed on the table. Breakfast would be ready when the guys came in from feeding the cattle and doing other chores.

Amber looked longingly at the bathroom door. A luxurious time in the tub in the family's only bathroom was not going to happen today. She went to her parents' bedroom, where her mother was sitting on the edge of the bed.

"Mom, how are you today?"

"I'm going to have a good day today," her mother declared as she moved her arms slowly to show her range of motion. "MS will have to take a backseat to my daughter's wedding.

"I'll just do my ablutions in here today. Would you bring in some soap and water?"

"Oh, Mom. I don't mind helping you."

Jean reached for Amber's hand and motioned for her to sit on the edge of the bed. "I feel good enough to take care of myself, and you need to get ready before you have your hair done. But, first I'd like to talk to you for a moment."

Amber sat down, her hand still linked to her mother's.

"This is an important day for you," Jean began. "I want to remind you to keep it in perspective. The wedding is just one day. Some things will go right today, and some things will go wrong. Keep in mind the overall purpose of the day. Don't let the wedding be more important than your marriage."

Jean paused for a moment and Amber squirmed a little. Her mother knew too well how she might get wrapped up in the details.

Jean continued, "I'm so proud of you. Kelly is a fine young man. He's worthy of your love and devotion. Amber, you must always give him your best. He deserves more than what's left over after your career and caring for us. And remember, he has a call to serve God. You must be his partner in carrying out his work."

Amber felt a stab of guilt. Was that what she was doing? Adding her marriage to Kelly to her to-do list?

"Now," her mother said. "I'm going to pray a blessing on you. Then you must go and lock yourself in the bathroom for a while. Don't worry about the rest of us, we can take care of ourselves today," Jean said as she smiled at Amber with impossibly kind eyes.

Amber's own eyes were wet when she left the bedroom. She never understood how her mother always managed to zero in on the exact places where Amber needed help. She'd given Kelly nothing except the leftovers of her time, energy, and focus ever since they'd been dating. That realization stung Amber. Things would change, she vowed as she turned on the faucets of the huge old porcelain tub and poured in some bubble bath.

Still, a thought nagged at her. She was marrying Kelly, but what was going to change? She'd be living in Bismarck during the week. She was working two jobs for Gates Insurance. Her family needed her help on weekends. Where was Kelly going to fit into her life? Sure, she'd be with him at the parsonage on the weekends, however, those were his busiest days.

Certainly, it would all work out, wouldn't it? She felt a finger of anger rise in her heart. What would God have her give up, anyway? She needed her job, and her family needed her. She and Kelly would get along as well as they could.

Taking a deep breath, she slipped into the fragrant, inviting water. By ten thirty that morning, Amber had regretfully kissed her mother goodbye. How nice it would have been for Jean to go with Amber, Brianna, and Kelly's mother, Nancy, to the beauty shop.

Jean didn't seem to mind being left behind.

"The most important thing is I'll be at the wedding. Besides, I need a nap more than a manicure at this moment," Jean told her firmly.

Maggie's Magic Makeover beauty shop was aptly named, Amber decided as she looked in the mirror. Somehow, the beautician had subdued her billowing golden curls and pulled her hair into an upswept hairdo. The effect was stunning, even to Amber. The new hairdo turned her usual perky look into something more elegant. As they worked the little hat and veil into a playful tilt on her head, she wondered what Kelly would think.

An hour later, Amber was at home standing in front of the mirror in her room. She absolutely loved her wedding dress. She had never gotten around to taking Aunt Kate's advice to look for a dress at the little downtown shops. Finally, Brianna had researched wedding shops online and insisted Amber visit one in a north-side mall on the way home from work.

One of the assistants had asked all the right questions and pulled out the perfect dress from a rack. Amber fell in love with the chiffon right away. Then she'd dug Kelly's measurements out of her purse and said yes to a tuxedo the clerk suggested.

A few nights later, as she sat in a circle of light at her desk working on a report, Amber had a news flash: her mother also needed a dress. The next day, she stopped at the bridal shop again, but the mother-of-the-bride dresses seemed too formal or fussy for Jean. Especially since she would likely be in her wheelchair during the wedding.

Amber rushed over to a nearby dress shop and picked out three dresses for her mother to try on when she went back to Cottonwood Creek for the weekend. Jean had settled on a navy dress with a short-cropped jacket.

Out in San Francisco, Brianna had sewn her maid of honor dress. After numerous phone and email discussions, they had agreed on a mango-colored, form-fitting gown that showed off Brianna's olive skin and great figure. Amber hoped the maid of honor wouldn't outshine the bride.

Keeping the event simple seemed harder than planning a large wedding. No, she didn't want numerous bridesmaids or flower girls. No fancy table arrangements. No tents or canopies. No live band. No dance.

Simple, simple, simple she emphasized. The planning wore on like a boring blind date. What kind of cake? How big? What color frosting? Music during the ceremony? Where to buy invitations? What, you mean there are special postage stamps for wedding invitations? When to send them out? Professional photographer or snapshots? Details. Details.

Chapter 33
Kate the Wedding Planner

R ows of white wooden folding chairs sat facing Cottonwood Creek as though waiting for a show to begin under the translucent blue, sunny sky.

As Kate Schulte tramped down the center aisle, a
general on the way to war, all one hundred chairs looked
straight ahead. Suddenly she turned and pointed at a half
dozen teenagers spilling from a van.

"You! Bring that table over here!" Kate commanded,
her pointing finger turning an arc from the teens to a spot
in front of the chairs. A couple of the teens looked over at
the white-haired woman, bewildered.

"Yes, you! I need some muscle power over here."

Two boys set down the band equipment they'd removed from the back of the van and started toward her,
while the others continued hauling out their instruments.

Once the boys had the table in place, Kate smiled
sweetly at them and pointed out the baskets of flowers that
must be brought to the altar area. Silence followed while
the boys, looking like mice trapped by a cat, glanced at
each other. Finally, Cole Jensen stepped forward.

"Um, we need to set up our instruments and get electricity out to the creek for the keyboard," he said hesitat-
ingly.

Kate looked at him and then at the load of equipment.
"Very well then, I'll just do it all myself," she said. A look
of self-pity crossed her face as she mopped her forehead,
although the morning was yet cool.

"Well, I guess I can help you while the others set up
our equipment," Cole said reluctantly.

"Good! Follow me." Reinvigorated, Kate tramped
off toward the church, where she'd already stacked more

items to enhance the supposedly simple wedding.

The wedding. Her wedding to plan. What a lovely time she'd had making arrangements so that two of her favorite people could have a wedding to remember.

She'd known Amber McLean since she was born. She quite clearly remembered the first time she'd seen the little button-nose, with her big green eyes and tuft of blonde hair. She'd teased Jean McLean about two redheads having a blonde baby, yet from the first day she'd been smitten by the girl.

In the following years, as the McLeans produced a string of four redheaded boys, Kate had appreciated Amber even more. Their farmhouse had practically jumped with energetic boys, but Amber remained sweet-natured and feminine. When Jean developed multiple sclerosis several years ago, Amber had taken on responsibility for her brothers.

Yes sir, she was a peach of a young woman now. A career girl. Got away from that cow manure and lived in Bismarck, Kate mused. She'd mostly watched Amber from a distance, yet somehow she saw the girl's struggles and how she overcame each difficulty. A day didn't go by that Kate didn't offer up prayers for Amber.

When the new young pastor, Kelly Jorgenson, had moved to Cottonwood Creek last year, she'd seen the possibility for the two young people right away. Not that she was a matchmaker. She had only hoped they'd spot each other.

Kate served on the committee to interview Kelly when he came out here to Dakota. She was taken by the young man right away. He likely didn't have a clue about what he was getting into moving out here from Los Angeles, she mused at the time. Still, she figured his forthrightness would help him survive and become a real asset to the community.

Not that she'd ever let him know how much she appreciated him. You couldn't give people too much credit. Let up for a moment and they wouldn't be toeing the line anymore. She'd certainly learned that from decades as a school superintendent. However, she had gone out of her way to let him know that closing Cross Church wasn't his fault. Besides, the building was being put to providential use.

This young band of musicians was also a product of Pastor Kelly's wisdom. His own past had made him sensitive to the dangers of the late night drinking parties that were popular with kids in these parts. He'd found the key to redirecting their energy by tapping into their musical interests. Every week he got them to jam together. Whatever that was. At least they weren't out horsing around at night any more.

Not that she liked their music. Why it lacked any melody and the drums gave her a headache. Not to mention, half the time she couldn't understand the words. Still, she had to concede that a lot more young people showed up in church on Sunday mornings and their enthusiasm warmed her prickly heart.

Today Kelly and Amber would be married at the same church where she'd once hoped to have her own wedding. Long, long ago, she thought with a sigh.

Kate grabbed hold of a white lattice arch. Turning to Cole, she said, "You're a good man to help me. Can you just grab the other end of this arch?" Cole looked at the heavy lattice arch that stood eight feet high. His eyes grew big.

"I think we better get some more help for this." He whistled and motioned for the other boys. Together they staggered to the edge of the creek with the unwieldy arch and then hauled baskets of flowers to the site.

"How did you get all of this out here?" Cole asked Kate.

"Oh, a volunteer helped me," she said, elusively. "You

can go on now. Do your own thing. I can manage the rest." Cole nodded and he and his friends wandered off to sort out their musical equipment.

Cole's story was another one for the books, Kate mused. A child unwanted by his parents, raised by his great-grandmother, for heaven's sake. Poor as church mice, but rich in the things that counted. It showed in what a fine young man Cole had become.

Kate had asked him to sing at her brother's funeral last year and she aimed to help him with college, just as she was helping Amber with the wedding. Sometimes young people needed a little boost in life. She just hoped word wouldn't get around that she had a soft heart. That wouldn't do at all.

While the boys set up their band equipment, Kate tucked greenery and white silk roses into the lattice and set a bouquet on the table which would serve as an altar for the wedding. She looked up at the sky. Not a cloud in sight. If the wind didn't blow like a fan set on high, the wedding would be picture perfect.

Soon after, Kate nabbed the boys again and ordered them to help her haul boxes back to the basement storage room. The church women arrived about that time with roasters full of hot food and ice chests stuffed with salads. Organized chaos reigned in the kitchen as the women deftly put together the final touches to the food. Outside, their husbands set up tables and chairs under the shady cottonwood trees.

The woman who baked the wedding cake backed her minivan up to the kitchen, and opened the hatch to reveal a cake at least three feet high. Kate clapped her hands in joy. The white fondant vision was decorated with white roses at the base of each layer and was topped by a tiny, classic bride and groom figurine. It was lovely. Just lovely.

A table was set up for the cake in the shade of the church, between the tables holding the punch bowl and the gifts. Kate clucked her tongue and clenched her hands as all the details came together. Her plan was working.

Ever since she'd found Amber and Kelly alone at the parsonage and they had announced their engagement, she had wondered if Amber was making any wedding plans. It was when the young couple was stranded at her house over Easter that she'd found out the truth. Poor girl had way too much on her plate to take on wedding planning. That's when Kate decided to step in.

Oh, she supposed she had driven Amber half-crazy, and Jean too. Most of the time, she hadn't bothered to ask what they wanted. She saw what needed to be done and did it. Amber had enough to do with finding her dress, sending out the invitations, and who knows what else.

Kate wondered again about Kelly's highfalutin friend from California. It seemed that she was going to be Amber's bridesmaid. Land's sake, what was the world coming to when the groom's best friend was a woman? At least Kelly hadn't asked her to stand up for him, Kate fussed. If she had a moment alone with Brianna Davis, she'd be happy to give her some advice.

Kate only hoped Amber and Kelly would spend more time together after they were married. To think Amber planned to work in Bismarck during the week and help her family on weekends. Kate didn't like that picture at all.

She looked around at the creek, the church, the flowered arch where the bride and groom would stand. Even though Amber insisted on keeping the event simple, it would be a beautiful and elegant wedding to remember.

Soon guests would begin to arrive. Kate leaned on her cane and lifted her rheumy gray eyes to the sky.

"This old woman has done all she can to bring these two together," she told the Lord. "The rest is up to you!"

Chapter 34
The Trip to the Church

A s Amber finished dressing, the endless wedding details made her dizzy. She looked in the mirror and took a deep breath. Her mother was right. This had to be about the marriage and not about the specifics of the wedding. Whatever happened today, in the end all that counted was that she and Kelly were going to be together.

She put on the new crystal and pearl earrings given to her by her Kelly's parents. After applying the pretty lip-gloss borrowed from Brianna, she looked at the name. Blushing Rose. How appropriate. Placing the tube into the beaded purse used by her mother at her own wedding, she spied a blue handkerchief Aunt Kate had given her. Something old, something new, something borrowed, something blue, she thought, snapping the bag shut.

Soon she was climbing into the backseat of the family sedan for the ride to her wedding. Glen drove and Jean sat straight in the front seat, looking elegant in her new dress. Her short hair was covered by a wig that she wore when she went out in public.

"Mom, you look very nice," Amber said. She leaned forward and patted her mother on the shoulder. "I'm so glad you're well enough to be part of my big day."

"Me too," said Jean. "An answer to a heartfelt prayer."

Just then, Amber's white Jeep roared around them, narrowly missing the sedan. Amber saw her brother, Daniel, at the wheel. The twins sat in the backseat and stuck their tongues out as they flashed by.

"Hey, what are those guys doing?" Amber shouted as she half stood in the back seat. She leaned over her father's shoulder and honked the horn. The other vehicle honked back and sped off leaving a trail of dust.

"Amber, be careful of your dress," her mother's voice was throaty with alarm.

"Brothers! That's the last time I'll let them drive my Jeep." Amber glared as her vehicle fishtailed across the washboard gravel road. She'd worked hard to purchase her beloved vehicle that her brothers were now abusing.

"They'll be okay. Calm down," her father, Glen, cautioned.

"They're so reckless and they have to tease me all the time," Amber sulked. "Dad, do you think they'd do anything to ruin my wedding?"

She sat back, worry creasing her brows.

"They better not," Jean said. "They'll have to answer to me. Glen, will you bring them over to me when we get to the church?"

"Yes, let's both talk with them," Glen replied. "They don't appreciate all Amber does for them." He gave Amber a sympathetic look in the rearview mirror.

Amber's lips turned up in a half smile as she repeated her wedding day mantra: "The marriage is more important than the details of the wedding." Even if her brothers put frogs in the punch or pushed someone into the creek, it wouldn't affect the rest of her life.

"I refuse to let them ruin my day, no matter what they do," she said aloud. "I only wish those rascals would behave. That's the best gift they can give Kelly and me."

Glen pulled the aging car up to the door of the church.

"Jean, if you wait here, I'll round up the boys as soon as I help Amber." He leaped from the car and opened the wide squeaky door for his daughter. She took his offered hand and stepped out. After arranging her train, she kissed him on the cheek and walked alone up the steps and into the church.

This was where she'd met Kelly one year ago this week. Amber entered the sanctuary. The sun was already high in the sky, but a row of tall cottonwood trees on the east side shaded the building, making it cool and dim inside. The afternoon she had met Kelly, light streamed in from the west and turned the room to gold. She'd never forget that enchanted moment.

Now as Amber walked to the center of the sanctuary, the chiffon of her dress whispered like angel's breath and the weight of her train seemed to be the only thing holding her to the floor. Downstairs she could hear an occasional clank of pans in the kitchen, mixed with the muffled voices of the women who were preparing the wedding luncheon.

Those sounds faded as Amber walked to the altar, arranged her dress, and knelt. She looked behind the altar at the picture of Jesus standing at the door knocking.

"Lord, you knocked at the door of my heart a long time ago. How can I thank you for being with me each moment since that day? How can I thank you enough for bringing Kelly into my life? Lord, I want to begin this marriage with clean books, so I ask you to forgive my every thought or deed that strayed from your perfect will for my life."

Amber rose and went to the piano. This is where she sat when Kelly first walked into her life. Although she hadn't played for a while, she let her fingers wander over the keys, picking out a song.

"Joy to the world, the Lord has come!" she sang, her head thrown back. Isaac Watts' Christmas hymn seemed appropriate on this June day. She smiled, suddenly filled with the joy she'd just announced and an urgency to get on with her life, to marry Kelly, embrace all God had for her....

A muffled cough from a far corner of the sanctuary stopped her mid-thought. Amber turned in surprise to see Kelly. They stared at each other for a moment, then broke out laughing.

"Have you been here the whole time?"

Kelly nodded, coming toward her. Still laughing, they gripped each other.

"I guess this is where it all began. Maybe we should plan to meet here every year on our anniversary."

Kelly picked Amber up and whirled her around until she became a blur of white. Setting her down, he looked into her eyes. Long moments passed. Tears glistened in Amber's eyes and then Kelly's.

"You are so beautiful today. When you walked in, I couldn't say a word, couldn't move at all," Kelly whispered. "I love you, Amber Rose. And I love you most in moments like these."

Before Amber could react, the church door flew open and the twins ran in.

"Everybody's looking for you two. Come on. You're late for your own wedding!"

Indeed, when they got to the churchyard, they found everyone assembled next to the creek. Most of the guests were already seated in the white folding chairs. Brianna paced at the back of the setting, her high heels digging into the sod. Kelly's father was checking his watch. Tiny Winger, the usher for the event, stood ready to help. Bonnie Jackson carried a camera and a bag of photo equipment, ready to snap a few memorable moments.

Amber and Kelly looked at each other. Kelly shrugged and grinned.

"Time must have gotten away from us in there. Let's get married," he said to Amber. "I can't wait to begin spending the rest of my life with you."

Chapter 35
The Wedding

Amber paused next to her father in the shade of the church as Kelly and his father walked to the outdoor altar. She quietly regarded the scene before her.

The sky was as blue as she'd ever seen it. The bright sun might have melted everything save for an occasional puffy cloud and a soft breeze. To the right, the footbridge led to the charming home where Kelly had proposed. Her new home. She was going to be living next to Cottonwood Creek again. A quarter mile to the south, a couple dozen cattle stood next to a fence watching the human pageant. Amber wondered if Mildred watched from the parsonage window.

She stopped breathing momentarily, remembering the first time she and Kelly talked. "My dream is to live by Cottonwood Creek forever," she had confided in him. In her mind she pictured a springtime walk along the creek as she searched for crocuses in the snow.

Until she'd spoken the words, she hadn't been aware of that hope planted deep in her heart. She'd been way too busy with her fast-track career. The wonder of the last few months was that she was finding herself and her calling. How could this happen, unless God himself was in the dream fulfillment business?

Rows of white chairs swept toward the creek and a new structure stood near the place where the creek bubbled over rocks into a little pool. Was it a gazebo? A giant arch? White flowers and greenery covered it. Aunt Kate's doing, no doubt about it. A dozen large baskets overflowing with pink peonies and lavender lilacs were lined up in front of the chairs.

Kelly's beloved Pastor McDougal stood at a small table near the flowered arch looking at his notes. Perhaps in his sixties, he seemed solemn and confident, as though traveling from Los Angeles to conduct a marriage by a prairie creek was nothing new.

The band members had set up their equipment to the left of the archway and altar area. They all wore white shirts with ties. Daniel played an electronic drum and Cole was on guitar.

Amber squinted. Was she seeing things? Three youthful looking musicians played the flute, violin, and cello. Where had they come from, she wondered. Then she realized the high school band director was seated at the keyboard, his fingers flowing over the keys, leading a jazzy instrumental. His head was up as he watched for cues to begin the processional music.

Aunt Kate had clearly outdone herself. This was no simple wedding.

Amber now focused on the gathering. Bonnie Jackson buzzed around taking candid photos of the crowd. Their mothers, Jean and Nancy, sat together in the front row. Her mother's wheelchair was stowed off to the side. Tim and Jim were in the second row, squirming in their chairs, the sun glinting off their unmistakable copper-colored hair. Then her eyes settled on Adam and she frowned. A girl sat next to him, but she couldn't tell who it was. Did Adam have a girlfriend?

She was delighted that her friends, the Rogers family, had driven in from Iowa. They were making the wedding part of a bigger family trip to Yellowstone National Park. A few people from her office, including Kimberly, sat together. She could see them pointing at the herd of cows. Amber was sad that Benson wasn't well enough to attend. However, she loved the bouquet of long-stemmed white roses that he and his wife, Claire, had sent.

What a kind thing to do, she thought. White roses, she knew, meant purity. At the last moment, she had decided to carry them for her bridal bouquet.

Most of those present were their church family, people who farmed or owned businesses in Cottonwood City. Most of the women wore dresses in summery colors and the men were in sport jackets or well-pressed short-sleeved shirts, their familiar faces tanned from the sun. A dozen of them crowded in the back row so they could quickly leave to help serve lunch after the vows were spoken.

Brianna gave her a thumbs up and held up the velvet box that held Kelly's wedding ring. Amber reached out and gave her a single white rose to carry instead of the wedding bouquet. Then they both stepped back into place, to watch for a signal from Pastor McDougal.

"Dad," Amber whispered as she clung to his arm. "I love you."

He looked down at her, his angular face creased with a smile.

"Sunshine," was the only word he could get out as he put his arm around her.

She noticed a tremor in his chin. "Thank you for being a good father. Remember, I won't be going far and we'll see each other often."

When Kelly and his father arrived at the front of the outdoor church, Pastor McDougal nodded, and the jazzy music paused. Slowly the crowd quieted as Cole stepped to a microphone.

"Sunshine," her father began again, not wanting to lose the moment. "You look beautiful today. I wish you every blessing heaven holds."

Cole's clear voice rang out with the first words of "Ode to Joy."

"Joy, beautiful spark of Divinity, Daughter from Elysium. We enter, drunk with fire, Heavenly One, thy sanctuary."

This is God's sanctuary, if there ever was one, Amber thought. A hundred people gathered on a pristine June day for a happy event, in a place filled with sky and water and green grass and the scent of all above.

Everyone stood as Brianna began her measured walk up the aisle. Her sophistication and narrow mango-colored gown attracted murmurs from the crowd.

Amber clung to her father with one arm, the other filled with the fragrant roses. Fighting nerves, she told herself to stay in the moment. However, the whole affair became a blur, so that she only caught occasional words of the beautiful song.

"Whoever has won a lovely woman, Add his to the jubilation!"

Amber blushed. She didn't consider herself lovely, though today she indeed felt like royalty in the soft white chiffon gown. The delicate weight of the train tugged at her shoulders, causing her to hold her head higher.

"You millions, be embraced. This kiss is for all the world! Brothers, above the starry canopy There must dwell a loving Father."

Kelly caught Amber's attention and smiled. His tan skin and blonde hair made him stand out in any crowd. He looked especially handsome in his tux. That same magnetism that brought them together now drew her forward. She beamed at him and staved off the desire to throw the roses aside and run up the aisle.

When they arrived at the front row, Amber made a quick decision. Murmuring to her father, she went to Jean and Nancy. After kissing their cheeks, she tugged at her bouquet and pulled out a rose for each of them. Back on her father's arm, they approached Kelly and Steve. The music concluded and Pastor McDougal signaled for the congregation to be seated.

"Dearly beloved," he began, his deep voice resonating. "We are gathered together in the sight of God, and in the face of this company of witnesses to join together Kelly Michael Jorgenson and Amber Rose McLean in Holy Matrimony, which is instituted of God. It represents to us the mystical union between Christ and His Church. Christ himself performed his first miracle at a wedding in Cana of Galilee. Saint Paul commended matrimony to be honorable, and therefore not entered into lightly, but reverently, soberly and in the fear of the Lord."

Amber's mind drifted as scriptures were read and Pastor McDougal talked to them personally. Before she knew it, Kelly was putting the ring on her finger.

She looked into his eyes and a current flowed between them.

When it was her turn to recite the formal vows, Amber simply slipped the ring on Kelly's finger. "I'll love you forever," she promised.

Flowing along with the turn of events, Pastor McDougal announced, "By the authority vested in me, I now pronounce you husband and wife. You may kiss the bride!"

Chapter 36
The Passion of Tiny Winger

Tiny stared at the wedding party gathered beside Cottonwood Creek. Amber and Kelly stared into each other's eyes and recited their vows. Tiny hardly noticed them. He couldn't keep his eyes from straying to the maid of honor, Brianna Davis. Tall, dark hair, olive skin. That stunning dress. And those shoes, all glittery on top, with five-inch heels. She looked like a picture from a fancy fashion magazine.

His own feet were out of view, on the far side of his bulging waistline. This morning he couldn't button his jacket and or squeeze his feet into his dress shoes. He decided to wear flip-flops with his old brown suit. He felt self-conscious. What the heck, a new suit and a pair of dress shoes sure might have made him feel better. What was he thinking?

Negative voices from his childhood paraded in front of him. "Fatty, fatty, two by four! Where'd you get those clothes, Winger? You can't come to my birthday party. Your dad's a drunk and your mother's a nut case."

Tiny's face colored, and he tugged at his necktie. It felt like a noose around his neck. For the most part, he'd left his painful childhood behind, and it surprised him now that circumstances brought the memories back so forcefully. However, this was Kelly's wedding day, and he wouldn't let the past ruin it.

His eyes strayed to the lovely vision in mango once again. What would it be like to have a beautiful woman smile at him or talk to him? Just thinking about her, let alone talking to her, made sweat pop out on his forehead. He reached into his back pocket and pulled out a hanky to mop his face, but it slipped from his butterfingers. He reached toward the grass to retrieve the white cloth and bumped his head on the chair in front of him, making a clunking sound.

The mango dream turned and shot a look his way. Those eyes could melt metal, Tiny thought. Better to forget about her. At age thirty-three, he had never been on a date. Ever. Miss Mango was out of his league.

Tiny patted the top of his head, wishing his comfortable green cap was in its usual place instead of on the seat of his Chevy pickup. This dress-up stuff wasn't for him. Kelly had said it would be a casual outdoor wedding. He didn't care where they held it, if people wore fancy dresses and five-inch heels, he didn't belong.

Give him a grease rag and work boots and Tiny was comfortable. He clawed at his collar and looked at Brianna Davis. She'd probably go back to California as soon as possible. Maybe he'd never see her again, so why even think about her?

Applause from the gathering brought Tiny back to the moment. Kelly and Amber were kissing. Tiny's head cocked to the side as he watched, somewhat shocked to see their embrace.

"Hey, hey, this is a new side of Kelly," he muttered under his breath. As usher, Tiny looked around to see if he could escort anyone. However, the crowd flocked toward the newlyweds.

He turned around and saw the ladies of the church carrying out a big white wedding cake. Platters of food covered the serving tables. Round tables with white cloths were scattered across the churchyard. Maybe he'd stroll over to the food table. He could always congratulate the happy couple later.

At least he had given them a wedding gift with a lot of meaning. He'd had his trophy walleye mounted. That was no inexpensive gift, for sure. The taxidermist even wrapped it in special paper with pictures of boats on it. Tiny smirked. At least he'd gotten something right.

The women shooed him away. Something about the bridal couple and their families should be served first. Tiny found a shady spot. From his vantage point, he could see that Brianna also stood off to the side. He hadn't considered that she wasn't family and she didn't live at Cottonwood Creek. Maybe she felt left out, too.

Plus, hey, at one time Tiny thought Kelly and Brianna were an item. It made him wonder whether that look she had sent him was scornful, or was it a cry for help. Maybe she needed a friend. Tiny couldn't help himself. He began walking toward Brianna, his flip-flops slapping against his heels with every step.

"Miss Davis, would you like a cup of punch?" He surprised himself with the question. His voice sounded deep and confident. Too bad he didn't feel that way inside.

Brianna gave him a startled look. She seemed to be trying to place him.

"I'm Tiny Winger," he offered. No recognition.

"Kelly's friend," he added. Still nothing.

"I run the Co-op."

"Nice to meet you," Brianna said, her cool dark eyes roaming beyond him. "Thanks. I plan to wait to have refreshments. Amber may need some help with her...dress... or flowers." Brianna turned and began walking along the creek away from the wedding party.

Tiny stood watching her stride off in her fancy shoes and then he shrugged. No big deal. He'd been insulted by others more important than a high-powered San Francisco businesswoman. He was a grease monkey. What did he expect?

Then, as he watched her magnificent dark hair bounce against her back, she dropped out of sight. A scream knifed through the air.

Chapter 37
The Mango Queen's Emergency

Tiny stood frozen for a moment. The Mango Queen must have stepped in a gopher hole, he thought. She now lay in a heap in the western wheatgrass that lined the creek. Finally, his brain engaged with his legs and he hurried over to where she sat. Her long hair hid her face as she bent over and rocked back and forth in pain.

He grunted as he knelt beside her. One quick look told him she needed more help than he could give. Studiously trying not to notice that her dress was hiked up a little high, he stood up and looked around. No one else had noticed her fall.

Tiny let out a shrill whistle, then called, "Hey! Hey, we need help over here! Is anyone a doctor? Miss Davis got hurt! I think she broke her ankle."

A few people hurried over. Bonnie Jackson and her sister-in-law, Mavis, knelt down beside Brianna.

"Sprained," said Bonnie.

"Broken," said Mavis.

"No! No! It's not broken. It doesn't even hurt much. Look, I can get up!" Brianna said, struggling to get to her feet. Letting out a guttural cry, she collapsed again.

"There must be an EMT somewhere in this crowd," Mavis said, looking around. "Tiny, go ask the kitchen ladies for some ice wrapped in a towel. Her ankle is already swelling."

Tiny almost tripped over himself rushing toward the church, where a half dozen women hovered over the tables.

"Hey, I need some ice. Someone fell and broke an ankle," he boomed.

"Who is it?" asked one of the women. They all gathered around Tiny.

"It's the maid of honor. Please hurry."

"She had those high heels on," one of the women said.

"I don't know what these young girls are thinking. It's a wonder more of them don't get hurt. I never did wear high heels," another said smugly.

"Highest heels I've ever seen. I'm not surprised she fell. Big city girl, isn't used to walking on the prairie," said a third woman, while others nodded in agreement.

"Please—just tell me where the ice is and I'll get it myself," Tiny pleaded.

All six women stood a little taller. "You'll not mess up our kitchen," the first woman said and rushed toward the door. The others pumped Tiny for more details.

A couple minutes later, he hurried back to Brianna with a scoop of ice cubes swaddled in a white flour sack dishtowel.

One of the women called after him, "Remind them that lunch is ready!"

He knew lunch was waiting. His stomach told him so.

When he arrived with the ice, Amber was kneeling on the ground examining Brianna's ankle, her soft wedding gown draped around her. Kelly held Brianna in an upright position.

"Seriously," Amber was saying, "You need to see a doctor. It's broken or badly sprained. You need x-rays to tell what's wrong."

"I have to catch a plane back to San Fran tonight. I just have to! Could someone take me to the local walk-in clinic?"

Mavis coughed. "You'd best go to Bismarck."

Brianna looked for a familiar face and spotted Kelly's parents. Steve shook his head apologetically.

"We're going to Bismarck, but we have to catch our flight in a few hours. We wouldn't be able to stay with you."

"Oh, how could this happen?" Brianna wailed as she lost all of her aloofness. Tears of fear and frustration welled up in her eyes.

When Amber and Kelly exchanged looks, Brianna's eyes got large.

"Oh no, you are not going to miss your honeymoon because of me. Don't even think about it."

Kelly lifted his hands to silence the conversation. He and Amber exchanged glances, and she smiled and nodded.

"First, let's be calm. Everyone take a deep breath." He bowed his head and prayed simply, "Lord, give us all wisdom."

Amber nodded encouragingly as he let the silence fill in again. The tall grass rustled in the afternoon breeze.

"This is not a real crisis," Kelly continued and almost everyone remembered the September 11 terrorist attack, less than a year ago. "This is a bump in the road."

Before the young pastor could say any more, Kate Schulte spoke up in her school superintendent voice.

"This is how it's going to be. Kelly and Amber will continue with their reception and honeymoon plans."

She hawkeyed the newlyweds and they nodded obediently. Then she turned to the band members who had strolled over to see what had happened.

"You, go play some music and make it peppy!" They rushed back to their instruments.

Kate looked over at the church. "Those kitchen ladies are probably having a meltdown. All the food is out in the sun. So, go on with you," she said as she waved at the newlyweds. "Pastor Kelly, you said this is a bump in the road. Now treat it as such."

"I admire your chutzpah!" Brianna blurted. As a businesswoman in San Francisco, she had worked with high-powered people. None of them wielded more authority than this stout, white-haired woman.

Kate looked intensely at Brianna, who quickly shrank back.

"Obviously you can't travel until you have a doctor's verdict. I will take care of your medical and travel arrangements."

Rubbing her ankle, Brianna turned to Kelly and Amber and said, "She's right. The only thing that could make me feel worse than I do now is if I ruin your wedding and honeymoon."

"You haven't ruined anything," Kelly said softly to his old friend.

Brianna looked again at Kate, Mavis, and Bonnie. Something told her she could trust these women. "I'll be in good hands."

Kelly pulled Amber to her feet and they walked toward the reception. Others followed. Kate stood quietly until the only people remaining were Mavis, Maury, Bonnie and George Jackson, and Tiny Winger.

"I assume you aren't so damaged that you'll be admitted to the hospital," Kate said imperiously to Brianna. "You can stay with me until you're able to travel. Tiny, you take her to the hospital in my car. Lord knows she's too dressed up to ride in your scruffy pickup."

The Jacksons started to protest that they should drive Brianna. Then, Kate raised her hand.

"After the wedding, you need to put things back in order. And make sure those teenagers get all their music baggage out of here!"

"She's right," Bonnie said. "We were going to take care of things after the wedding."

The only one who hadn't responded was Tiny. He

stared at the people in the buffet line in the churchyard and sighed. Kate didn't seem to notice that he was distracted.

"Well, don't just stand there, go get my car," she said to him.

Tiny headed to the car, resentment welling up in him. Kate had conscripted him like a piece of military equipment. Hey, every person here would probably say he was a good guy. He helped everyone who came to the Co-op, took care of his mother, and helped with the youth group, but it was another thing to lift a finger for bossy people like Aunt Kate or snobs like Brianna Davis.

Instead of going directly to the car, Tiny angled off to the food-laden table. Brianna could wait a few minutes. He was starving. He picked up a plate and slapped some potato salad on it, followed by some kind of fancy chicken wrap. He gulped the food, grabbed a cup of punch, and swished it down.

Only then did he head for Kate Schulte's black boat. She'd left the keys in the car, so he started it and slowly glided across the prairie grass to where Brianna sat. As he drove up, he could see she looked pale even with her dark skin. He almost felt some compassion for her.

Kate stood with her hands on her hips waiting for him.

"Took your time," she challenged him as she dabbed at her forehead with a hanky. Tiny gulped with embarrassment as he realized she and the others had watched him hit the food table.

Kate barked at the others to help Brianna into the back seat of the car. Then, she smiled in a most charming way and slammed the car door shut.

Tiny drove Kate's car back through the churchyard. It was a tradition in North Dakota that whenever wedding guests clinked their glasses with their silverware, the bride and groom had to kiss. Tiny watched now as Kelly and Amber kissed and the crowd clapped and cheered.

Chapter 38

The Limo Driver

Tiny was anxious to get on the road, but they had a few stops to make before the trip to Bismarck. He drove down the road a quarter mile and turned in at the parsonage to collect Brianna's purse and luggage.

Leaving her in the car, he let himself into the house and puffed up the steps to the second floor. At the top of the stairs, he looked into the room on the right, which spanned the width of the house. Kelly's room. A big heart-shaped glittery sign hung from the ceiling proclaiming, "Kelly & Amber Jorgenson." Probably the work of Kelly's mother and Brianna.

Tiny turned left and found a smaller bedroom where a large suitcase and a big shiny black purse lay on the bed. Figures, Tiny thought. Brianna's purse was as big as most peoples' suitcases. Immediately he felt disgusted by his attitude. He'd never met anyone who pushed his buttons like Brianna. His good nature had gotten him through a lot of hard times, so why let that Mango Queen bother him this much?

"Lord," he muttered under his breath, "give me patience."

He grabbed the purse and suitcase and lugged them down the stairs. At the bottom of the stairs, something brushed against his flip-flop-clad feet.

"Aug! Oh. It's you, cat. Let's see. Mildred. Hi, Mildred." The gray feline ignored him, put her tail in the air, and walked to her food dish.

"Oh, you want some food? I'm going to be your chef for the next week." Tiny spied a bag of cat food near the dish and poured some into the bowl. "Happy chow time," he said as he hauled Brianna's bags to the door.

At the car, he handed Brianna her purse and put the suitcase on the rear floor so she could prop her injured leg on it. As he settled into the driver's seat, ready to start the engine, a small voice spoke up from the rear.

"Tiny? Um, before we make a long trip, um, I need to use the powder room."

"Powder room?" he asked.

"You know, bathroom. I really need to!"

Tiny groaned and hefted himself out of the car. He opened Brianna's door and together they made a three-legged trip to the house and up the four steps from the door to the kitchen. Tiny was amazed at how scrawny Brianna was when he hoisted her up the steps. He could feel her ribs beneath the silky fabric of her dress.

At the door to the bathroom, Brianna peered in and then forced a smile.

"I can handle the rest myself," she said as she hopped in and locked the door.

Mildred wound herself around Tiny's leg and begged for more food. He peered into the fridge. "Yogurt? Cheese?" he asked the purring cat.

After what seemed like a long time, the bathroom door opened, and Brianna gave Tiny another determined smile.

"Hey, Brianna, you didn't eat anything. I could go back to the wedding and get a plate for you," he offered eagerly, thinking he might also pick up one for himself.

"Wedding food? Yuck. No thanks," she said, "There are some pink containers in the fridge with my food in it. Would you take one out for me?"

Tiny pulled a plastic carton from the fridge. "You gonna eat this?"

"That is a highly nutritional culinary supplement that helps me maintain my weight." Her eyes wandered to Tiny's ample waist.

"Looks like dog food," he said, holding it up to the light for a closer examination.

Brianna's Taser-like look stopped any further comments from Tiny, but she still needed his help. She stretched out her hand to him. When they reached the steps, he picked her up and carried her out to the car. After she was settled in the backseat again, he asked if there was anything else she might need. She shook her head and lay back with a moan.

Tiny pushed himself into the front seat.

"Before we leave for Bismarck, I need to stop by the Co-op and make sure Rusty can close up for me. Then I'm making a quick stop at home to change out of these monkey clothes."

They also stopped at the churchyard when two women wearing aprons flagged down the car. They threw open the door and filled the front seat with containers of food.

"For your mother," one said. The other woman winked as she shut the door.

Tiny pushed on the accelerator, aware that most of the wedding party had stopped to watch the car drive off. He felt like a chauffeur driving a black limo with a diva in the backseat.

"Now I know God has a sense of humor," he muttered.

Chapter 39

The Reception

Kelly and Amber sat down under the canopy of giant cottonwood trees. Nature had decorated the churchyard with impossibly green grass and stands of wispy lilacs, while bushy peonies nodded along the church's foundation.

"Other than Brianna's accident, this is like something out of a storybook," Amber murmured. The day was turning out way better than the dream she had of being a bride with a briefcase.

They sat at a table with their parents and Pastor McDougal. Brianna's chair remained empty. Amber glanced around. Tiny and someone else were helping her bridesmaid to Aunt Kate's car. Her twin brothers sat with friends at the kids' table. Daniel and the other band members had left their instruments and strolled toward a table reserved for them.

Women from the church set platters and bowls of food before the bride and groom. However, before they could take a bite, a clinking sound rose from another table. Kelly looked at Amber, a question in his eyes.

"Old North Dakota custom. They won't stop until we smooch." She stood and pulled him up for a kiss. Whoops and cheers erupted across the lawn.

"I'd rather do this in private," Kelly whispered, his forehead resting against hers.

Most of the talk at their table centered around Brianna's accident, as they reviewed all that had happened since they'd said "I do" less than an hour ago. Amber noted that her mother looked as tired as the wilted rose that laid near her on the table. She barely nibbled her food.

The newlyweds didn't eat much, either. Every few minutes, the wedding guests began clinking their glasses.

Each time, Amber and Kelly cooperated by kissing.

Finally, Amber whispered in Kelly's ear, "Let's wander around and greet people."

To Kelly's surprise, she led him away from the crowd and toward the lovely arch. He understood why when they reached the other side. Adam and his friend were sitting close together on the grass, legs sprawled in front of them, laughing and picking at the food on their plates.

When Kelly and Amber rounded the corner, Adam jumped to his feet and pulled the slender blonde girl to her feet. Amber stopped short, a jolt of surprise going through her. When had her younger brother grown into a man?

Adam looked like a lanky younger version of their father with a full head of copper-colored hair and shoulders broadened from hard work. He wore a string tie with a dressy western shirt and kept his right hand reassuringly at the girl's back.

"Brother, you've been holding out on me," Amber said with a wide smile.

"Amber, Kelly, I'd like you to meet Lori Sanderson."

"It was a beautiful wedding," the young woman said, holding out her hand. Her blue eyes smiled confidently into Amber's. She wore her hair cropped short and had a row of piercings in one ear. Most of the women in attendance wore dresses, but Lori had on a pair of cropped white slacks and a pretty blue tunic that matched her eyes.

"Lori is from Cooperstown. She works at the nursing home in Cottonwood City," Adam explained.

"I received my LPN license and started work last week. I'm staying with my aunt over in McClusky until I can get my own place."

"Well, congratulations," Kelly said, shaking her hand. "And as one newcomer to another, welcome to Cottonwood Creek."

"I'm sorry I didn't help the bridesmaid." Lori blushed.

"We went back to the car to get your gift and missed the whole thing." Adam pawed the ground nervously, leading Amber to wonder if they had sneaked away for a few private moments.

"Well, it turned out fine. Don't worry about it." Amber assured Lori. Still, she couldn't resist interrogating her brother. After all, he had shown up at her wedding with an unfamiliar girl. It seemed like her business to find out more.

"So, Adam, how long have you two been dating?"

"We used to see each other at high school basketball games. Lori was a cheerleader and I picked her out right away." He gave Lori a lopsided grin.

"Our first two dates were for his senior prom and then mine," Lori offered.

"Really! You keep a good secret, Adam," Amber commented. Why hadn't she known this? Did her parents know?

"Lori went away to school. We only saw each other during school breaks. We didn't make any commitments. Until now."

"Now?"

"We prayed about it, and said if we're meant to be together, let Lori get a job here. And she did." They both were bashful when talking about being a couple.

There must be something to this, Amber thought. It took courage for Adam to bring a girl to a family wedding. And Lori must like him a lot or the string tie would be a deal breaker.

"Have you met the rest of the family?"

"I think Adam has been hiding me from them," Lori confided.

Amber nodded. "With good reason. You might want to meet our parents and avoid our brothers."

Adam laughed "That's what I had in mind."

Amber looked up at Kelly. "We better finish saying farewells."

"Where are you going on your honeymoon?" Lori asked.

Amber looked askingly at Kelly. "I haven't a clue."

"Wanted to surprise Amber and keep her, ah, brothers from messing up the plans."

Adam shrugged and Amber realized it had been a long time since he'd been part of any tricks her other brothers played on her. Maybe he was all grown up.

"We even worried that they planned to embarrass us at the wedding, but so far nothing has happened."

Adam shuffled his feet again. Aha, Amber thought. Something was planned. However, she could hardly put him in a headlock to get information from him, so they moved on.

Before they could walk very far, the girls from the youth group descended on them. After admiring Amber's dress and gushing over the wedding details, they pelted her with questions.

"Will you be at youth group from now on?"

"We'd like to sing together in church, would you help us?"

"Do you give piano lessons?"

Feeling like a princess surrounded by her court, Amber once again realized that there was a role in Cottonwood Creek waiting for her to fill. She tried not to make promises she couldn't keep, but she did promise to keep their requests in mind.

One of the highlights of the reception was introducing Kelly to the Rogers family, who had traveled all the way from Iowa. When Felicia asked how things were going with work, Amber was reminded that she had yet to tell Kelly about Slate's advances.

Felicia seemed to read Amber's thoughts, as she nodded slightly when Amber gave her standard plastic answer that everything was fine.

"When you're back from your honeymoon, we must talk."

They thanked a few more people and headed to the front steps of the church where their parents had gathered to say goodbye. As they rounded the corner, they saw a team of miniature horses hitched to a tiny black buggy.

"Kelly, aren't they cute?"

Kelly broke into a big smile. He'd been partial to miniature horses ever since his first visit to the Jackson farm.

Daniel came forward, led them to the buggy, and insisted they get in. Maury Jackson tapped the reins on the diminutive horse rumps, and they moved forward with a jolt. Kelly grabbed Amber tightly, afraid she'd slip right out of the little buggy. She held on to her hat and veil as they drove around the churchyard and up the road.

The band cranked up their amplifiers and played while the crowd sang out, "Love and marriage, love and marriage, go together like a horse and carriage." They made so much noise, Kelly figured people could hear it five miles away in town.

They had correctly supposed her brothers would have some fun with them at the wedding. However, their caution was disarmed with the unique gift of the buggy ride.

Finally, the buggy stopped. Kelly climbed out and helped Amber down. The Rogers girls waited nearby, eagerly hoping to have a ride. Amber nodded at Maury, who waved them over to the carriage.

Tim, Jim, and Daniel stood beaming at them. Amber grabbed each of the twins, hugging them and kissing their ruddy cheeks. She also hugged Daniel, who had masterminded the plan.

"That ride was a wonderful gift we'll never forget! I love you guys."

Kelly followed behind, warmly shaking their hands. He had brothers now, he thought. His relationship with Kyle was rooted in the past, but these new brothers were in his future.

It was time to leave for their honeymoon. Turning, they saw their parents waiting for them on the shady north side of the church. The farewell was emotion-packed. They each went to their own parents for a few private words.

Jean drooped in her wheelchair. "Mom, I hope this hasn't been too much for you."

"Don't worry about me. I'm just tired," Jean whispered. Behind her, Glen nodded.

"Don't worry about a thing, Sunshine. We'll go home now and rest up. The wedding was more wonderful than I ever thought possible."

After embracing their parents, Amber and Kelly traded places.

They were each gaining new family. For Kelly, becoming part of the McLean clan was only the next step in a good relationship. However, Amber hardly knew her new in-laws. She realized it must be painful for Nancy and Steve to watch as their son assimilated into a new family so far away from them. Especially after losing Kyle.

As Kelly said goodbye to her parents, Amber took Nancy and Steve's hands.

"Thank you so much for Kelly. I want you to know that I look forward to being part of your family. And I hope you know you're gaining a daughter rather than losing a son."

Nancy smiled and nodded as she squeezed Amber's hand tightly. Steve patted her on the back, then pulled out his handkerchief.

"I look forward to having a daughter, and I'm so glad he found you," Nancy told Amber. "We hope you can come out to California to visit soon."

"Me, too. I can't wait to spend time with you."

"Your church community is wonderful," Steve commented as he looked around. People lingered in the shade of the great cottonwoods, while the clean-up crew worked together. Laughter and conversation filled the air.

Amber and Kelly discreetly rounded the corner of the church, hoping to drive away unnoticed. However, her brothers had one more surprise for them.

The boys had covered Amber's white Jeep from front to back with colored frosting, balloons, and tin cans. A sign reading, "Just Married! Honk!" filled the back window. Eager to get away, Kelly and Amber drove off with all the decorations waving and clattering.

Chapter 40

Just Married! Honk!

Yet another passing motorist honked as Kelly and Amber hummed east on Interstate 94.

Amber sighed. "I wish the 'Just Married! Honk!' sign would rub off the back window. I'm glad to let everyone know we're married, but I don't want them all tooting their horns at us."

Settling back, she let her mind lounge in memories of the day. "What was that quote Pastor McDougal shared?"

"You mean how the wife is supposed to be obey her husband?" Kelly asked slyly.

"He didn't say that!" she responded as she whapped him on the arm. "Something by Martin Luther about friendship in marriage."

"The quote is, 'There is no more lovely, friendly and charming relationship, communion or company, than a good marriage'. He always finds the perfect quote to sum up his message."

"I really like that. I'm going to tape it on the bathroom mirror. Every morning it'll remind me of how blessed I am. As if I could forget." She patted Kelly's arm lovingly.

Privately, Kelly wondered where she would put it. On the mirror at her apartment or the one at the parsonage? Her work issues still weren't settled.

Amber continued. "I was relieved when Tiny and Bri were on their way to the hospital."

"Me too. The sooner that ankle is treated, the sooner she'll be back on her feet. Literally. Still, it was funny to see Tiny driving Bri around in a Cadillac. It looked like Bri was a movie star and Tiny was her chauffeur."

Amber giggled. "Oh, I'm sorry the accident happened, but it was super funny to see them driving off together."

Then she grew serious. "Kelly, do you think we should have delayed our honeymoon to take care of Bri?"

"No," Kelly answered a little too quickly. He had his own guilty feelings about leaving one of his best friends behind with a medical problem.

"Remember, Bri is very independent, and you know everyone will help her," Kelly said, reassuring himself as much as his bride.

"Besides, it's out of our control. Let's keep praying for her and see what God brings out of this. As for delaying our honeymoon, do you want to postpone our time alone together?"

"No way!" she said, trying to pat her hair into place. The upswept hairdo was slowly coming undone as her golden ringlets found freedom.

Another vehicle beeped its horn as it passed.

Amber peeked at Kelly out of the corner of her eye. "Don't you think it's time to tell me where we're going on our honeymoon? After all, my brothers can't mess up our plans anymore."

"I don't know, maybe they're hiding in the backseat." Kelly feigned a worried look.

Amber peered behind her seat. "Nope. We're alone. Tell me where we're going."

"Okay. We have reservations at a Minnesota lake resort for a few days. Then we're off to the Twin Cities for the rest of the week."

"Mmmm. That's wonderful."

"Thank my parents. They thought we needed time alone together."

"Your parents are sweet. I loved going to the beauty shop with your mother and Bri this morning." Amber snuggled into her seat. "Tell me about the resort."

"We'll be staying in a yurt." Kelly replied. "The outhouse isn't too far away. They provide flashlights to find it in the middle of the night."

"Sounds wonderful," Amber repeated absently.

Kelly tried not to smirk.

Her head jerked up.

"What's a yurt? Did you say outhouse?" she asked with alarm.

"A Mongolian tent, but I'm teasing you. We're going to a beautiful resort near Detroit Lakes. Honeymoon suite. Crystal clear lake. Classy dining room."

"Mmmm, sounds perfect. Do I dare ask where we're staying in the Twin Cities?"

"At a hotel near the Mall of America."

"That's my kind of vacation. We can shop and you'll love the rides at Camp Snoopy. Maybe we could check out Como Park and the Minneapolis Institute of Art."

Kelly ran his hand through his hair. He hoped to spend the whole time at the hotel.

"We might be too busy to go to the Mall," he suggested.

"Fat chance." Amber responded joyfully.

"We do have tickets for a Twins game."

"A ball game for you and shopping for me." Then she began brainstorming. "I wonder if we can get tickets to the Guthrie Theater and...."

"Hold up, Amber!" Kelly interrupted. "I don't want a to-do list on our honeymoon. Let's, ah, save time to be alone. I want to simply hang out with you."

"You mean no schedule?" Amber asked, doubtfully.

"That's right. And you might want to turn off your cellphone."

"It seems reckless to not answer the phone. What about Bri, or if our parents have an emergency, or there's one at work?"

"Amber, be reckless! We can check on Bri and give our folks the hotel numbers in case of emergency. The world won't end if the office can't reach you."

Amber shivered, remembering that Mammon Global was only a few miles from the Mall of America. Kelly was right. It would be great to forget the rest of the world for a few days.

"I can hardly imagine having a whole week of free days." A dreamy smile crossed her face as she lay her head back against the seat again.

"I remember a day when I was little. I had taken my dolls out under that big cottonwood behind the house. It was hot. I can still hear the sound of bedsheets flapping in the wind on the clothesline. We had a dog named Rover and he was there."

Kelly nodded for her to continue.

"It may be my best memory," said Amber ruefully. "A couple years later, the twins were born, and then Mom got really sick. One day she was so weak that Dad carried her to the car and took her to the hospital. Something changed in me after that. My innocence was gone."

Kelly felt the weight of her memories.

"And you've been responsible ever since."

Amber sighed and relaxed in her seat. "I love the idea of being reckless with you." She leaned over and turned her phone off.

Kelly pulled her hand to his lips and kissed it, unable to fathom that his love for her could grow any deeper. Yet it had in the last few moments.

He glanced at her profile, the golden hair, the up-turned nose, her delicate, determined chin. Yes, there was a God in heaven, and he had blessed Kelly with the best.

A minute later, he stole another glance and saw Amber's eyes had closed. At that moment, Kelly wanted to hold her in his arms and never let another worry crease her brow. Thinking of the popular Christian song Cole Jensen sang during the wedding, he whispered, "Amber, I'll always be here."

When Kelly was growing up, he took for granted that he'd spend his whole life near his twin brother, Kyle. Now, his eyes automatically went to the dashboard and felt a shock when Kyle's photo wasn't there. It has been on the dashboard of his pickup since the day he bought it. Today he was driving Amber's vehicle.

A lump formed in his throat. Kyle should have been his best man today. Kelly couldn't believe how time had hurdled forward for the last seven years, propelling him into the future, while Kyle lay in a nice cemetery, in a tidy grave. He could see the headstone in his mind.

"Kyle, buddy, I know you're up there singing with the angels, and I'll see you again someday. I want you to know that I'm trying to live life the best I can. I'm doing it for you, as well as for me. You'd like Amber. I know you would. And Brianna is doing fine."

Kelly didn't speak aloud, couldn't have even if he wanted to, however, his lips moved as he stared into the windshield. He would never, ever, take his time with Amber for granted.

When he looked over at her, she had awakened and was watching him. A sweet smile played across her lips and compassion filled her eyes. As if she read his thoughts.

After they arrived in Minnesota, Kelly called Aunt Kate to check on Brianna. When Kate answered, she curtly told him Brianna was fine. Then, before slamming the receiver down, she told him not to call about another woman again while he was on his honeymoon.

Then Amber tried calling. Marge answered and handed the phone to Brianna.

"I'm glad to hear from you. How's the honeymoon?" Brianna sounded cheerful, but breathy, as though she were in pain.

"The best," Amber responded. "Still, it'll be better if we know you're doing okay."

Brianna reported that Tiny Winger had taken her to the emergency room in Bismarck. An X-ray revealed that the smaller bone in her lower leg, the fibula, was broken. She had a walking boot, and needed to remain in North Dakota until she saw an orthopedic surgeon.

"I'd like to talk more, if Aunt Kate wasn't glaring at me. I'll give you a full account when you get back. Say hi to Kelly for me and have a beautiful time."

Next, Amber called the farm. Tim picked up the phone, impatiently said they were all fine, and hung up. When she called back, he answered again. "Mom said to tell you she's fine," he said and hung up again.

At first, it took all of Amber's willpower and encouragement from Kelly to not call the office. However, as the days went by, she found it easier to let go. For eight sweet days, the couple focused on each other.

Chapter 41
Home from the Honeymoon

Kelly and Amber arrived home from their honeymoon late Sunday afternoon. As they pulled to a stop in front of the parsonage, they spied Mildred peering out the window at them.

"Looks like my roommate survived without me," Kelly said.

"Now, you'll be living with two females."

Kelly eyed her. "I'm looking forward to every second."

As they pulled up at the parsonage, she bounded out of the car and dragged her purse, shopping bags, and travel kit up the steps to the house. Kelly followed slowly behind.

When they walked in, Mildred stared at them for a moment, then turned and walked away with her tail in the air.

"Mildred, don't you want to say hello?" Kelly asked to her backside.

"Who can understand cats?" he asked Amber. "She should be glad to see us."

"Maybe she liked being by herself." She looked around and then put her arms around Kelly's waist and hugged him. "This is my new home. Our home. We're going to be so happy."

They could see into the dining room. Wedding gifts filled the table, sat on the floor and leaned against chairs. Amazingly, Mildred hadn't bothered them.

"Oh, aren't the gifts beautiful?" Amber said. "Not only because they're wrapped in pretty paper, it's because they're from so many lovely people."

"When do you want to do the gift opening?" Kelly asked as he eyed the overcrowded dining room. "How about tomorrow evening? Maybe your family can come over."

"I'm going back to work tomorrow."

"Aren't you taking an extra day off? We just got back!"

"I can't be away any longer," Amber responded.

Kelly felt disappointment down to his toes. The honeymoon was over.

"Tell you what, let's do the gift opening when I get home on Friday evening," Amber suggested. "If you make sure the house is tidy, I'll figure out how to feed everyone. We can invite my family over. And Bri and Aunt Kate."

"Okay," he said reluctantly. "I'll miss you every second when you're away."

As he hugged Amber, he noticed Mildred sitting in the doorway between the kitchen and dining room about the same time he noticed an unpleasant odor. When he took a step toward the cat, she once again turned and sashayed away. This time Kelly followed her as she walked to the middle of the living room and sat down.

"Oh no!" he said. "There's a dead mouse in here!"

Amber rushed to the scene.

"Yuck!" she said, covering her nose. "That thing has been dead for a few days. And look, there's another one over there."

She giggled. "They must be Mildred's wedding gifts to us."

Kelly felt disgusted. Peering around the room, he said, "There doesn't seem to be any more corpses, I mean wedding gifts. I'll clean this up."

Mildred purred as she looked up at him. He knelt and stroked the top of her head.

"Your taste in gifts stinks, Mildred. Literally," he spoke kindly, but honestly, to her. "Still, I understand it's probably the best kitty gift you could give us."

Mildred seemed to smile and wink at him. Then she rolled on her back, ready for a tummy rub. Kelly obediently stroked her gray fur.

Later, while he took care of the mess and checked for other signs of mice, Amber unpacked and filled the washer with dirty laundry. She opened the drawers to the French provincial dresser Kelly had inherited from his grandparents and put away clothes she had kept at her parents' farm. Most of her other things would remain at her apartment in Bismarck.

Then she raced downstairs and hugged Kelly.

"You won't believe the pretty sign your mother and Brianna made for us. It's hanging in the bedroom." Then she was gone, speeding down the road to check on her parents and brothers.

The washer swished, the dryer hummed, and an empty suitcase sat at the bottom of the stairs. Kelly had married a whirlwind. All he had managed to do since they arrived home was bring in the luggage, pet the cat, and haul two mice to the shelterbelt for burial. He and Amber definitely ran at different speeds.

Kelly listened to the phone messages and wrote them down. The last one was from Marge Selby. He gave her a call. Yes, Brianna was still there. She had an ortho appointment on Tuesday, and after that, she could probably fly back to California. Marge was making honey chicken for dinner. Could Kelly and Amber come over?

Kelly said they would be in Schulteville by six-thirty. After he hung up, he called the McLean residence to let Amber know.

"Oh, Kelly. I'm making dinner for my family. I thought you could come over here."

"Guess I should have talked to you before I made plans," Kelly said. "I could call Marge back and decline her offer, but I'd really like to see them. How do you think Aunt Kate and Brianna got along?"

"I've been wondering, too. I'll finish making dinner and swing by to pick you up as soon as I can."

Kelly agreed to Amber's plan. When the dryer stopped, he folded a load of clothes and put in the next load. Holding up a piece of frilly feminine laundry, he wondered if it should be thrown in the dryer or hung up. It would be too embarrassing to call Amber back and ask her what to do with her underwear. Neither did he want to leave it for late in the evening.

He sighed and looked for advice from Mildred, who had been following him around like a lost puppy. When she blinked her eyes in total disregard to his question, he draped Amber's delicate items over a doorknob.

"Let's look at your food supply," he said once the dryer was running again. When he opened the garage door, Mildred flashed past him. Kelly flipped on the light. Mildred crouched by the cat food bag. He usually kept the bag in a metal container. Now the lid was off. A virtual pantry for rodents, Kelly thought unhappily. They could have scurried into the house if the door had been left open for even a minute.

He grabbed the bag and hauled it out of the garage. He half expected a parade of mice to hop out of the bag carrying nuggets of cat food, but didn't wait around to see. Instead, he closed the garage door and went into the house.

Kelly was excited to tell Amber his discovery. She had handled the mouse affair like a farm girl well acquainted with rodents. Still, they would both be relieved if they didn't find any more mice in the house.

Amber wheeled into the driveway late. Kelly was waiting on the steps and jumped into the Jeep without saying a word. He considered it rude to be late, and he hoped their hosts would understand. Of all the kind, sweet people he didn't want to inconvenience, Marge was at the top of the list. He also cringed at the vision of Aunt Kate rebuking their tardiness. Yet, he had made the date without consulting Amber.

After a charged moment, they both said, "I'm sorry!" at the same time. Then they began to laugh.

"I tried to hurry," Amber explained. "I was trying to make the meal, and everyone was talking to me at once. I had to find something personal for Mom in her closet. The twins needed help with a 4-H project and before I knew it..."

"It's okay. Next time, I won't make plans without checking with you," Kelly said. They grasped hands and Kelly leaned over and kissed her before Amber accelerated.

He glanced toward the garage as they whirled around the driveway and out to the road. Mildred still sat next to the food bag waiting for an escapee to appear.

He wondered if there was a sermon in that bag. How often do we become trapped by too much of a good thing, like a mouse caught in a bag of cat food with a cat waiting patiently nearby? It wouldn't be the first time Mildred inspired a sermon.

"Honey," he said as they sped toward Schulteville, "I found out how the mice got in the house."

Chapter 42
Trip to Schulteville

As the newlyweds sped off to the impromptu dinner at Kate Schulte's home, Amber popped her favorite Christian music into the CD player and belted out, "Let there be praise, let there be joy in our hearts!" Once again, Kelly thanked God for his life, his wife, and at this moment, her perfect pitch.

When Schulteville appeared on the horizon, a distant leafy fort, he slowly dialed away from his wife's joyful cacophony. Hilly country and a small lake sat beyond the village. Two landmarks rose above the tree line. The first was a row of the gray metal elevators, and the second was the brown-shingled steeple of Cross Church.

The steeple confirmed a spiritual lesson that Kelly lived by: God gives second chances. Even church buildings can begin again, he thought as he focused on the steeple. Since Easter, the old church had found new life.

The aging building located in a dying town could have met a dismal end. Instead, with the help of God, Wayne and Marge Selby were turning it into a blessing. Wayne had given the building a fresh coat of white paint and moved his carpentry business into the sturdy structure. A banner across the front now read "Cross Church Carpentry."

Kelly had stopped by several times. He enjoyed the fresh scent of sawdust permeating the air as Wayne built church pulpits and other furnishings to ship across the United States. His was one of the first business owners in the area to set up a website. His motto was, "Jesus was a carpenter, too."

People enjoyed stopping by Wayne's business. A radio played country and gospel music. The coffeemaker perked all day. A miniature refrigerator held cold bottled water. Farm women dropped off baked goods to share with others. Men stopped by, took off their caps, swigged coffee, and discussed everything from raising kids to harvesting wheat.

Instead of being open one hour on Sunday, the building was now open six days a week. Wayne often prayed with those who came to visit. Sometimes he picked up a worn copy of the Bible and thumbed to Proverbs when giving advice, or to a Psalm when offering comfort.

What everyone, including Kelly, saw as the end to Cross Church turned out to be another beginning. He wondered why change was so feared when God often used it to bring about good.

His thoughts returned to the present as Amber came to the end of a song. They slowed and turned off the narrow paved county road onto the gravel main street of Schulteville.

When the Jeep rolled to a stop in front of the Queen Anne, Kelly and Amber could see Aunt Kate and Brianna sitting on the veranda.

"Are you ready?" Kelly asked Amber.

"No," Amber responded, a sudden shyness in her voice. Kelly noted that her cheeks were turning pink. "I've heard that Aunt Kate likes to embarrass new brides. You know how she can ask the rudest questions."

"Ah," Kelly answered. "Attacking the blushing bride..."

"Yes, exactly," Amber moaned.

Kelly laughed as he opened the door.

"Listen," he said, trying to get his bride to loosen up. "If she makes a fuss, I'm going to give you the kiss of a lifetime right in front of her."

"Oh no! You can't do that! Promise me, Kelly."

He climbed out of the Jeep, went around to the driver's side, and opened Amber's door. As he helped her, he whispered in her ear. "You are my Golden Girl and the love of my life. Not even Aunt Kate is allowed to give you a bad time."

Amber smiled up at him as they shared a look that could only transpire between two people in love. Then they walked up the sidewalk hand in hand.

"Land's sake!' Kate crowed. "It's the newlyweds. Come up here and let me look at you." She gawked at them like a hawk watching its prey. The couple remained silent under her gaze.

"Well, what's the matter? Can't you say hello?"

"Aunt Kate, Brianna, it's so good to see you!" Kelly boomed. "How are you?"

"We're fit as fiddles," Aunt Kate declared, as she waved off their concern with her hanky. Then she settled deeper into her chair, her eyes sparkling with mischief.

"Tell me all about your honeymoon." Kate's false teeth clacked.

Amber turned a brighter shade of pink. Kelly searched for something safe to say.

"Aunt Kate! That's not your business." Marge stood at the screen door, with her arms folded.

Kate's mouth flew open, and then shut, as she realized she'd been called out on her snoopy ways.

"I'll help Marge," Amber said. She gave Brianna a bright smile as she slipped through the screen door.

Kelly sat down. Aunt Kate had an embroidery frame in her lap and Brianna held a sketchpad.

"What are you working on?" he asked Brianna.

"I've been drawing Schulteville today." Brianna held up the pad. Whimsical buildings reached to a cloud-puffed sky. "It's lucky I brought my art kit, because it's kept me occupied. I've worked on sunflowers for several days.

"See?" she said, flipping pages that revealed a variety of yellow flowers.

"I only wish I had more time, so Aunt Kate could teach me how to embroider."

Kelly stared at his old friend. She wore a faded plaid shirt. Her cast stuck out of a pair of baggy beige trousers. Her hair was pulled back in a ponytail, and there wasn't a trace of mascara or lip-gloss on her face. Was this the same girl who had meltdowns over broken fingernails and skipped classes on bad hair days? He remembered how she skipped school one time, because she didn't think her shoes matched her outfit.

Today her urbane sophistication was gone, yet she looked radiant and at peace.

"May I say you look great considering all you've been through?"

Aunt Kate cleared her throat, plainly not comfortable with Kelly's friendship with Brianna. Kelly could understand her concerns. A year ago, he might have expected to marry Brianna someday. Now his friendship with Brianna was nothing like the deep love he felt for Amber. Brianna had experienced that kind of love with Kyle, and Kelly hoped she would find it again someday.

"I feel really good. My ankle still hurts, but something wonderful has happened to me on the inside. Aunt Kate, Marge and Wayne have been so kind to me. I guess that sometimes you need to let go and let God. I didn't have any choice this time."

Kelly was astonished at the change in Brianna and he couldn't wait to hear more. However, at that moment his sweet bride opened the door and announced that dinner was ready.

Chapter 43
Dinner with Friends

Kelly had eaten dinner at Aunt Kate's a number of times. The formal affairs made him nervous. Last Easter, he'd dumped a dessert on the floor and broken the china plate. While his mother set a nice table, his family's lifestyle was California casual rather than Midwest formal.

When Amber opened the screen door and announced dinner was ready, he helped Aunt Kate out of her rocking chair. Brianna rose from the chaise lounge, grabbed a pair of crutches, and hobbled into the house.

Kelly was surprised to see the table set with a grass-green woven cloth, vintage green and white plaid dishes, and paper napkins.

"Do you like it?" Kate beamed. "I showed Brianna all of the dishes gathering dust in the china closet. She wondered why I don't use them. Why indeed, I asked myself."

Amber clapped her hands, exclaiming over the appealing table. Kelly noticed that the dining room drapes were pulled open, revealing the flower-filled side yard under a colored-glass transom. He commented on how cheerful the room seemed.

Kate pursed her lips. "Oh, that's Brianna's meddling. She told me that she likes this house, but I should join the twenty-first century."

"Aunt Kate, that's only half of what I said," Brianna exclaimed. "I also said you should redecorate, because your house is excessively yellow.'"

Kelly almost choked. Aunt Kate did have a fondness for yellow. Dingy yellow wallpaper in various patterns added no charm to the otherwise lovely rooms.

He sneaked a look at Aunt Kate. Although she was trying not to smile, Kelly could see that Brianna's impertinence pleased the older woman. He and Amber had sent up a few prayers for Brianna and Aunt Kate, as they wondered if the strong-willed women would clash. Now it appeared they had connected in an unexpected way.

Marge brought out honey chicken, a pasta dish, tossed salad, and homemade biscuits. Brianna regaled her friends with humorous stories of her trip to the emergency room.

Kelly observed that Brianna ate the salad, picked at the chicken, and avoided the biscuits. He wondered if she was still on some kind of extreme diet or too busy telling stories to eat.

"There we were at the hospital registration desk. By then, my bridesmaid dress looked like it came from a secondhand store. Tiny had changed out of that awful brown suit into his filthy cap and a t-shirt with a hole in it. The clerk frowned at Tiny and asked if we had insurance.

"I said, 'Yes, I have insurance,' and then she looked at Tiny and asked him if he'd fill out the forms. I said, 'I'll fill out my own forms.'"

"When she suggested my husband do the paperwork because I was in pain, I said, 'This man is not my husband. I hardly know him.' All the clerk said was 'Oh!'"

Kate cackled and the others laughed aloud.

Brianna began another tale. "When Tiny brought me back here, I was woozy with pain meds and exhausted from the day. Kate took me in there and got me settled in bed," she said as she waved at a bedroom behind a pair of curtained French doors.

"I fell asleep right away and woke up hours later, disoriented. It was black as coffee and I could feel a presence. It scared me! I lay there hardly able to breathe. The window was open and I could hear sounds from outside. However, whatever scared me wasn't outside. It was closer than that.

"I was never one to believe in ghosts or spooky things, yet something was there beside me. Then a loud snort scared the snot out of me! I was ready to grab the pillow and start whapping. Thank goodness, I remembered there was a small table beside the bed. I reached over and felt around until I found the light switch and turned it on."

Amber leaned forward. "What was it?" Her green eyes were as big as the dinner plates.

"Aunt Kate," said Brianna. "She was sleeping next to me." Everyone roared with laughter, except for Aunt Kate.

"Well, I put her to sleep in my room, for pity's sake," she explained, her false teeth clacking. "Where was I supposed to sleep? I just crawled in the other side at bedtime and didn't give it another think."

After the laughter died down, Brianna continued. "The next night, Kate insisted I sleep in her bed again, and she crawled in later in the evening. This time I was awake, and we talked and talked. It reminded me of..." Brianna stopped speaking. Her smile remained bright as tears glittered in her eyes.

"It reminded me of when I was a little girl and stayed at Grandma's house. We'd sleep in the same bed and talk until all hours. Because my parents moved so much, it was hard for me to make friends at every new school. Grandma was my best friend."

Those gathered around the table sat hushed in the poignant moment.

Kate broke the silence.

"Well, now you're one of my girls, just as Amber is." She patted Brianna's hand. Looking around the room, the spinster explained, "If you don't have any children of your own, 'tis all right to adopt someone else's."

Kelly wondered how many lives she had improved throughout the years. Perhaps there was a soft heart under her stern exterior.

After dinner, the party moved to the living room and Brianna continued talking.

"Tiny was so kind to me and I was such a crab that day. I owe him an apology, but for some reason he hasn't been by."

Chuckles filled the room. Kelly doubted Tiny would ever mention Brianna's name again, let alone stop to see her.

Over a dessert of fruit and cheese, they discussed Brianna's return to California.

"I hope the surgeon will say I'm healed up enough to fly home," she said. "Wayne and Marge will take me to the appointment. However, I need a place to stay until I can make plane reservations."

Turning to Amber, she asked, "Could I stay with you for a few days?"

"Of course, you can stay with me as long as you need to."

"When I first came here, I couldn't wait to get back to San Francisco, but now I hate to leave," Brianna said, looking around the room. "You've all been so kind to me and I feel like we're family."

She sighed. "Yet, it's time to go home."

Wayne cleared his throat. "We usually read a devotional each evening and pray with one another. Would you join us this evening, Pastor Kelly and Amber?"

When they nodded, Wayne went to his desk, put on his glasses, and picked up a small book. He sat next to Marge and began to read.

"Robert Frost said, 'Two roads diverged in a wood and I---I took the one less traveled by. And that has made all the difference.'"

Wayne's glasses sat low on his nose. "When you walk through a wooded area, it's difficult to see very far ahead.

As the path curves, you don't know what is around the bend. A log fallen across the path? A beautiful waterfall? A bear with her cubs?"

He continued, "Every day we come to crossroads in our lives and must decide which way to go. We can find direction in God's word. Jeremiah 6:16 says, 'Stand at the crossroads and look; ask for the ancient paths, ask where the good way is, and walk in it, and you will find rest for your souls.'"

Wayne looked up. "In other words, do some investigating before you make a decision. Pray for wisdom and direction. Ask other people what worked for them. Based on what you've learned, step out in faith. This is the path less traveled, as well as the path of confidence and peace."

Wayne pushed his glasses further up on his nose.

"We have some prayer needs here. Let's pray for a good outcome at Brianna's appointment tomorrow. And for the newlyweds that God will continue to bless you and your marriage. Any other requests?"

"My mom. She needs a miracle," Amber said. Kelly felt a stab of regret. He hadn't even asked about Amber's trip to the farm or about Jean's health.

They bowed their heads and raised prayers to their Friend, whom they believed was surely present with them. Kelly peeked at Brianna. Her eyes were closed in earnest prayer.

As they drove home later, Kelly and Amber talked about the surprising turn of events.

"I confess I went to Schulteville expecting the worst," Amber commented. "How remarkable that a friendship has blossomed between Aunt Kate and Brianna."

Kelly smiled. "We hated to leave Brianna last week, yet God was in control."

Amber nodded. "It went like the devotional Wayne read tonight. We took stock of the situation at the wedding, asked advice from our friends, prayed for wisdom, and set out on our path. And God took over."

Then she quietly murmured, "If only it was always that easy."

Chapter 44
Roses for Amber Rose

The honeymoon is over, Amber realized as she arrived at work on Monday morning. Her email inbox was clogged and mounds of files covered her desk. Kimberly had sorted the mess into stacks and put a sticky note on each one. PHONE CALLS. CLIENTS. SPIT.

The phone calls included all those Kimberly had fielded at the front desk, the ones that couldn't be sent to another staff member. The client folders held the histories of clients who were making new claims.

SPIT was another story. Her coworkers had met Benson's new marketing ideas with disdain and quickly dubbed the strategic planning in-house training as SPIT. They regularly made comments about the "SPIT fire" or asked, "Are we within spitting distance yet?"

Amber didn't take the jokes personally. She agreed that if something worked well, it was best not to change it. Yet, the insurance industry was in a necessary transition. For now, she would lead the process and fervently hope Benson would soon be well enough to come back to work and relieve her of the job.

A couple hours after arriving, she was summoned to the front desk. Assuming Kimberly wanted to have a quick cup of coffee, she made her way to the lobby. A large bouquet of red roses graced the front desk.

"For you," Kimberly exclaimed. "The romance continues."

Amber opened the card. The message read, "Always on my mind." She beamed as she carried the bouquet back to her office and shoveled out a place on her desk for the vase. Then for a moment, she let her mind drift back to the honeymoon. How she wished they could be like the Jewish newlyweds in the Old Testament who took a whole year off to settle into married life.

Amber dialed the parsonage and waited to hear Kelly's voice. Instead, the standard recording clicked on.

Speaking low, she left a message. "Kelly, you're such a romantic. You're always on my mind, too." She hung up and breathed in the scent of the flowers.

The rest of the day was hardly a bed of roses. Like a racehorse, she kept focused on completing one task after another.

The sun was low in the June sky when Amber pulled into her apartment parking lot. Although it was her first night away from Kelly since they were married, she wouldn't be alone. Brianna was already at her apartment.

She was happy to offer their friend a place to stay. After all, it was because Brianna had been in their wedding party that she was in North Dakota with a broken ankle. Still, having her stay at the apartment was a reminder that Amber's married life was a lot like her single life.

"Hi, Girlfriend," Brianna greeted her as she walked in the apartment.

"How did your medical appointments go?" Amber asked as she stowed her briefcase.

"Good news. My ankle is healing, and I can go home. I need to follow-up with a doctor in San Francisco. I fly out at five-thirty Wednesday morning."

"I'll drive you to the airport and make sure you're safely onboard," Amber responded.

The women smiled shyly at each other. As much as they had talked on the phone and exchanged emails before the wedding, they had never found time to develop a friendship in person. Even when Brianna arrived for the wedding, there was little time spent together.

Holding up a bag, Amber said, "I hope you're hungry. I picked up Chinese." Sitting cross-legged on the floor by the coffee table, she pulled aromatic cartons out of the bag.

Brianna, who had been lying on the couch, sat up.

"As soon as I'm home, I must get back on healthy food."

"What's not healthy about Cashew Chicken?" Amber asked.

"Probably nothing, but I'll stick with my nutritional packets." Then, waving a fork in the air, she added. "Mm, this tastes as good as it smells. I hope my clothes still fit when I get home. I couldn't resist Marge's cooking last week any more than I can resist this."

"Oh, don't worry. What happens in North Dakota stays in North Dakota. Any extra weight will be gone by the time your plane touches down," Amber teased. "Hey, you know what Kelly did today? He sent the most gorgeous bouquet of roses."

A frown crossed Brianna's face.

"Kelly must be changing. He's never been big on flowers for some reason. I remember Nancy saying that she had never received flowers for Mother's Day or her birthday."

"I'll have to remember to send her a bouquet when her birthday comes around. He's never bought flowers for me before, either."

Just then, the phone rang. "It's Kelly," Amber said as she picked up the receiver. "Kelly, I was telling Brianna about the flowers you sent today." She paused and cocked her head.

"You didn't order red roses for me? If you didn't, who did?"

Chapter 45
Girlfriends

A mber hung up the phone and turned to Brianna.

"The flowers weren't from Kelly. Who else would send them?" she puzzled. "Benson! He sent white roses for our wedding."

"What did the note say?" Brianna asked.

"Always on my mind.'"

"That's seems mysterious and romantic. Not something a boss would send. Could it be an old boyfriend?"

"No way. Kelly was my first serious boyfriend."

Amber went to the kitchen and brought back a carton of mint chocolate chip ice cream and two spoons. Brianna ignored her spoon for a couple minutes, then she absently began eating as they sat on the couch discussing the flowers. They exhausted every possible scenario as the ice cream carton emptied.

Finding no answers, Amber concluded, "I'll have an uneasy feeling about those flowers until I know for certain who sent them."

"I'm feeling a little sick myself." Brianna laid down her spoon. "For more than one reason."

"You're picking up my bad eating habits," Amber said with a laugh. "Why did you start eating those nutrition packets? It can't be to lose weight, you're already so thin."

"My mother was always on one diet or another. She insisted that I watch my weight. I always wanted her approval, or maybe just some attention. We moved a lot, and wherever we lived, Mom got involved in the arts community. She was never home."

"So you began to diet to win your mother's approval. Not good. Do you see much of your parents now?"

"No. They moved overseas about the time I got a job in San Francisco. We had moved to Huntington Beach just as I started high school, so that became my first real home. Now I can't go home anymore.

Amber was quiet for a minute before responding. "That would be hard. My parents live on the family homestead. I can't imagine what it's like not to be able to go home again."

"It wasn't until we'd lived in California for a couple years, and I began dating Kyle, that I felt like I belonged. I totally gave my heart to him. I still have nightmares about the night he was killed."

Amber felt sympathy for Brianna. No matter how someone looks on the outside, you never know what they're dealing with on the inside, Amber thought.

"After Kyle died, Kelly and I went through the same emotions at first," Brianna continued. "Then he decided to seek a relationship with God like Kyle had. As soon as he became a Christian, he found his footing.

"If you could see that, why didn't you do the same?

"I couldn't give my heart to God. It was too much like giving it to Kyle. I didn't dare trust anyone, even God, ever again."

"You trusted Kelly." Amber countered.

"True. But that was different."

"You've found your footing now," Amber said.

Brianna smiled. "All the while I was in college, I was waiting for something else to go wrong. Finally, when I began doing well in the design field, I decided security was in success."

We have another thing in common, Amber noted. Security issues.

"Now I know I had based my confidence on something false. Then my parents and Kelly left California and my business partner moved to Sweden. All my security was gone. Again. That's when I fell apart."

"Was that last December when you called Kelly and said you were coming out here?"

"He had what Kyle had. Finally, I knew it was what I wanted, too," she replied earnestly.

Amber smiled. "When Kelly urged you to trust God, it must have taken a lot of courage."

"Listen, I was truly alone in this world at that moment. In the Denver airport. In the middle of an unending snowstorm. It was like hanging from a window ledge and hoping someone could save me." Brianna's usual aloof expression was gone, replaced by an animation Amber hadn't seen before.

"After talking with him, I sat on the floor at the airport with a lot of time to think. There was nothing to lose and everything to gain by testing out this God thing."

"The Lord is faithful to those who trust him," Amber said.

Brianna brightened. "What a change God is making in my life. You helped, too."

Amber was surprised, wondering how she fit into the equation.

"Last December, Kelly said you had invited me to live with you. You hadn't even heard of me before that morning. That meant a lot to me.

"Of course, things smoothed out after that. Jontel came back to San Francisco. I love working with him, even if he is somewhat odd. I found a church tucked away near our studio and began attending Bible studies. I didn't jump in head first, because I still had some trust issues. Still, I kept dipping my feet in the water."

"That offer to live with me was genuine, although it was a leap of faith for me, too. Yet, here we are, friends and roommates."

Brianna nodded. "Life has some surprising twists."

"Speaking of which, tell me about your week in Schulteville. How did it really go with Aunt Kate?"

"Oh, she can be quite a trip!" Brianna said. "I'm so grateful to her. Beginning when I fell at the wedding, she took charge of things. She welcomed me into her home. Isn't there a scripture about taking in a stranger?"

"I was a stranger and you invited me in. Matthew 25:35. Memorized it when I was a kid." Amber said. "Aunt Kate is half full of pickle juice and half full of honey. She can insult you, then turn around and do something grand, such as planning my wedding and paying for much of it." She shook her head in disbelief.

Brianna was leaning forward, her eyes shining.

"You know what really got to me? Although Kate is bossy, she treated me like family. Me, the girl who felt like she had lost her home. I soaked it up like a sponge in a bathtub."

The following evening, Amber brought salads home from a nearby restaurant after a twelve-hour day at the office.

"You put in longer hours than I do!" Brianna exclaimed, as she dug into her salad.

Amber noticed that she didn't bring up her nutrition program.

"Now, tell me about your family. Your mother---." Brianna didn't know what to say, because it was obvious that Jean McLean had health issues.

"She's forty-five and she developed multiple sclerosis after the twins were born. She has classic symptoms: Fatigue, balance, and vision problems. She goes through relapses and remissions, but this is the worst she's ever been."

"One of our neighbors in California had MS. Everyone tried to support her."

Amber nodded. "People want to help. After a while, they wear out. When you have a long-term illness, you're in for a marathon, not a sprint. It's been tough, although she never complains. In fact, her prayer life is awesome."

"Still, your whole family must be affected by this," Brianna observed.

"We are. By the time I started high school I was in charge of the household. I even took emergency medical training, thinking I could help her." She wagged her head sadly.

"It doesn't work that way. The twins can't remember when she played the piano or worked in her garden. Dad struggles to pay medical bills. Now I'm gone and he's the chief cook and housekeeper. It's good that Adam decided to farm, because he takes on some of Dad's responsibility."

"You're still pretty involved in her care."

Amber nodded and smiled sadly.

"Now what?" Brianna asked. "You're married. You have a job that keeps you away from Kelly. Your family needs you. How are you going to juggle all of that?"

Amber shrugged. "I love my job and we need the income, and I'm still the oldest child and the big sister. Doing things like shopping for groceries or my brothers' school clothes, or driving them to the dentist takes some of the stress off my parents."

"I guess it's none of my business, except Kelly is like a brother to me," Brianna circled around a topic she didn't want to bring up.

"What?" Amber asked as she idly picked up her doll, Rusty Ann, and began stroking its yarny hair.

"Maybe I'm missing something, however, it looks like Kelly is going to get the leftovers."

A troubled look came over Amber's face. "That's exactly what my mother said."

Chapter 46
Tiny Goes Jogging

The figure jogging over the rise looked like a mirage through the west window, a pinpoint on the horizon, wavering and distant. It was the kind of spectacle you see out of the corner of your eye and think it's merely a water drop or a green fly on the window.

Kelly was standing at the dryer folding clothes. His shirts hung from the bar he had wedged in a space over the ancient washer. The bath towels lay in a pile, folded precise and square, like he did his boxer shorts. They were easy compared to the oddly shaped underthings his wife wore. Fold them in a triangle? Roll them up? Wad them in a ball? He shrugged. At least he now knew better than to put them on a doorknob to dry.

Mildred jumped up on the dryer and planted herself on the warm stack of towels.

"Move, Mildred. No wonder there's cat hair all over the house." The kitty purred and settled on the towels anyway. As Kelly went to move her, he glanced out the window again. His smooth jaw grazed Mildred's fuzzy gray cheek as he leaned forward for a better look.

The mirage had moved closer, and for all the world it looked like Tiny Winger wearing a tank top and running shorts. Moreover, was that a sweatband in place of his grimy green "Your Friendly Co-op" cap?

His gait was slow, and every time his feet touched the ground, his ample girth rippled and dipped. Kelly wondered how he could make his legs, as big around as trees, move with any kind of rhythm and grace.

Kelly shot down the steps and out the back door. He rounded the corner of the garage in time to see Tiny leave the pavement and jog down into the tall grass of the ditch. Then he disappeared like a UFO off a radar screen.

"Tiny!" Kelly shouted as he ran over to the ditch. There was his friend sprawled, arms extended, face down, the color of his clothing blending in with the grass.

"Tiny! Are you okay?" Kelly knelt beside his friend. Tiny raised his head. His face was as round and red as a blood moon. "I didn't know it was so far out here," he huffed and dropped his head again.

"You jogged all the way out here?" Kelly asked incredulously. He'd never known Tiny to move faster than a slow walk.

Tiny looked up. "It's part of my new weight-loss plan." His face dropped into the grass again.

A couple years earlier, before he became a pastor, Kelly might have spoken the first thing that came to his mind, something like, 'You crazy fool.'

Now he said, "Perhaps you need to rethink this."

"Nope," Tiny responded as got up on his hands and knees. "I'm going to get in shape if it kills me."

After Kelly pulled his friend to his feet, Tiny made a beeline for the water faucet on the north side of the house. He turned it on full blast. A dribble of water came out of the garden hose. Desperate, he held the hose over his head and let the small stream trickle through his hair and down his face.

"Don't you even have a bottle of water with you?"

"Did. Drank it and threw it in the Watson's trash pile when I went by."

"I'll go get you some water and a towel."

Kelly sighed again and trotted into the house. He shooed Mildred off the pile of towels and grabbed the top one for his friend to use, hoping Tiny wouldn't notice the cat fur on it. He also pulled a bottle of water out of the fridge and rushed back outside.

Tiny took the towel and dried his head and face with it before spitting out what looked like gray cat hair. He looked accusingly at Kelly.

"Cat hair all over the house, lately," Kelly apologized. "Cats shed this time of year."

Tiny twisted off the bottle cap and took a swig.

The two sat down in the shade at the old picnic table. The last of its paint had worn off years ago and its main use now was as a place to clean fish or game. Kelly could clearly see fish scales on it.

"When did you begin this weight loss program?" he asked.

"A few weeks ago. Quit drinking soda pop, and eating chips and donuts. Decided to exercise."

"How's that working for you?"

"Lost five pounds the first week. Seven more after I started jogging." Tiny gave a moon-face smile as he crushed the plastic bottle in his palm.

"That's impressive," Kelly said enthusiastically. "Did you see a doctor before you started all of this?"

"Sort of. Doc Boveen stopped by to get his tires rotated."

Kelly groaned. Doc Boveen was the local veterinarian.

"Yep. He gave me great advice. Said, 'You can't yank a horse out of the pasture and expect it to run a race at the county fair.' I figured that was true for me, too. I started by just jogging around the track at the school."

"That's wise, but maybe you should go, you know, to a people doctor and get your weight and blood pressure and those kinds of things checked."

Tiny looked dubious. "Heck no. I've got a scale. I know what I weigh, and I know how much I want to lose. Why go to a doctor and run up a bill to find out what I already know?"

Kelly ran his fingers through his hair. "Hard to argue with that logic," he said dryly.

They sat quietly for a few moments, while Tiny cooled down.

"So," Kelly hesitated, eyeing his friend's emerald-green shirt and shorts. He had to know. "Where did you get your running clothes?" Tiny's legs looked even more like tree trunks from close range. Tree trunks coming out of a leafy green tree.

"These clothes? When I started my fitness program, I decided a new set of clothes was in order. You wouldn't believe what a bargain they were. Got 'em online. What do you think?" he asked as he held out his shirt.

"They're outstanding," Kelly replied evenly. "I admire your determination.

"Yep. I'm pumped. That's why I decided to jog out here today." Tiny eyed the road. "It was farther than I expected."

"Hey, I'll give you a ride back to town."

"I'd love a ride." Tiny got up, stretched, and jogged in place.

Kelly looked away. The sight was too much to take in. Then he had a thought.

"Have you given up brown sugar sandwiches yet?"

Tiny looked stricken. "Oh, I don't know if I can take it that far," he said. "That would really be going off the deep end."

Chapter 47
The Gift Opening

With Amber's demanding schedule, the couple didn't have time to open weddings gifts until three weeks after the wedding. Then they decided to make a party of it. Guests included friends who had helped with the wedding and Amber's family. It was a way for them to thank everyone, and let them share the fun.

Some gifts were still arriving. Earlier that week, Kelly was surprised when two delivery trucks pulled into the yard on the same afternoon.

First, Adam's red pickup rolled in. Daniel was riding in the passenger seat and an upright piano was tied on the back.

"What on earth?" Kelly exclaimed as he hurried to the door.

The brothers made a slow, wide swing around the driveway, then shifted into reverse and backed across Kelly's lawn. When the back bumper almost touched the steps of the seldom-used front door, Adam killed the engine and hopped out.

"This here piano is a gift from Mom and Dad," he explained. Kelly quickly opened the note Daniel handed him. It read, "We hope the music this piano produces will bring much joy to your home. Mom and Dad McLean"

"It's the one Amber learned to play on."

"But it's always been in your living room," Kelly protested.

"Yep," Adam responded as the two brothers deftly set up a ramp to the house. Kelly noted that the piano was already on a dolly. He realized that their years of farm work had prepared them to be handy at a lot of jobs.

Adam and Daniel pushed and pulled. Riding on the dolly made the piano even taller, so that it barely fit through the door. Kelly spotted for them, telling them to go a bit to the left or right, and steadied it as it slowly moved across the ramp and over the threshold. Then he raced around the house to the back door and cleared a place for the venerable antique on the east wall of the living room. It fit nicely between his desk and the French doors leading to the sunroom.

After Amber's brothers pulled out, Kelly ran a dust rag over the piano and sat down at his desk again. Soon a second truck drove up. The deliveryman was the owner of the local hardware store. He opened the back of his van to reveal a new gas grill, a gift from Kelly's folks.

"Your father called," Hank explained. "He said to pick out a good grill for you, so here it is. Top of the line." Hank proceeded to explain how to start it, how to change the gas tank, and even gave out his secret recipe for the world's best hamburgers.

Kelly couldn't wait to call Amber and tell her about the excitement. She'd be thrilled to know they now owned a piano and a grill. Instead, when he reached her with the news, Amber burst into tears.

"You realize letting go of the piano means my mother has given up hope of ever playing again," she sobbed.

Kelly wanted to comfort her, but wasn't sure what to say. The truth was, Jean McLean hadn't been able to play for a long time and was now spending more time than ever in her wheelchair.

Between sniffs, Amber said, "When Brianna was here, I told her how Mom always thinks of others. This is one more example..." Her voice trailed off.

Kelly held the phone close to his ear and stared at the piano. He could imagine Amber sitting at the keyboard, her face lit up and her hands roaming over the ivories. Her lovely voice seemed to fill the room.

Kelly finally spoke. "It's like your mother to give away something she loves to someone who will love it even more."

She sniffed. "You're right about her. The piano will always be bittersweet because it will remind me of her in so many ways. She inspired me to play, because I'd hear the joy she had as she played and sang. And now..." Amber was tearing up again.

"We can't lose hope." Kelly encouraged her. "Your mom may go into remission. She may even play again."

On the other end of the phone line, a hiccup escaped. "Maybe she'll want the piano back," Amber said.

"And we'll gladly give it to her."

"I'm going to tell Mom and Dad that."

Kelly heard her take a deep breath.

"Are you going to use that new grill when our guests come over Saturday night?"

The grill. The idea of barbecuing a hunk of meat on it enticed him.

"Hank gave me his secret hamburger recipe," Kelly said. "Do you think I dare give it a try? I mean, you know my cooking skills are pretty basic."

"Oh, you can't ruin grilled hamburgers unless you burn them or serve them raw. Or put anchovies on them."

"Let me write that down," Kelly joked.

"You'll do fine and it's okay to tell everyone you're experimenting. Ask for advice."

Kelly smiled. He was going to be a grill master, he just knew it.

"I'll pick up buns, and make baked beans and coleslaw. The whole bottom tier of our wedding cake is in my parents' freezer. They can bring that over for dessert."

Amber was thinking aloud. Kelly liked it when she did that.

"I'll sweep the deck. We can have the picnic out there, and open gifts in the house later. I'll bring over tables and chairs from the church."

With their plans all set, the young couple settled down to another night separated from one another and the anticipation of a weekend together.

Chapter 48

The Gift Fish and Sunflower Plates

Kelly and Amber agreed that the gift opening party went well. It was now after midnight and they lay facing each other in the moonlight. The scent of clover drifted through the open bedroom window.

"People liked my burgers." Kelly sounded pleased and unaware that he'd turned most of them into charcoal briquettes.

"Mm," Amber murmured. "What kind of comments did you receive?"

"The twins both said they reminded them of the burgers they had at summer camp."

Amber didn't have the heart to tell him that her brothers had said the food at camp was, in their words, historically bad. Kelly was a novice at the grill, but certainly would master it.

"I'm troubled that my folks weren't here very long. I hope Mom gets better soon."

Glen and Jean had missed the meal and only stayed through an hour of gift opening. Jean had also needed extra help to get into the house.

Kelly gave her a sympathetic look. Their concern was mutual.

Amber's eyes fell on the red glittery sign Brianna and Nancy had made for them before the wedding. They had decided to tack it to a wall. Smiling, she recalled how much fun Nancy and Brianna had together. No wonder Brianna had wanted to be part of the Jorgenson family.

Her eyes drifted to the stack of bed and bath linens they'd carried upstairs.

"Aren't we blessed to have generous friends and family members? Their gifts were so thoughtful."

"I didn't know we'd be getting that much stuff. We won't have to buy towels ever again. And I have to say I'm happy to have a full set of silverware."

Amber sighed. "I wish we had made time to do a wedding registration."

"You're thinking about Aunt Kate's gift."

"Don't get me wrong, I like Fiesta dinnerware," Amber said. "But twelve place settings in sunflower yellow?"

They lay quietly for a moment.

"Maybe we can learn to love them," Kelly answered.

"Would Kate be offended if we exchange them for a different color?"

"Does the sun come up in the morning? Yeah, she'll be offended. Hey, maybe Bri can help us. Remember how she told Kate her house was too yellow?"

"Except, ironically, Brianna has developed a love for sunflowers. She might think we should keep the plates."

Kelly groaned. "Let's sleep on it."

"First, we need to talk about that fish from Tiny." Amber's eyebrows were arched in her you-get-the-point look.

"You don't like it?"

"It will never hang in our house. Trust me."

"Do you want to break Tiny's heart? He's gone out of his way to help. He's a true friend. Plus, he spent a lot of money on what he thinks is the perfect gift."

"I wouldn't want to hurt Tiny's feelings. It's just, Kelly, we can't have that walleye hanging in our living room."

"Why not? Jesus liked fish. He said we should be fishermen."

"I think Jesus meant we're to be fishers of men, Pastor Jorgenson."

"At least it's the real thing and not one of those hideous talking ones."

Amber smiled. Her husband had a way of helping her see the bright side of life.

"I love you," she said as she reached over to give Kelly a kiss.

A moment later, the phone rang.

"Timing is everything," Kelly moaned. He struggled out of bed and over to the phone on the other side of the room.

He answered, then listened silently. Running his hand through his hair, he shook his head at Amber, and said, "When will you be here?" A few seconds later he hung up.

"Sweetie, what is it?"

"Your mom is having terrible pain. Cramps in her arms and legs. Glen is taking her to the hospital in Bismarck. They want you to go along."

"Did you say I would?"

"Didn't have to. He said they'd be by in a few minutes to pick you up."

Amber scrambled out of bed and slipped into the jeans and tank top she'd worn for the gift-opening party, the party her mother had mostly missed. After running a brush through her hair, she flew downstairs to search for her purse and a light sweater.

Amber stopped short at the bottom of the steps when she saw the piano in the living room. She had barely glanced at it when she got home, because there had been little time to prepare for the party.

She paused to finger the familiar keys, as emotions billowed up from the deepest part of her soul. The piano was one of her mother's treasures, making it an extraordinary gift. Why was she willing to give it away? Had her mother given up ever playing again?

Amber saw headlights turn onto the road leading to the parsonage. Soon her parents would pull up. She felt stiff and wooden, unable to move toward the door.

The many things she'd done to help her mother, from taking the emergency management course to a thousand loads of laundry, passed through her mind. Nothing she'd done was enough, because it hadn't prevented this moment from happening.

Amber took a deep breath and closed her eyes. She could picture her mother when she was young and lithe.

"Mom doesn't deserve this," she whispered to God. "If you had to let someone be sick, why couldn't it have been me?" When she opened her eyes, she saw a wooden cross that hung on the dining room wall.

Behind her, Kelly put a hand on her shoulder. "It's time."

Choking back tears and unable to look at Kelly for fear of losing control, she pulled her loose golden curls back. The lights from the sedan flashed in the dining room window as the car pulled to a stop at the backdoor.

"Pray that God gives me courage," she croaked, as she moved toward the door.

"Courage for all of you, and healing for Jean," he said quietly. "And that we can live peacefully here at Cottonwood Creek."

Amber turned and gave him a rueful smile before she disappeared down the steps.

Chapter 49
The Diagnosis

A mber spent the rest of the weekend at the hospital with her mother. Kelly stayed home to prepare for the Sunday service. Afterward, he drove her Jeep to Bismarck and spent the night with her.

On Monday morning, Jean began a round of tests. Amber went back to work, though her thoughts and emotions were a few blocks away at the hospital. Kelly sat with Glen as Jean was wheeled from room to room for various tests. First, a standard medical exam, then blood tests, an MRI, and something called an evoked potential test.

Finally, late that afternoon, her father called Amber. The doctors wanted to meet with Jean and her family. Amber dropped what she was doing at work and managed to slip into the hospital room as the doctors began outlining the results from the day's tests.

"It looks like we have your immediate symptoms under control. However, as you know, the disease is progressing. We think it needs to be dealt with aggressively. Rather than continue testing here, we recommend setting up appointments at the Mayo Clinic in Rochester, Minnesota."

"What is the prognosis?" Amber asked numbly. Might as well get it all out in the open.

"As you know, multiple sclerosis is a debilitating disease and we have no cure for it. Left unchecked, it can become more aggressive. However, with the right treatment, we may be able to slow it down and even bring it into remission."

The lead doctor looked directly at Jean. A man of about fifty, he was reputed to be the best neurologist in the region.

"Given your young age and the quick progression, we highly recommend a more aggressive treatment. If we can get this under control, you may be able to live a long and relatively healthy life."

Jean nodded, tears in her eyes.

"That is my prayer. I want to get well. I have twin boys at home who still need a mother."

She looked at Amber and then back at the doctors. "I couldn't even help at my only daughter's wedding. If there is a way to stop this nightmare, please help me find it."

"Then it's settled. We'll send your test results to Mayo and get those appointments set up as soon as possible. You might want to plan to spend a few weeks there. Until then, you can go home."

Hope flooded Jean's eyes. Kelly and Glen murmured their thanks.

Amber looked up at the ceiling. How she hoped her mother would get better, but she knew her parents would probably need to sell the farm to pay for the treatment.

Once Jean was checked out, the two couples left the hospital and stopped at a cozy restaurant for an early dinner. After that, Kelly rode back to Cottonwood Creek with his in-laws and Amber pointed her Jeep toward the office.

It was almost midnight before she arrived at the apartment and slipped into bed. She turned on the radio, hoping it would make her drowsy enough to fall asleep. A man was speaking in a low, encouraging tone. Amber snuggled into her pillow to listen.

"See, I am doing a new thing! Now it springs up; do you not perceive it? I am making a way in the wilderness and streams in the wasteland.

"This prophetic word from Isaiah 43:19 foretells of deliverance for the Jews, but its promise holds true for us today. Believer, get hold of the promises of God. Believe our Lord can make a way where there seems to be no way."

The speaker's words went through Amber and she sat up in bed.

"Oh Lord, would you make a way where there seems to be no way for my mother? Please make Mom well again. Please help her through this hard time. Please keep her body from wasting away. And Lord, I know it's beyond what their insurance can pay, so will you help with finances, too? Please?"

A song began playing that reinforced the comforting message. She recognized it and sang along. "God works in ways we cannot see, he will make a way for me." As she expressed her renewed faith, peace filled her.

She lay back down and reached to turn off the radio. Before she could touch the button, the radio voice said, "Signing off for tonight, with this inspiration from 1 Peter 5:7: Cast all your anxiety on him for he cares for you."

"Okay, Lord," she said, as she turned off the radio. "I'm going to trust you and seek your answer to my parents' problems."

Her concerns reached a tipping point a few weeks later.

Jean was now at Mayo Clinic, six hundred miles away. Glen had driven her there and promptly returned home because summer was his busiest time of year. Glen's sister, Sandy, drove from Chicago to stay in Rochester with Jean during her treatment. As a nurse, Sandy had racked up extra vacation time. In addition, the women had been good friends ever since Glen and Jean married.

Amber felt torn. She couldn't be with Kelly or at the farm when her project at work was ramping up. To add to her stress, other agencies were contacting her for advice on strategic planning. Unable to refuse their requests, she worked even harder to help her clients, run the strategic planning at the Bismarck office, and assist agencies from as far away as Pennsylvania.

She had only made it back to Cottonwood Creek one weekend since her mother was hospitalized. That time, she'd spent as much time as possible with Kelly. However, with her father and brothers in the midst of summer work, she was needed at the farm.

The guys usually pitched in with cooking, cleaning, and laundry, but during harvest, routine flew out the door. Amber spent most of the weekend preparing crock-pot meals and putting them in the freezer. She threw piles of dirty denim in the washer and mopped the kitchen floor.

Late Saturday afternoon, she took a break and strolled out to the mailbox, soaking in the mid-summer air that shimmered with heat and smelled of harvested grain. In the distance, she could hear the hum of farm equipment out in the field. Grasshoppers leapt about, while honeybees buzzed around the uncut clover of the ditch. The grass that grew alongside the driveway waved in the breeze and tickled her bare legs.

When Amber was younger, she had helped with harvest. She could still feel the sweaty satisfaction of stepping down from the grain truck after delivering a load of wheat to the elevator in town. She had also shoveled her share of oats into the granary.

Her brothers were now all old enough to take on the outside jobs. The hard work was good for the twins, she decided. They were played out by the end of the day, and only spent a few minutes with their computer games before crashing into bed.

Back at the house, she sorted the mail and dropped bills on the metal desk in the corner of the living room. That is when she saw the stack of envelopes held together with a rubber band. Slumping into the creaky office chair, she opened each one. They were all medical bills.

Amber put the stack away, a sick feeling filling her stomach. Her worries about her parents' financial problems seemed to be true. They owed thousands of dollars. She wondered why her father hadn't said anything. Was he too ashamed? Too proud?

She decided not to confront him yet. His focus was on bringing in the harvest and more income. At the same time, she needed to confess that she'd found the bills. Could she hope for a reasonable explanation or would her worst fears be confirmed?

Driving back to the parsonage, Amber decided she couldn't tell Kelly what she found before talking with her father.

Chapter 50
Funny What Marriage
Can Do to a Guy

The next Monday morning, Amber spun out of the gravel driveway so fast that the dust hung in the air for minutes, like mist in the early morning sunlight. Kelly watched her leave. When he could no longer see the dust of her departure, he turned from the window and sat down on the couch next to Mildred.

"What do you think, Mildred? Will she make it to work in Bismarck by eight o'clock?" he asked. Mildred ignored the question and continued bathing herself in the sunlight streaming through the east window.

Ten minutes to Cottonwood City, another ten to Highway 83, and then an hour to Bismarck. Well, not quite an hour the way she drove.

Kelly wished cell phone service in the Cottonwood area would improve. He wanted to call her and say, "Come home. I need you." Maybe it was better that he couldn't pick up the phone and talk to her. After all, unlike him, Amber didn't have the day off.

"Yes, she'll arrive right on time. Amber is never late for work," he told Mildred. His voice sounded hollow. No, he thought, the whole house seems hollow without Amber.

Funny, what marriage could do for a guy. Her presence changed every part of his life, bringing joy, laughter, fresh ideas, and sweet private moments. Take this morning. After a romantic wake up call, she'd made fresh-squeezed orange juice and bagels for breakfast.

He grinned as he thought about how she discovered little things about him, such as his craving for oranges. Having grown up in Southern California, his family picked fresh citrus fruit from the trees in their backyard. A juicer sat on his parents' kitchen counter all year round. Since Amber figured that out, she'd been bringing home bags of oranges for him.

She was also sensitive to the ache in his heart for Kyle. Losing his twin brother was something that never moved far from him. Soon after they arrived home from their honeymoon, he found her arranging a picture of Kyle over his desk, along with an ornate metal cross. Next to it, she put a plaque Pastor McDougal had given them, with the quote from their wedding ceremony, "There is no more lovely, friendly and charming relationship, communion or company, than a good marriage." Their informal engagement photo snuggled next to it. How thoughtful of her to surround his workspace with items dear to his heart.

Amber had hung pictures here and there, put new scatter rugs in the entry and the bathrooms, and got rid of the red-checked kitchen curtains. She even agreed to hang the trophy walleye that Tiny Winger had given them for a wedding gift. How many women would want that over the fireplace mantel?

Kelly was mesmerized by Amber's speed at making decisions and accomplishing tasks. He tended to analyze every side of a project before beginning work on it. They were total opposites in that respect, but he'd come to see them as two halves of a whole. She needed him to slow her down a bit. He needed her to stay focused. She completed his life and he hoped he completed hers. Each discovery made him love her more. Their times together were electric.

Sadly, those moments were rare. After the honeymoon, not much had changed from their dating days. She still worked in Bismarck and spent Saturdays at her parents' home. At least, that's what happened when she was able to come home for the weekend. Her job was consuming her like a fire burning up whatever it touched. And hanging over them was concern over her mother's prognosis.

In some ways, Kelly still felt single. His time alone with Amber was sandwiched into a few cherished moments each weekend. The only time they reserved for themselves was late Sunday afternoon and evening. Barring pastoral or family emergencies, they simply considered themselves "booked."

Sometimes they drove back to the restaurant where they'd spent their first date. Most often, they preferred to stay home. They had explored the banks of Cottonwood Creek and, holding hands, admired wild rose bushes and spotted meadowlarks. This past weekend they had stood on a rise viewing a field that looked like an ocean of sunflowers.

Kelly sighed and looked around the living room. Monday was his day off, and he struggled to fill the time. He should mow the lawn today and finish the laundry.

He was thankful that Tiny had become a good friend. They had cooked up some fun times this summer with the youth group. Playing badminton on the church lawn was a favorite. One time, before the creek turned green with algae, they went swimming and built a campfire. Still, his friendship with Tiny or the youth group wasn't a substitute for time with his Amber.

"I need to quit feeling sorry for myself, Mildred," Kelly said more to encourage himself. "Maybe I need to accept Amber being away. We still have a terrific relationship."

He blinked. Did Mildred arch an eyebrow at him?

"I guess you wish she was here more, too. It's true. No one can fill Amber's place, not you or Tiny or anyone else."

Later that day, he drove into Cottonwood City and found Cole Jensen working the counter at Your Friendly

Co-op. Because business was slow, Kelly got a soda from the machine and sat down to talk with the young man.

"I heard you decided on Minot State," Kelly opened the conversation. Going to college in Minot meant Cole was giving up several scholarships that would have helped him pursue degrees in pastoral ministries and sacred music.

"I need to stay within driving distance in case Grandma needs me." There was an edge of resignation in Cole's voice. Sadie wasn't doing well. Arrangements had been made for her to move into the nursing home in town before Cole left for school.

"It's the least I can do for her," Cole continued. "She raised me and gave me a good home." He looked away, sadness showing across his face. "It looks like we'll have to let go of the house," Cole said. "We can't keep it just so I can come home on weekends. The doctor said it's unlikely that Grandma will ever be able to live there by herself."

Kelly sucked in his breath. Cole had been homeless before Sadie took him in. Now, except for a dorm room, he'd be homeless again. No wonder he sounded discouraged. His security and dreams had vanished.

"You're making some hard decisions," Kelly commiserated. "As far as the school goes, I assure you, things will shake into place. Don't give up on your goals, just get your freshman year out of the way and see what happens."

Cole remained quiet.

"I wonder, would you be interested in coming to live with Amber and me? I know you'd probably only be around for weekends and holidays, but I could use your help."

He was recklessly stepping out on a limb. He and his bride had never discussed having a housemate. They had enough trouble finding time to be alone without someone else living with them. Yet, Cole had a serious need, and Kelly was certain Amber would have made the same offer.

Cole shrugged and looked at him sideways. "Really? Then this would be my home." He seemed to turn the idea over in his mind a few times, before smiling.

"We have a spare room. Although it isn't big or fancy, the room is yours from now on. You can park your extra stuff there or in the basement."

Cole looked up. "One of Grandma's friends offered me a room, too. But, to be honest, I'd rather stay with you and Amber."

His voice took on an excited tone. "When I'm home, I can do my laundry and help with the dishes. And I can help with the youth or the music on the weekends."

He'd already called the parsonage home, Kelly noted. He clapped the boy on the back. Then in a rare and spontaneous display of affection, Cole threw his arms around him.

"You're the best!" he said.

It was the finest man hug Kelly had ever received. Now all he needed to do was break the news to Amber.

Chapter 51
The Award

Benson called Amber that same day. He began by announcing that he was feeling much better and hoped to begin spending a few hours a day in the office. Next, he gave her some startling news.

"Kimberly's been routing the mail to me," he said. "It seems there are accolades building up for you."

"What do you mean?"

"A local organization plans to recognize you as the 'Young Business Woman of the Year.' You'll be invited to an awards luncheon and written up in newspapers and magazines. That's great publicity for Gates Insurance."

"I didn't apply for anything like that."

"I did," Benson responded.

Why, the old fox must be feeling better, Amber thought.

"Not only that, Slate Nadoff called. He can't say enough about your work. I know he wanted to hire you earlier, and you didn't want to move to Minneapolis. You might want to reconsider now, because he's going to make you another offer."

"What might that be?" Amber asked softly, almost unable to speak.

"You could work out of our office most of the time. Only travel on occasion."

"Doing what?"

"It's the same job that was open at the Mammon Global office in the Twin Cities. They never filled it. He thinks you're the only one for the job. He says most of the work could be done online and through teleconferencing. What do you think of that, Amber?"

"Not much. I've been waiting for you to come back so you can take over the strategic planning project."

Benson laughed. "My dear, this is an assignment for a rising star, not a burned-out one. We'd shuffle things around so you'd have a bigger office. You might even be able to hire an assistant.

"As I understand it, the financial rewards would be significant," he emphasized.

"I haven't been offered it yet."

"You will be. Slate will be in Bismarck soon."

There's the deal breaker, Amber thought. She didn't want to work for Slate under any circumstance, even if he was usually five hundred miles away. When she started to tell Benson that she could never work for Slate, he cut her off.

"You know, you're like a daughter to me. I would prefer you remain with the agency, but I can't deny that this is a brilliant opportunity. You're always worried about your family and now your mother needs specialized treatment. Maybe this is the answer to your prayers, Amber."

Was it? Usually her answers to prayer were accompanied by a lovely peace. This time, her heart thumped as she considered the possible career step.

The idea of working with Slate made her break into a sweat. What exactly would he expect from her? She'd had only the briefest professional phone and email exchanges with him since the incident a few months back, so it was hard to gauge what it might be like.

Amber hung up, grabbed her purse, and stumbled from the office. She needed to get some fresh air and perspective. Custer Park was the logical place to go. Hugging her purse, she strode toward the tree-shaded park that was dominated by a sculpture of a bald eagle.

Glancing to the right, she saw the sign for an ice cream shop. In a weak moment, she stopped and purchased a root beer float. Then she found a bench in the far corner of the park.

It was quiet except for the happy sound of children splashing in the pool across the street and the din of traffic. Immersed in the quiet, she begged God to give her direction. However, the heavens seemed particularly still.

She didn't have to decide today, she consoled herself. Yet, she couldn't delay long. The whole divide between her career and her calling was getting more difficult. Whenever she embraced the idea of giving up her career, something like this award and job offer popped up.

Setting aside the empty container, Amber fingered the beautiful antique diamond ring Kelly had given her. She needed to talk to him. Flipping open her phone, she called and reached Kelly on the first ring.

"Hi. I just called to say I love you."

"Well, I love you, too, Amber Rose. What's up? I usually don't hear from you during the workday." He was excited to tell her about Cole coming to live with them, hoping she approved.

"Benson called this morning. For some reason I've been selected as Young Business Woman of the Year."

"No kidding. That's wonderful."

"It was a complete surprise. Apparently, he and some of my coworkers nominated me for taking on the strategic planning project."

"I'm so proud of you!"

"He had other news, too. He said Mammon Global wants to hire me for the same position that was open earlier. This time I could work out of Bismarck."

Kelly remained silent.

"Benson said he'd hate to lose me, however, since it's such a wonderful opportunity, he thinks I should take it."

"I didn't think you applied for that job?"

"I didn't. It's unfolding in the most amazing way. Kelly, can you come to Bismarck tonight so we can talk about all of this?"

"Sorry, it's Wednesday. I need to be at church."

Of course, Amber thought. How could I be so out of touch with my husband's schedule?

"Kelly, here's what I need to discuss. With all these things happening, how do I know when God is leading me? I'll need to decide soon. I mean, we will have to make some decisions."

"Do you remember when Wayne did that devotional about finding direction? He quoted from Jeremiah about asking God where the good way is, and then walking in it."

"I remember. It ends with 'and you will find rest for your souls.' Kelly, I've been praying so hard, hoping I'd get a heavenly green light to move back to Cottonwood Creek. Instead, this career stuff unrolls like a red carpet. It's confusing."

"I don't know what to say," Kelly answered. "Except, give God more time."

She could hear discouragement in his voice. And sadness. If she jumped deeper into her career, Kelly would be impacted as much as Amber.

Late that evening, she called Felicia Rogers to discuss the job offer. Felicia had a wealth of Godly wisdom, plus she and Ted had witnessed the incident with Slate. Amber laid out the whole scenario.

"What does Kelly say?" Felicia had asked after Amber explained the offer.

"I called him with the news, but we won't be able to talk it through until this weekend."

"How do you feel working with Slate?"

"I know he can be a wolf," Amber responded. "But, he's been a gentleman since the incident. Besides, I'll be in Bismarck most of the time. He won't be within shouting distance."

"We flagged Slate as a treacherous character. We have as little to do with him as possible. Be wary. He may think you're agreeing to more than a position with the company."

"That's one of my concerns."

"What did Kelly say when you told him about Slate's advances?"

"Well." Amber paused. Suddenly, it seemed obvious that she should have explained the incident to Kelly right away. "I haven't been able to tell him," Amber confessed.

"Because you're afraid or ashamed?"

"Both. I'm trying to forget it happened. Telling Kelly would bring it all back."

"If Kelly knew, would he approve of you working more closely with Slate?"

"Put that way, no. But there's more to the story. I have financial obligations that push me toward accepting this job."

"And Kelly knows about these obligations?"

"Wow, you're asking a lot of hard questions," Amber hedged.

"Amber, I've been married a long time. When you have a big decision to make, you must sit down with all the information and decide together."

"We'll talk it out this weekend, however, it's still my career and my obligations that must be filled, and I'm the one who must deal with Slate."

"That's partly true. You don't want to forget that whatever you decide will affect Kelly's life and career as well. I guess that's why they call marriage tying the knot. Your lives are tied together.

"By the way, thank you for inviting us to the wedding. We loved Kelly and Cottonwood Creek. You're surely blessed by both."

"Very blessed," Amber agreed, feeling that they were getting back on solid ground.

Then Felicia offered some final wisdom. "Remember, God leads and the devil pushes."

After they hung up, Amber considered her friend's chastising words. She needed to tell Kelly why she wanted to accept the position. And why she didn't.

Chapter 52

The Newlywed's
Part-Time Marriage

Late the next Sunday afternoon, Kelly and Amber sat at the dining room table, heads bowed together. Kelly read figures as Amber's fingers flew over a calculator. The Jorgensons were trying to figure out their budget.

It was a quiet interlude after a hectic weekend. Amber's father had left that morning. In a few days, he'd bring Jean home. Both Amber and Kelly had worked at the farm all day Saturday in preparation. He finally had time to explain his discussion with Cole. As he expected, she compassionately approved his offer.

"Honey, we've gone through these numbers three times. If I quit work and come back here, we will barely get by. If I keep my job as an insurance agent, we'd be more comfortable. However, this new job will allow us to put money away and help my family," Amber said.

She hadn't actually seen the official numbers for the position with Mammon Global. However, a rumor had spread around the office that she was being hired at a significant salary. She was already getting congratulations.

Amber had talked to Kelly about the job with Mammon Global and they had reviewed the job description. Then, they'd looked through their income and expenses. She knew it was time to take Felicia's advice and be fully open with him.

"I want to tell you a couple other things that have bearing on this decision."

He laid down his pen and raised his eyebrows.

"One reason to refuse this job, is I don't want to work with Slate Nadoff."

Kelly folded his arms and looked at her questioningly. "When I was in the Twin Cities, he started off acting nice. He showed me around the office. It was all so impressive. Then that evening, he began drinking and made a pass at me while we were at dinner with the whole group. The Rogers saw what was happening and gave me a ride back to the hotel. That's how we became good friends as fast as we did."

"That must have happened before our wedding. Why didn't you tell me this earlier?"

"The whole thing was so disturbing. I didn't want to think or talk about it."

Anger flashed across Kelly's face at the thought of some guy hitting on Amber.

"How has he treated you since then? And why would you consider working for him after this happened?"

"He's been respectful," she said tentatively. "The next day he ignored me. I'm not sure he remembered the...the incident. If the Rogers hadn't been there, I might have believed it was my imagination. Now he's offered this dream-come-true job."

"Dream come true? I thought your dream was to live here. Sit by the fire in the winter and pick crocuses in the spring. And be available for your family."

Amber hung her head. "Well, yes. Someday. I need to take the job because I've learned that even before this long stay at Mayo, my parents had a lot of debt. They don't know that I learned about it, so please don't say anything to them."

"Wouldn't it be better to talk with them and not make assumptions?"

Amber shook her head. "That would hurt their pride so much."

"Their pride?" Kelly's face hardened and he ran his hand through his hair. "What about us? You're sacrificing our life and dreams, so you better know the whole story. The last thing I want is a part-time marriage."

"I too, Honey," Amber consoled. "But it isn't that bad. We're together on weekends."

"Like I said, a part-time marriage. If money is so important, I can pick up an extra job to help make ends meet. They're always looking for school bus drivers," Kelly recalled.

"That wouldn't begin to solve the problems. Besides, you shouldn't be getting a second job. I'd feel terrible if you were distracted from your call. People need you."

"And your call, Amber? Which calls louder, your career or coming back to live here?"

"Of course, I'd like to be back here. You don't understand, though. My family was always on a tight budget. We didn't have extra money for anything. I like having an income. I don't want to give it up."

Kelly had never seen her green eyes blaze as intensely.

"Your parents are financially comfortable. You've never had to worry about making ends meet. I have had to do that most of my life."

Kelly felt as edgy and restless as Amber sounded.

"That's the bottom line isn't it, Amber? Career doors are opening and you've made up your mind to do what you please."

"Do what I please? No, Kelly, it's what I must do." Amber stood up and stared out the dining room window, her back to Kelly.

He had an idea. "Let's go for a walk down by the creek."

Chapter 53
Two Pigs in a Puddle

The midsummer heat thickened the air and perfumed it with the scent of sage as Amber and Kelly trudged through the tall grass. Bees and other insects buzzed lazily around wildflowers. The couple had put on boots to walk through the prairie grass. The spring runoff was long gone, and only a couple feet of green water lazed along in the creek. From the bank, they could see a fish just under the surface.

Although they were officially having their first marital argument, they held hands. Kelly stroked the top of Amber's soft hand with his thumb. They walked silently, their irritated thoughts calming as they swished through the grass. At the edge of the church property, Kelly helped Amber through a barbed wire fence. The neighbor's pasture spread out before them. Here the grass was cropped short and fertilized by the cattle that stood bunched together on the other side of the pasture.

After walking some distance, they found a spot along the creek bank and sat down. Kelly took out a small bag of chocolates and offered it to Amber. Taking a couple pieces, she popped them in her mouth.

She'd never looked more beautiful. Her face was flushed from the hike and the sun glinted off her golden hair as it blew in the breeze. She dazzled him as much as the first time he saw her.

"Amber, remember the day we met?"

She nodded.

"You seemed like an angelic being that day, and even said something that sounded mystical or prophetic. 'There is power in the name of Jesus and there is power in the

Word of God. But when you praise his holy name, something more happens. The glory of heaven joins you.'"

"You remember my exact words?"

"I was stunned by the mood in the church that day. It was as if a holy presence surrounded you. I wanted it to surround me, too. It seemed a little bit like heaven."

Amber remained silent, a wistful look on her face.

"After that, a vision grew in my heart for us. A higher calling." Kelly felt as though he was unzipping his heart and showing Amber what was inside. "I believed, still believe, we won't be an ordinary couple bound by ordinary problems, like budgets. We're meant to be partners in ministry. Together we can be extra-ordinary and much more than I could ever be alone. I saw us, I mean I see us, as overcomers helping people conquer the pain, doubts, and circumstances they face."

Kelly pulled at some grass as he looked out over the creek and gathered his thoughts. He decided he might as well say what he'd been thinking.

"I don't want to bicker with you, Amber. I want to live in that golden light you brought to the church that day. I miss you, Amber. I miss you in places we've never been together."

She looked at him, confused.

"On Sunday mornings, you sit in the pew, while I dream of you leading the congregation in worship. You're usually not here when the youth group meets, but I see you being a close friend and mentor to the young women who attend Cottonwood Church."

His thoughts and dreams poured from deep within.

"When I'm called into an emergency or crisis, I wish you were with me to help bring comfort. Although there is no paycheck for that kind of ministry, the rewards are huge."

"Essentially, you're inviting me to give up my world and become part of yours?"

The question surprised Kelly. Had she not heard how much he needed her? How he had faith that God would work out the circumstances? Isn't that what he had said? What was all of this about your world and my world?

"No," he said, slowly. "I'm inviting you to join me in making 'our' life together. It will look way different than what your world or mine look like right now. Can't you see there might be a better way?"

"I remember the day we met in the church," Amber mused. "I had spent a long time waiting in God's presence alone. That happens so rarely. I love those times of refreshing, and I'm glad, very glad, you came along that day."

She looked at Kelly tenderly and spoke softly.

"Your vision for us is lovely, but Kelly, we have to be practical. I can't quit work. We can't live on love."

Kelly set his jaw. He'd just poured out his heart, and he felt as rejected as if she had refused his marriage proposal. In fact, he fumed, it was a lot like that. She was refusing to make a life with him.

"Please keep this in mind, Amber. I've never cared for leftovers."

"Leftovers!" Amber looked as if he'd just slapped her.

"That's what I'm getting here. If, and I do mean if, you have time after your career and your family, you're sure to schedule me in."

She got up and dusted herself off.

Angry now, Kelly impulsively added, "By the way, Brianna sends her regards."

"What's that supposed to mean?" Amber stood with her hands on the hips of her cutoffs.

"It means I spend more time talking with Brianna then with you. For that matter, I spend more time with Tiny than I do with you."

Kelly jumped up and began striding across the pasture. Amber hurried to catch up.

Then a peculiar sound began behind them. He turned around to see a small herd of black-faced cattle galloping toward them. Panic replaced his anger as he recalled a story about how bulls could attack and gore a person. Maybe these were bulls.

He needed to run, yet he stood riveted to the ground as the herd closed in.

Amber rushed toward him. "Jump!" she shouted as she grabbed his hand and headed to the creek bank. They both made a leap into the shallow creek and regained their bearings.

"Wade!" she called. Still holding hands, they struggled through the water, their boots squishing in the muddy bottom.

The cattle came to a halt on the bank, watching curiously as the humans splashed to the other side of the creek. Once it appeared the cattle wouldn't follow them into the water, Amber began laughing.

"Why are you laughing? They were going to attack us!" Kelly said.

Amber laughed harder. "They wouldn't. They're just big, friendly calves."

"Then why did we have to jump in the water?" Kelly cried as they waded upstream away from the four-legged stalkers.

"Even friendly beasts can knock you over, especially in a herd. Besides, we needed to break up the ice forming between us."

Her love for him showed in Amber's green eyes.

Kelly pulled her close. "I love you, Amber Rose Jorgenson."

"I love you, too, Kelly Michael Jorgenson. More than I can say."

Kelly released her and tried to climb up the steep bank, anxious to get safely on the other side of the fence, away from both the menacing calves and the argument.

Then he began to slip backward. He grabbed at some stray roots and missed. Back he fell into the creek with a splash.

Amber laughed as she offered him a hand. Kelly knew what he had to do. He pulled her down into the water with him.

"How does it feel?" he asked as the dirty water saturated her clothes. They both sat up to their waists in water, their feet splayed in front of them.

"Like we're two pigs in a puddle."

"That sums our lives up pretty well, Amber."

Chapter 54
Advice from the Past

"Two pigs in a puddle, huh?" Kelly asked as he pulled Amber up from the muddy creek bottom.

A nostalgic look crossed her face.

"Sitting here in the mud reminded me of a book about a pig that Mom read to me when I was little. Those were happy days. It's hard to watch what has happened to our family since then. That's why it's so important that I can help them."

"I know they're in a tough place, Amber. I just don't know if your parents would want us to sacrifice our lives for them. There must be another way."

Amber nodded and touched his face with her fingers, which were slick from the slimy water. Relieved that their spat was over, Kelly and Amber squished their way back to the house. They sat on the outside step while they unknotted slimy shoestrings, and put their wet boots on the deck to dry. Soggy clothes were dropped in the washer on the way through the laundry room.

"Where are you going?" Kelly asked after they were again clean and dry. She was pulling out her car keys. "We haven't resolved anything. Besides, I was thinking about grilling brats for dinner."

Amber touched his face again and sighed. "I want to check on the boys. With Dad on his way to Minnesota, you never can tell what might be going on there."

She wrapped her arms around Kelly.

"We can talk about it again later. Right now, I have an obligation to my family, and I need some space to think and pray."

A few minutes later, Amber looked in her rearview mirror as she pulled out of the yard. Kelly stood watching her leave.

"What am I doing? Why can't I stay and work things out with Kelly?"

Amber considered putting the Jeep in reverse. She'd back up, jump out and hug Kelly. They'd laugh and kiss. Everything would be okay. Instead, she scanned the highway and drove away.

The farm was unusually quiet when she arrived. Even Rover Three lay restfully in the shade, refusing to give up his Sunday nap to greet her.

"Where is everyone?" she asked him. He thumped his tail a couple times, and then lay his head on his paws.

Inside the house, she found a note scribbled across the back of an envelope. "Gon to state fare with Adam and Lori. Dad knows. Me and Tim did chores. Daniel went with his friends. Jim"

Wow, they went to the state fair in Minot without even telling me, Amber thought. How can I be responsible for my brothers if they don't tell me what they're doing?

The farmhouse was seldom this quiet and empty. Amber looked in the fridge and found an ample supply of food. A pan full of brownies stood untouched on the counter. No reason to linger in the kitchen, she decided. Standing at the door to the enclosed porch that served as a laundry room, her mouth fell open. The boys had even put their folded laundry away. There was no reason to delay spending time with God.

Going into the living room, she sat in her mother's green chair. She smiled as she remembered how Kelly dubbed it Jean's power seat. Her mother had prayed in this room until a sense of peace always lingered.

Quietly, she began to talk to the Lord about all that had happened. She cried when she remembered Slate's advances and the disgust she felt toward him. She remembered the satisfaction of working with her clients and the challenges presented with her role as a strategic planner.

She prayed for Benson's recovery. She thanked God for Kelly and listed all the wonders she'd found in their love.

Finally, she laid out her concerns about her family, and the opportunities and challenges in her career. Then she sat waiting, hoping an answer would come.

The room was a timeless tribute to the 1980s. The same green carpet and pale paisley wallpaper remained. Priscilla curtains covered the tall windows. The old metal desk still sat in the corner. The space where the upright piano had stood was empty.

Her eyes strayed to the bookcase and landed on the family Bible. Getting up, she took it off the shelf and sat down again. It opened to the family history recorded in her mother's handwriting. Marriages. Births. Deaths. Their family had experienced them all.

When she flipped to another page, a sheet of paper fell out. Her mother's precise handwriting gave the date as years earlier. "First cutting of hay underway. Meatballs for supper. Strange event of the day, Amber said a man in white visited her while she played in the yard. (I didn't see or hear a thing.) He put his hand on her head and said God has a special plan for her life. That girl either has a vivid imagination or a special calling on her life."

Something electric seized Amber's chest. She had completely forgotten about the visitor on that day long ago. Now, she recalled the love and joy he brought. As a child, she'd taken his message to heart, although it had slowly faded over the years. She'd been playing with Rusty Ann. That's why finding the doll had evoked a strong response in her a few months ago.

Even now, she tucked the doll into her bag when she traveled. Whenever she saw the little yarn-haired doll, she was reminded of the same love she'd felt that day.

"God has a special plan for my life. Deep down I've known that. It means I can trust Him. I truly can," she said aloud. Amber saw herself rushing back to Kelly, could see them walking through life together.

Then her heart sank. What about her family? She glanced at the desk where she'd spied the stack of bills a few weeks earlier. She shouldn't, couldn't, and wouldn't abandon her family. Certainly, God didn't want that.

Pacing back and forth across the room, she prayed for a heavenly vision, a booming voice, anything to give her direction. Sitting back down in the green chair, Amber picked up the family Bible again. Peeking inside the front cover, she saw her grandmother's signature at the top and a message written underneath.

It read, "To anyone who reads this, may you know that in our family 'We speak as those approved by God to be entrusted with the gospel. We are not trying to please people, but God, who tests our hearts.' 1 Thessalonians 2:4."

Wow! That has been the essence of our family, thought Amber. It's part of my heritage, this being entrusted with the gospel. Being called to live for God.

"Lord, I'd love to believe it's your will for me to come back to Cottonwood Creek. I'd be content with owning just a couple pairs of jeans and eating peanut butter sandwiches every day."

She stood and looked out the window as she continued her conversational prayer. "I can do with less, however, you made me an organized person, a bean counter, who likes security. I don't want to look in the checkbook and worry about how to pay bills. I don't want to watch my parents struggle anymore."

She placed her hands on her hips. "I'm being given a chance to be more financially secure and help my family. I know the Bible says you test our hearts, however, I'm going to run a test of my own."

Pacing across the room to the desk, she declared,

"If you really are calling me back here, then I must see some proof that my parents' financial problems are being solved."

The stack of bills she'd seen a few weeks earlier was no longer on the desk. She rummaged through the drawers, but they weren't to be found.

"You have a great sense of humor, Lord," she said with bewilderment. "I didn't expect the bills to literally disappear. I need more realistic proof than that."

Finally, she got back in her Jeep and drove to the parsonage. Kelly was just getting off the phone when she walked in the door. A smile played around his mouth. He looked happier than he had in weeks.

"Kelly, I'm sorry I left like that. Forgive me?" Amber wrapped her arms around him and leaned her head on his shoulder.

"Forgiven," he said. "We'll get our lives figured out."

Amber closed her eyes, expecting a kiss. Instead, Kelly said, "While you were gone, Brianna called. She and Kate Schulte have become great friends, like they've adopted each other."

"Brianna," Amber mused. "I haven't been much of a friend to her. I don't even know how her ankle is healing."

"You won't believe why she called," he said, the smile on his face broadening.

"Try me."

"Brianna might move to Schulteville."

"Right. And there's a man in the moon."

"Seriously. She and Kate may set up a bed and breakfast at Kate's house."

Amber sat down, a flood of emotions washing over her. She was startled to realize the bond between Brianna and Kelly was growing again. And while she was always driving off with her briefcase, Brianna was ready to pack her bags and move here on blind faith.

Chapter 55
A Visit from Slate

Amber had trouble sleeping the next night. She tossed in her bed as she considered the career course being set before her and her longing to go back to Cottonwood Creek.

Once she drifted off to sleep, she dreamed a man was following her down a long hallway. She kept walking faster and faster. Although she tried to dodge him, he remained only a few yards behind her. She pushed open a door and went through, only to find he was in the room. He held out a bouquet of flowers to her.

Amber awoke with sweat beading on her face. It was only a dream, she realized while looking around the dimly lit bedroom of her apartment. Crawling out of bed, she went out to her tiny balcony and sat in the seldom-used lawn chair she kept there.

The nightmare had shaken and revolted her, partly because the hallways looked like those at Mammon Global. Was the man who followed her Slate Nadoff? It dawned on her that Slate might have been the one who sent her flowers a few weeks earlier.

Normally, the cool night air would have calmed her. Instead, her heart hammered in her chest. "I can't let my imagination get the best of me. The Lord is my protector!" she whispered. Slipping inside, she locked the patio door and checked the deadbolt on the front door.

The next morning, when Amber arrived at the office, Kimberly told her that Mr. Nadoff from Mammon Global would be in later, and that Benson Gates planned to attend the meeting.

When Amber didn't respond, Kimberly asked if she was okay.

"I didn't sleep well."

"I don't know how you can sleep at all with what's going on in your life. New bride, mom in the hospital, extra work at the office, and now, you may be moving into the big time."

Her friend's assessment didn't calm the alarm bells going off in Amber's mind. Still, she tended to business, going through emails, answering phone calls, and wading through paperwork.

A couple hours later, Kimberly buzzed her. "Slate Nadoff has arrived. He and Benson are talking in his office."

"How does he look?" Amber asked with Benson in mind.

"Benson looks like he's recovering from cancer. The other one. Wow. Tall, dark, handsome. For a full five seconds, I considered running off with him."

"Kimberly!"

"I know it was a crazy idea. Me, with a husband and two dogs."

She sighed. "He charmed me into getting him a coffee. Since he didn't seem like the foam cup type, I gave him a Gates Insurance mug. How I hate washing those mugs."

Just then, there was a rap at Amber's door.

"Benson, you're back!" she cried as her boss walked in. He had lost a lot of weight and all of his hair, but his eyes still sparkled.

"Now that my treatment is over, I'll be coming in a few hours a day. While I'll still need to rest, getting back to work will be the best medicine."

Amber beamed, until Slate stepped up behind him. Then she looked down and fiddled with something on her desk.

"Amber, it is delightful to see you again." Slate was standing before her, holding out a manicured hand.

She looked up at him as his eyes swept over her body. She dropped her hands to her side, unwilling to shake his hand, and giving as little eye contact as possible.

"I am here to make the job offer." Slate's voice was as silky and smooth as fine chocolate.

"Let's move to the conference room and start the interview," Benson said, motioning them through the door.

Amber was relieved that Benson planned to sit in on the discussion. It was unsettling to have Slate show up after her vivid dream. She prayed Benson would help her notice any red flags in Slate's proposal.

As they walked down the hallway, Kimberly pulled Amber aside. "Your father just called. He said they're on their way home. He asked if he could fax a list of things for you to pick up that she'll need right away."

Kimberly handed her the list. "That treatment must be expensive, huh?"

More expensive than you can imagine, Amber thought unhappily, as she trailed down the hall behind Slate and Benson.

The rest of the morning was spent reviewing how the project was working region-wide. Slate praised Amber's work and waxed eloquently about the award she was to receive. Otherwise, he remained focused on business the entire time. Amber decided perhaps she had only imagined the once-over he gave her earlier. She began to relax.

Before delving into the job description, they decided to break for lunch. Outside the office building, Slate led them toward his rental car. She shuddered, remembering how he had given her a ride to dinner when she was in the Twin Cities.

Once seated in an upscale restaurant, the conversation drifted away from business. Amber leaned back in her chair and sipped water as Slate and Benson discussed hobbies.

"Don't have too many hobbies," Benson responded to a question from Slate. "I've spent most of my time building this business. Played a little golf until this cancer hit. How about you?"

"I like fly fishing," Slate said with a self-satisfied smile. "I especially like a fish that will give me a good fight. There's great satisfaction in reeling it in." Although he was looking at Benson, the comment made Amber uneasy. Was he talking about fish or about her? She remembered they had ordered fish at that restaurant.

No matter how businesslike he'd been this morning, the alarm bells kept ringing in her head. Paranoid, you're getting paranoid, she told herself.

After lunch, Benson began to wilt with fatigue, so he went to his office to rest. Amber took a moment to look at the information Kimberly had given her. There was a long list of supplies to purchase for her mother. Several appointments were already set up. Dollar signs seemed to march before her eyes.

Surely, it was significant that on the same day her mother was coming home, Slate was offering a better job. From every appearance, God was opening a door for her. However, if that was true, where was the peace of God that she'd known in the past?

Neither Slate nor Benson questioned whether she would accept the offer. Her salary would triple. Triple! She would receive generous benefits, and being able to work out of the Bismarck office made the offer even more enticing.

Everything in her past had prepared her to handle this new role. Hadn't she carried bigger and bigger loads for years? She was like a pack burro climbing a mountain road.

Except when she was with Kelly. What a contrast between how she felt when she was with him and how she felt right now.

When all the working arrangements were laid out, Amber found herself back in her office staring at her computer, ready to fill out employment forms.

Slate stood behind her. "Go to the next screen by clicking on the left," he instructed, laying a hand on her shoulder.

Amber flicked her shoulder. "Please don't touch me," she said, her voice low.

"Excuse me. I do not mean to be familiar. I am only trying to help you."

A minute later, he leaned over the desk and pointed to a couple of dried roses that lingered in a waterless vase in the corner of her office.

"Did you like them?"

"The roses?" she asked in surprise. "You sent them?"

Slate smiled in an ingratiating way. "Yes, my dear, I sent them."

"Why would you do that? Why would you send me flowers right after I came back from my honeymoon? And why would you say in the card that I'm always on your mind?"

"Because I am always thinking of you and me. Together. By now, your honeymoon must be over. I bet you've had an argument or two?"

Her argument with Kelly the previous Sunday filled her mind. Slate couldn't possibly know about that could he?

"Perhaps you are ready to consider other personal options?"

"My personal life is none of your business."

His hand found her shoulder again.

Just then, Benson and Kimberly appeared at her office door.

"What's going on in here?" Benson demanded.

Amber looked up in surprise and relief.

"You are interrupting a private conversation," Slate said, dismissing Benson and Kimberly.

"Not so fast," Kimberly said. "Someone pushed the intercom button. The whole office has been listening to your conversation for the last couple minutes."

Amber looked down. Slate likely had bumped the button when he leaned over her desk. He now backed away.

"Are you okay?" Benson asked Amber. She opened her mouth, but no sound came out.

Kimberly stood, hands on hips, and glared at Slate.

There are moments when time seems to stand still, moments when a person's vision clears. That is what happened to Amber on that August afternoon.

She realized her heart was clenched as tightly as her teeth in overwhelming frustration. Then the freedom and joy she felt with Kelly washed over her, beckoning her to be reckless. Giving her courage. A profound faith gripped her. Whatever they faced, the Lord could take care of her, Kelly, and her family. Maybe the only real security was in trusting God.

Amber stood up and smiled, as she made a fateful decision.

Turning to Slate, she forcefully said, "You are despicable. You're polished on the outside and a sewage pit on the inside. I will never work for you. My husband and I plan to serve God. And you, you ought to be very afraid of Him. Now, leave my office!"

He sneered at her and then stepped quickly from the room. As Kimberly bustled out to escort him down the hall, cheers broke out across the building. The intercom had remained on to the entertainment of the rest of the staff.

Amber pushed the button off and looked up at Benson.

"I resign. I'm going home to Cottonwood Creek, Benson," she said as she gathered her purse and tossed her briefcase in the corner.

"Amber! You can't mean that," Benson pleaded.

She paused, distressed by the thought of failing Benson, then straightened her back.

"You've been wonderful to me, but my future isn't here anymore. I'm giving you my two-week notice."

Startled at her own words, she wondered if two weeks was enough notice. No, don't get wishy-washy, she told herself.

"Look, will you give a message to the committee that nominated me for the award? Tell them thank you, however, I must decline," she said as she slipped past him and out the door.

She'd never felt so free in her life.

Chapter 56
A Royal Dream

Amber walked down a long hallway paneled in rich inlaid wood. The wood was rubbed shiny and smelled of lemon oil. Soon, a woman appeared wearing a green sari. Red thread ran through it and gold tassels waved from the ends of the sleeves. She held a garment on her arm.

"When you see the king, you must wear this," said the woman, whose skin was the color of milk chocolate. Her almond eyes were rimmed with long dark lashes. Even her voice seemed exotic to Amber.

"What king?" Amber asked uncertainly.

The woman gave a low chuckle. "Why, your Father, of course."

"But my father isn't a king, he's a farmer," Amber protested.

The woman shook her head dismissively before draping a white robe over Amber's shoulders. It was made of heavy white brocade with a silk lining. White pearls were sewn in swirly designs all over the fabric.

This wasn't purchased at Kirkwood Mall, Amber thought. Handmade by a skilled seamstress, it was something royalty might wear. Even her beautiful wedding gown couldn't compare with it.

The woman turned and extended her arm toward a set of tall wooden doors with brass handles. Two titan men pulled open the heavy doors.

Amber took a step forward. The robe made her feel elegant, even regal. She straightened her shoulders. With her head held high, she walked through the doors, with no idea of what or who was on the other side.

The large room looked like a library. Chandeliers, each with hundreds of crystals, hung along the ceiling.

The walls were paneled and the windows covered in heavy velvet curtains. An enormous fireplace on one wall held a cheery fire. Shelves of books rose to the ceiling. Faded green overstuffed armchairs and lovely tables were strewn around the room.

Amber's feet sank into the Persian rug with each step forward. At the center of the room, under one of the chandeliers, a man sat at an ornate wooden desk.

Her eyes wandered to the bookcases. Is that my Rusty Ann doll up on that high shelf, she wondered? As she stared at the doll, it seemed to nod at her.

"Come in, Daughter." The man's voice was gravelly. He was perhaps in his fifties and seemed to be reviewing a ledger. A mane of hair reached his shoulders and he wore a royal blue jacket, white shirt, and a black bow tie.

Amber suddenly felt weak. When she reached for a chair, the two strong men magically appeared and guided her to it. Once seated, she took a deep breath. From a sitting position, she could see the man's feet. He wore red high-topped tennis shoes.

Following her glance, he said, "Sneakers are one of the wonders of the world. So comfortable." Amber was still puzzling over his comment when he picked up a paper, swiftly reviewed it, and began speaking again.

"Daughter, you've been very busy with your job."

How nice that someone is paying attention to my life, she thought, but I don't like the way he said it. What was wrong with trying to be there for Kelly, Benson, her parents, and her clients?

He looked up at her, his eyes crinkled as he smiled.

"Being kindhearted is a good characteristic. However, you tend to overdo it."

"I used to be kind," she confessed. "Now I'm not so sure. I just told Slate off. Called him a sewage pit."

He chuckled. "One of your finest moments. I hoped you would have the self-respect to walk away from that offer. It opens the way for the next step."

"The next step?"

He leaned forward.

"Daughter, I don't think you understand your place in my kingdom. Your calling. There are things that only you can do for the kingdom."

He was touching the heart of her struggle between career and calling.

"I'm trying to be a good daughter, wife, and employee. Isn't that what a Christian does?"

"My Daughter, you must choose now whether to live in my kingdom or whether to struggle with worries about finances and that disastrous marriage of yours."

Disastrous marriage? We're newlyweds, she thought. We love each other.

Then she remembered how she put off planning the wedding last spring. How she'd kept secrets from Kelly. How they bickered over the budget.

If their marriage wasn't in trouble yet, it surely was headed that way.

Reality was beginning to take hold of Amber. She settled into the high-backed chair and began to listen earnestly.

"The gift of music flows from your fingers at the piano. Your voice is as clear and pitch-perfect as the angels. Although you haven't discovered it yet, your talent for working with young people may be your best gift. I've equipped you well.

"Now, I've summoned you, because I have an important question to pose."

What can he possibly want to ask me, Amber wondered.

"Will you wear my mantle from now on?"

Amber fingered the white brocade. It felt weighty, yet was incredibly soft and supple. What was the difference between a robe and a mantle, she wondered.

"Beloved," he said, eerily reading her mind, "a mantle is more than an item of clothing. It signifies you are part of my family. When you wear it, you will have my protection and the authority to act on my behalf."

"I don't understand."

"You will have a rich and rewarding life if you walk in my plans. They are better than you can imagine, better than what you can try to accomplish by yourself. You worry about bills now. If you work for me, you will never have lack. Haven't I provided you with everything you need? Good health? An education? A Godly husband and family?"

Amber stirred to respond, but he interrupted her.

"Daughter," his voice had grown gentle, as he revealed a confidence. "Kelly is already living in my kingdom ways. He knows I'm providing for his needs."

It was true. Kelly was never too concerned about money and he always had what he needed. She was the bean counter in the family.

"It's not only Kelly and me. I'm also helping to provide for my family. They're struggling. Mom isn't well and they have medical bills. The twins need braces. And the cattle prices are never good."

"Your parents are my precious children, too. They are not your concern."

Not my concern, Amber thought. "Not my concern?"

"Daughter, do you like it when your brothers drive your Jeep carelessly?"

"No." She remembered how recklessly they drove on the way to her wedding. Her shoulders slumped as she realized where this was going. He was saying she'd been in the driver's seat of her life instead of giving God control.

"I'm calling you to walk in a dimension where you represent me." His words were warm and kind. "As you do that, I will meet your needs. Even as you face difficult days, your mantle will always have a silver lining."

Amber looked down at the white flowing mantle that covered her.

"You will sense when you're wearing it, and you'll flow in my power to bring grace, love and peace to others. When you're wearing it, you will always be covered with my protection.

"Now, it's time to decide if you want to take on your rightful role as my heir, as my daughter."

How could she refuse this man who lived like a king and called her daughter? She glanced up at the doll on the shelf, as she stroked the rich white brocade and fingered the silver lining.

"Silver lining, silver lining..." Amber whispered as she stirred from her dream. She looked around at the institutional white walls that surrounded her and stroked the cloth in her hand. It wasn't brocade and silk, but coarse cotton.

"She's coming around," a voice said.

Amber turned her head at the sound. A woman and man stood at her side. Nurses? Doctors? Where was she?

"Can you hear us?" the man asked, leaning over her, his face serious.

"Yes," Amber answered.

"I'm Dr. Keaton. Do you know your name?"

"Of course. Amber Rose Jorgenson, daughter of a king."

The two attendants looked at each other. "Do you know what day it is?"

"The best day of my life!" she answered.

One of the attendants began scribbling in her note-book.

"Mrs. Jorgenson, you were in a car accident on Highway 83. On the way to the hospital in the ambulance, you stopped breathing and were resuscitated. You've suffered a concussion."

"Oh," she replied, as she fingered the white sheet. "Kelly. Where's Kelly?"

"Your husband has been notified. He's on his way."

Amber felt light-headed, like when she was a kid and inhaled helium from a balloon.

"Do you have any pain?"

"I'm sleepy, but my Father will take care of me." She said waving her hand airily, before drifting back to sleep.

The attendants again looked at each other and Dr. Keaton shook his head.

"Yes, well, for now we're going to give you something to help you rest," the man said. "It looks like you'll need a lot of rest."

Chapter 57
Down by the River

Kelly had begun to dread his days off. For most of the summer, he'd filled them by going fishing with Tiny or mowing the lawn. However, Tiny wasn't available today. There was no need to mow the lawn, since the August grass already had the crisp dried look of fall. What he needed was Amber's companionship.

Still, the idea of driving over to a park on the Missouri River appealed to him. He packed a few items for a day trip. A bottle of water, some sunflower seeds, a notebook, and his Bible were all he needed.

He fed Mildred and slipped out of the house wearing a gray sweatshirt and a cap.

Thirty minutes later, when he drove through Riverdale and over Garrison Dam, the morning promised a fine summer day. He turned south and headed past the fishery and campgrounds filled with tents and motor homes. The pavement ended in the parking lot of a primitive campground.

Kelly locked the pickup doors and strolled down a narrow, steep path toward the river. He brushed through thickets of short, willowy trees. At the bottom of the slope, the dirt path gave way to a trail carpeted in sand as fine as sugar. Weeds tore at his pant legs as he continued west across a low area and then up a sand dune. The landscape reminded him of the beloved beaches near his home in southern California.

He was puffing by the time he'd climbed the last dune. His sneakers filled with sand and he slipped with every step up to the crest. At the top of the rise, the sand gave way to the brilliantly blue river.

Kelly stopped and stared at the surprising vista. On the other side of the river, rugged brown and rose-colored cliffs towered above the water. A small forest of leafy green trees seemed to climb out of the riverbed. He sat down on a water-washed log that had to be forty feet long. There was no one else around.

The longing in his heart for peace had drawn him to North Dakota, and this day and place were exactly what he had hoped to find. Drinking in the quiet, discouragement drained from his soul. It felt like he'd been swept from his daily life and deposited on this beach alone, yet not lonely.

"Lord," Kelly whispered. "This place leaves me in awe."

A light breeze rustled through the cottonwoods and water lapped against the shore. Across the river, a cow bellowed and another answered. A small herd moved to the water's edge. Time seemed to stand still as the animals drank their fill, then wandered single file into a gully and disappeared.

The beach was only about thirty feet wide, but it stretched around a curve and out of sight. Kelly took off his shoes and socks to dig his feet into the cool damp sand. The tracks of deer, raccoons, and three-toed birds crossed the beach from the sand dunes to the water's edge. Seagulls flew silent reconnaissance overhead. As he strolled along the beach, his tracks added to the sandy mosaic.

The fine sand sparkled like diamonds with veins of black coal threaded through it. He found a couple of old campfires mostly washed away with the tide. It made him happy to know others had explored this place, which curved on and on in endless sand and sky and water.

Back at the log, his shoes were right where he left them. He sat down, drank from his water bottle, and opened the bag of sunflower seeds.

Drowsily he watched the sunlight reflect off the water in a million golden arcs that shimmered on the surface. Kelly sat up. Across the river, a bird flapped against the breeze and soared past the cliffs. A bald eagle.

He remembered another time, another wild place, another soaring eagle. He had just completed high school and was struggling with the pain of losing his twin brother in a senseless gun accident. In that mountainside encounter, he'd understood that he had a choice. Did he want the kind of peace his brother had found, or did he wish to continue down a path of destruction?

Broken, he decided to reach out and give God a try. After whispering a prayer, he'd opened his eyes to see a bald eagle soaring higher and higher until it vanished in the clouds above the mountaintop.

Now, he watched this eagle making ever-widening circles.

Some might think he was foolish for believing the eagles were signs from God. Yet, Kelly could look at the years since that mountaintop experience and see the hand of God in his life. He knew he'd been delivered from a grief-filled, destructive life.

He had been living by the very word of God since then. The scripture found in Jeremiah 29:11, "For I know the plans I have for you, plans to prosper you and not to harm you, plans to give you hope and a future," had become very real to Kelly.

Now, he began laughing aloud and jumped to his feet. Faith and joy rose up in him and he began walking up and down the beach, declaring words of victory.

"Lord, you didn't bring us this far to leave us. You have plans for Amber and me. You said you would never leave us nor forsake us. How could I ever forget that? Help us find a way to live together and do the work that you've called us to."

Kelly let out a whoop, surprising a gull hidden in the brush. It called out in alarm and flew away.

"It's okay, buddy, you can have the beach to yourself again," he shouted to the gull. "I need to go home and call Amber Rose!"

He dried off his feet and pulled on his shoes. After taking a last look at the shimmering water, the jagged buttes, the puffy clouds sailing overhead, he hurried back across the sand dunes.

When he arrived at the parsonage, Kelly was still excited. He found it only mildly surprising that the sheriff's car was parked by the back door. It wasn't the first time someone from the sheriff's office had stopped by to notify Kelly of someone who needed pastoral help.

They got out of their vehicles. The sheriff looked grim, Kelly thought.

"There's been an accident. It's your wife."

Chapter 58
Prayers for Amber

Kelly staggered backward. Suddenly, he was eighteen again, his brother lying dead beside him. Emotional pain engulfed him as though he'd been set on fire.

Then the earth tilted. Everything went black for a moment before light exploded around him. He himself was silently exploding, his body parts floating away like a scene from a space movie.

The sheriff continued to talk, but Kelly couldn't process what he was saying. He was nothing without Amber, nothing except matter floating in the universe. Crumpling against the pickup, he slid down to the bumper.

Kelly looked up and croaked, "Amber." His voice sounded like an old man coughing up chewing tobacco. His throat closed, strangling him. My life is over, he thought.

The sheriff laid a firm hand on Kelly's shoulder as he bent down to look in his face. His eyes were compassionate. "Pastor, are you okay? Is there anyone I can call for you?"

Kelly shook his head. "Did you say she is in Bismarck?"

"Yes, the accident happened on Highway 83," he explained patiently again. "She's been taken to a hospital in Bismarck."

"Is she..." Kelly couldn't finish.

"She's alive."

As Kelly stood to his feet, he was surprised to see Tiny drive into the yard.

Tiny surveyed the scene, rolled down his window and asked, "What's up?"

"Good to see you," the sheriff greeted him. "I came out to tell Pastor Jorgenson that his wife was in an accident."

"Oh no! Was Amber in that accident south of here? I heard about an accident on my police scanner. Thought Kelly and I would drive down that way and see if we could help."

"I have to get to the hospital in Bismarck," Kelly whispered.

"Hey, hey, I have a full tank of gas. I'll take you."

"Make sure you have your phone and medical information," the sheriff quickly advised Kelly. "I'll call and alert the highway patrol and hospital that you're on your way."

Kelly nodded his thanks, and then walked numbly into the house. Mildred followed him around, meowing the whole time.

"Mildred, Amber's in trouble. Say your prayers that she'll be okay."

The first few miles of the trip seemed to take forever as they slowed for towns and corners. "Can't you drive any faster?" Kelly asked.

Just then, a patrol car pulled out in front of them and its red light went on. Tiny chuckled. "See that patrol car? That's our escort. We're going to get there in record time."

Kelly scrunched back in the seat and gripped the door handle.

"What was she doing on Highway 83 in the middle of a workday?" he asked. "It doesn't make sense." He looked at the ceiling of the pickup, hoping to suppress tears that threatened to pour down his face.

"We can only wait to find out," Tiny said, clearly uncomfortable with Kelly's emotions.

"Lord, protect Amber. Save her life," Kelly mouthed over and over.

Where the highway curved north of Wilton, both vehicles slowed and pulled over. Amber's Jeep lay overturned in the ditch.

"Stop! I have to see," Kelly cried out. He jumped from the pickup as soon as he could.

The front window of the Jeep was broken out and the top crushed in like a soda can. No one could survive this, he thought. He spied Amber's phone in the grass. Looking around, he had a sick feeling. Within a few miles to the north, she would have been out of cellphone range. Was she trying to phone him when the accident happened?

"Let's go," Kelly said as he turned toward the pickup.

At the hospital, Kelly stepped into the room where Amber lay. She had stitches across her forehead. Cuts and bruises covered her beautiful face. Her hair was matted with blood.

"Your wife had to be resuscitated by the ambulance crew." The doctor let the words sink in for a moment. "By the time they arrived here, she was awake and talking, which is a good sign. However, she wasn't making much sense."

"Amber spoke? What did she say?"

"Something about being the daughter of a king."

Kelly frowned. "How bad is it?"

"Initial tests show she has a concussion. We're watching her closely. The first twenty-four hours are critical. I'll be able to tell you a lot more tomorrow at this time. For now, we want her to rest."

Kelly went into the waiting room and gave Tiny the update. "It could be a long wait and I need to make some urgent phone calls. You don't have to wait here..."

Before he could finish his sentence, Tiny responded. "I'm not leaving you here alone." With that, he plunked back down on a chair in the waiting room.

Kelly nodded his thanks. While he made calls to Amber's family, Tiny called Maury Jackson and Kate Schulte and asked them to pray.

When Kelly called Gates Insurance, Benson had left

for the day. Kelly relayed the news to Kimberly. As soon as she heard that Amber had been in a serious accident, she began to cry.

Trying to hold it together himself, he told her, "I need to know why she was driving toward Cottonwood Creek on the day of her big interview."

"Amber refused Nadoff's offer and told him off," Kimberly said between sobs. "She said she would never work for him. She was going to work for God. I'll tell you what, the office was in an uproar when she left."

"She just walked out?"

"Yep. She resigned from the agency, too." Kimberly took a deep breath. "Where is she?"

"She's in the hospital here in Bismarck with a head injury."

Kimberly offered to contact Benson and help in any way she could. "Amber's the sweetest. I'll be praying real hard for her."

While Tiny left to move his pickup to a long-term parking lot, Kelly called his parents.

His father answered.

"Pops," Kelly uttered, before he broke down. "Pops, it's Amber. She was in a bad accident." Haltingly, he poured out the story.

Even though his father was over fifteen hundred miles away, Kelly found his words to be like a comforting arm wrapped around his shoulders. A few minutes later, he felt strong enough to make a final call.

Telling Brianna was almost harder than telling Amber's parents. He knew too well how the news might affect her, might tear at her emotional scar tissue as it had his own.

Instead, she astonished him by being remarkably calm and quick to assess the situation. "Kelly, you're going to need some help. I'll be on the next plane to Bismarck."

Chapter 59
Anxious Days

Kelly wouldn't remember much about those anxious days as he waited by Amber's bedside. What he recalled were the people who appeared in Amber's time of greatest need.

The first surprise was when Jean and Glen walked slowly from the hospital elevator. Kelly sprang from his chair and rushed to greet them.

"How's Amber?" Glen asked. "Can we see her?"

"You can, but she's asleep," Kelly said as he gripped their hands.

"She has a concussion. Her forehead is stitched up. Plenty of bruises," he blurted out. "Thank God, no broken bones. They're watching her closely. However, they don't expect to know much before morning."

While they went to Amber's room, Kelly walked aimlessly up and down the hallway. Tiny came and laid a hand on his shoulder.

"Now that the McLeans are here, I'll head back to Cottonwood Creek. I can stop out at your place and feed Cat if you like. Let me know if you want me to bring anything when I come back tomorrow."

Kelly nodded numbly, unable to think of what he might need.

When Glen and Jean came out a few minutes later, they were shaken but resolute. Kelly sat down with them in the waiting room, comforted by their presence. Jean's simple and abiding faith shone like a candle in a dark room.

"How did you get here so quickly?" Kelly asked. When he had phoned the farm with the news, Adam had assured him that he would contact Glen and Jean. They were driving home from Minnesota, but Kelly was too shook up to ask how close they were to Bismarck.

"We were about a hundred miles out when Adam called," Glen explained. "When we got to the exit at Bismarck, we turned left toward the hospital, instead of going right toward home."

Kelly considered the timing providential. If the couple had arrived earlier, they might have happened upon the accident scene. It gave him the chills to think of them finding Amber's smashed-up Jeep.

"Jean, you're walking. That's remarkable."

"I'm full of hope. The medications and treatment I received are working," Jean said. "I should have gotten more help a long time ago instead of thinking the MS would just go away. I'll need to stay on a program of therapy and medications."

"God has answered a lot of prayers lately," Glen stated. "A couple weeks ago, I submitted all of our medical bills. Yesterday, we received word that many of them will be paid after all. Now Jean is in an experimental program that will cover a lot of medical costs."

"That's good news," Kelly said, his voice flat. Under other circumstances, the news would have been worth a celebration, but Kelly couldn't work up any happy emotions.

Glen looked down. "We've depended on Amber's help through some troubled years. I only hope..." He couldn't finish his sentence.

Jean spoke up then. "I'm not afraid to ask for another big answer to prayer. It's raining answers to prayer lately. Such as, for years our specialty breed of cattle have been a liability, but now there's a growing interest in them."

Glen picked up the story. "Adam has been working with a cattle organization that is interested in contracting with us. We're close to signing papers with them."

"These answers give me faith and hope that there will be one more. Let's pray that our Amber will come through this and be fully restored," Jean added.

Kelly spent the night at the hospital, fitfully sleeping in a chair by Amber's bed. The next morning, he was surprised when a nurse alerted him that they had visitors.

Benson and Kimberly were standing in the waiting room.

Kelly rubbed the stubble on his chin and finger-combed his hair. He noted that Benson seemed weak from cancer treatment and wore a baseball cap on his hairless head.

"I went shopping with Benson's credit card." Kimberly was perky as she handed him bags filled with a teddy bear, chocolates, and a robe for Amber.

"By golly, this accident about broke my heart," Benson confessed to Kelly. "Amber is like a daughter to me. I shouldn't have expected so much from her or pushed this whole thing with Mammon Global. I feel responsible for the accident."

Kelly shook his head. "No, don't blame yourself. Amber adores you and she wanted to help you."

He then asked for Benson's version of what happened at the office before the accident. The older man looked miserable as he told the story, ending with Amber informing him she was resigning and going home to Cottonwood Creek.

"She resigned?" Kelly's heart soared. That meant Amber had decided to come home to Cottonwood Creek.

Then his heart fell. When he arrived home from his trip to the river, she might have been there ready to begin a new phase of their life. Instead, the sheriff's car waited, and that dream seemed farther away than ever.

"Don't worry, she'll be okay," Kimberly soothed, though tears filled her eyes.

"I didn't sleep much last night," Benson confessed. "Went into the office at dawn this morning. I have a proposal for Amber."

Kelly groaned. How could the man think of work at a time like this?

Benson pulled some papers from his pocket. "According to my figures, about half of Amber's clients live north of Bismarck. I want to propose that she takes all of those clients and opens an office in Cottonwood City. She could work part-time."

The idea shocked Kelly. In all their discussions, they'd never considered this option.

"I think Amber would like that idea," he said quietly.

The third surprise happened later that day when Kelly glimpsed a handsome couple walking down the hallway. As they came closer, he thought it looked like Brianna and Tiny. He closed his tired eyes, and when he opened them again, indeed it was the most unlikely couple on earth. As he watched, they laughed and talked like old friends.

Brianna was as tall and elegant as ever, though she wore a pair of denims and a knit top instead of her usual fashion-model clothing. Tiny continued to amaze him. Although still a hefty size, he had lost a notable amount of weight. His grimy green cap was gone, and he had definitely stopped at Riley's barbershop in Cottonwood City. He wore a button-down shirt, khakis, and new tennis shoes.

Kelly closed his eyes again, but the mirage didn't go away. "If only Amber could see this," he murmured to himself, as they embraced him in a bear hug. King Solomon was wrong, he thought, there could be something new under the sun.

"I planned to come to Bismarck today and spend time with you," Tiny explained bashfully. "Then, Kate Schulte called and asked me to pick up Brianna at the airport."

"I was glad to see Tiny again," Brianna reflected. "I hadn't thanked him for bringing me to this same hospital the day of your wedding."

Kelly's heart overflowed at the outpouring of help from friends and family. However, it didn't change his concern for Amber. Her well-being hung over his head like an axe ready to fall.

Brianna and Tiny planned to stay for the afternoon, so Kelly left them to keep watch. The chapel offered quiet respite from the constant hospital noise. As soon as he entered, Kelly knew Amber would love this place. He dropped to his knees at the altar and took in the stained glass windows and white candles.

He wasn't sure of how long he had been kneeling there, pleading for Amber's life, when he felt a tap on his shoulder. Cole Jensen knelt beside him. He was surprised to see the young man, who should have been over a hundred miles away at college.

"You've helped me so many times. I'm here to return the favor," Cole told him. With that, Cole laid his hand on Kelly's shoulder and prayed confidently for Amber to be restored. Kelly leaned forward and rested his head on the altar railing, accepting the blessing and hope that enveloped him.

That evening, Kelly held Amber's hand and told her about their visitors. Although he didn't know if she could hear his voice, he found comfort in talking to his true love.

And then Amber began murmuring. Surprised, he leaned close to hear her words.

"There is power in the name of Jesus and in the word of God. But when you praise His holy name, the glory of all heaven joins you."

Her eyes remained closed as she breathlessly chanted the phrase again. He'd heard those words before. In fact, they were the first words she had ever spoken to him. Then her eyes fluttered open and she smiled through her bruises.

A miracle was unfolding.

"Kelly, guess where I've been," she whispered.

"Where?" he asked.

"I think I was in heaven."

Just then, a small corps of medical staff came in and there was no small amount of activity in Amber's room for the next couple of hours. The staff was elated that Amber had fully awakened. She could see, hear, speak and move her limbs.

"How bad is your headache?" she was asked every few minutes.

"What headache?" she replied each time.

The staff seemed mystified by her recovery. A series of tests was scheduled to see what exactly was happening. However, Kelly didn't see any mystery, he saw a miracle.

Amber was back and they were going to be fine. His heart wanted to shout with joy. Instead, he lifted his hands in praise.

Chapter 60
The Thanksgiving Day Guest List

Perhaps the best way to understand the next few months in Amber and Kelly's lives is to examine the guest list for the Thanksgiving Day dinner they hosted that year.

Please note that the list had more changes than a ballerina's dress rehearsal. Amber didn't mind, though. Before sunrise on Thanksgiving morning, she buzzed around the parsonage kitchen taking caramel rolls out of the oven and hefting the twenty-pound turkey into it.

For breakfast, she made fresh-squeezed orange juice for Kelly and double-checked the supply of bananas, which Cole ate by the bunch. She peeked in the fridge to make sure the pumpkin pie was still there. She'd probably always be wary of food disappearing, even though her hungry brothers weren't around.

Amber studied the oak dining room table. Extended with two card tables, it reached all the way into the living room. It was festively draped with tablecloths and covered with yellow, red, blue and green Fiesta dishes.

After being released from the hospital, Amber had rested for several days, then began settling into her new life at Cottonwood Creek. One of the first things she did was take a fresh-baked peach pie to Kate Schulte. By the time Kate was eating her second piece, she agreed that exchanging some yellow pieces of the dishware for other colors was a good idea.

Now, satisfied with the table set for dinner, Amber poured a cup of coffee and took a sample caramel roll to the breakfast nook to review the guest list and what food they had offered to bring. At the top of the list:

Mom & Dad. Scalloped Corn. Amber couldn't remember the last time her mother had felt well enough to make her prized Thanksgiving side dish. Thinking about the sweet, creamy corn infused with cheese and baked with a golden crust made her mouth water.

Jean was doing well with her new therapy and medication routine. Although she might never ride a bicycle again, she was much better able to care for her family and enjoy life. She continued to spend part of each day resting in her green prayer chair.

Amber continued to peruse the guest list.

Tim, Jim & Daniel. She couldn't wait for her brothers to arrive. Kelly had a surprise for them. He had unearthed his first computer and classic games. The sunroom had been turned into a game room for the holiday, complete with lots of snacks.

She'd be happy to see Daniel again. He now attended a two-year college, where he was learning auto body repair. Restoring Amber's Jeep was one of his projects.

Adam. And Lori! Their names had been scratched out and reentered a few times as their plans kept changing. As of now, they would have dinner at Cottonwood Creek, and then drive to Cooperstown to spend the rest of the day. Adam had confided to his big sister that he planned to give Lori a diamond for Christmas.

Their romance had gone from zero to eighty in no time. A lot like Kelly and me, she thought. Lori would make a wonderful sister-in-law.

Cole and Sadie. Both names were now crossed off the list. Cole wanted to bring Sadie to dinner, but she was too frail. Instead, he decided to dine with her at the nursing home. Later, he'd come back to play video games with the guys.

When Kelly was finally able to tell Amber that he had invited Cole to live with them, she had welcomed the idea.

Cole had moved his few belongings to the parsonage in early October.

Kelly, Amber, Cole and a crew of others had cleared out the little home in the country where he and Sadie had lived. With Sadie's instructions, they had picked out her most cherished items and decorated her room with photos and mementos. Cole's belongings were packed into his room at the parsonage, his dorm room at college, or were in the trunk of his car.

The happy news was that every week when Kelly visited Sadie, she told him what wonderful care she received. With her sweet spirit, it wasn't surprising that she had made many new friends. Even Kate Schulte called often and, of course, many friends stopped by to see her.

Cole stayed with Kelly and Amber on weekends and holidays. He fit right into their family. Remembering her own lean college years, Amber always filled a cooler with food when he left for Minot on Sunday evenings.

Cole had arrived late the evening before with dark circles under his eyes. Now, he was sleeping late this morning, getting some much-needed rest.

Tiny and his Mom. Scratch his mother. Tiny had called last night to say she refused to leave the house for Thanksgiving dinner, but he'd be there with enough sodas for the whole crowd.

Aunt Kate. Cranberry sauce. Kate Schulte was bringing cranberry sauce made from a family recipe. Kate had implied that her ancestors had picked their own berries from the family's cranberry bog out East. Very special.

Marge and Wayne. Crossed off. They had flown to Florida for time with their grown children.

Brianna Davis. Cheesecake. No, Brianna hadn't learned how to cook. Instead, she ordered cheesecake from her favorite outlet in California.

Amber looked up as she heard Kelly come in and take his boots off. Soon he peeked around the corner. He had also been up early, in spite of holding Thanksgiving Eve services the evening before.

"How was your predawn walk?" she asked as she slid out of the breakfast nook to greet him. He hung his jacket on a hook and wrapped his arms around her.

"It reminded me of last Christmas morning when I took a walk. That's when I gave up on ever finding that phantom girl with the angelic voice and curly golden hair. Now, less than a year later, we're married. I have a lot to be grateful for."

"Me, too," she said as she snuggled in his embrace.

Sometimes, letting go is the only way to allow God to work in our lives, Amber mused. She had walked out on a major career opportunity a few months earlier, only to find God had a superior plan for her life. In the end, she hadn't had to choose between a career and her calling.

Kelly buried his nose in her curls. "You smell like a caramel roll."

"No doubt. And in a few hours, I'll smell like a turkey."

Kelly gave her another hug.

"Amber Rose," he whispered in her ear. "We're living the dream. When the accident happened last August I thought I'd lost you forever. And here you are. Miracles still happen."

They stood for a moment, lost in memories of the emotional journey they had traveled. Amber had awakened from the coma with few aftereffects, although the doctors sent her home with warnings to rest, and to call if her headaches increased in strength or frequency.

However, she hadn't experienced any headaches. Now, the only sign that she'd been in an accident was the scar across her forehead.

"The accident sure changed things," she said. "And not just for us. It motivated Brianna to move here."

After spending a few days making sure Amber was okay, Brianna had flown back to San Francisco, sublet her apartment, and returned to North Dakota. Aunt Kate had invited her to move into the yellow Queen Anne house in Schulteville. Soon, she was working out of her second-floor studio and tearing wallpaper off Aunt Kate's walls. Kate's Bed & Breakfast was scheduled to open on Memorial Day Weekend the following year.

Brianna and Tiny were an item now, in a complicated way. Tiny liked to say, "Hey, hey, the Mango Queen. What a dream!"

It was hard to tell if their relationship was serious or not. Either way, Tiny was looking buff these days, and was considering opening a gym in Cottonwood City. He and Brianna frequently double dated with Amber and Kelly, who remained bemused by the new romance.

Amber had accepted Benson's offer of opening a Gates Insurance office in Cottonwood City. It was located on Main Street right next to Maggie's Magic Makeover beauty shop.

For the time being, the insurance company had suspended any work on strategic planning. Mammon Global had fired Slate Nadoff after the news spread about his unwanted advances toward Amber. Since then, several other women had come forward with similar stories. It was rumored that he was now doing infomercials for a rodent control product.

Brianna had helped Amber remodel her new office to be welcoming to clients and organized for efficiency. The grand opening at Gates Insurance North was held in early November. It was the event of the month in the Cottonwood area.

The company had supplied dozens of cookies and a huge supply of coffee and punch. With pride, Amber handed each visitor a calendar so appealing it was destined to hang in many homes. Her name and contact information were visible on each page.

The event helped Amber gain more clients, and Brianna had received job offers from people looking to update their homes and offices.

Amber was thrilled to work fewer hours. She relished her newlywed life and happily spent time with her family. Her role at church was evolving. You could find her surrounded by teenage girls at church every weekend. After the beginning of the year, she also planned to be part of the church music program.

Another sign of the changes in her life was that the ringtone on her phone now played a worshipful praise song instead of a Sousa march.

This Thanksgiving morning brought home to her the many blessings she was enjoying. All of her senses seemed alive, and she no longer felt as though she was made of plastic.

"Kelly, I appreciate every single moment with you. Sometimes it scares me to think how close I came to making the wrong choice."

"Me too. Especially today, I'm thankful for God's leading in our lives."

He paused as an odd look crossed his face. "Right now I could use some more leading."

"What do you mean?"

Kelly laced his fingers through Amber's and cleared his throat.

"Amber, do you remember that next week we're talking to the youth group about dating and saving yourself for marriage? And how you can't trust your feelings?"

Amber groaned and then grinned. "Listen, that evening you can lead the discussion. I'll nod in agreement to whatever you say."

Now it was Kelly's turn to groan. "How do I get myself into these things?"

"For now, let's get ready for our guests. I want to enjoy every minute of this day," Amber said as she dished up a caramel roll and a glass of milk for Kelly.

Throughout the whole conversation, Mildred sat snoozing on the living room sofa. Perched on the fireplace mantel was a scruffy doll with yarn hair. Over the mantel, Tiny's prize walleye kept watch.

On the other side of the room, above Kelly's desk, the words, 'There is no more lovely, friendly and charming relationship, communion or company, than a good marriage' foretold the continuing story of Amber's choice.

About the Author

Gayle Larson Schuck is a native of North Dakota. She holds a Bachelor of Science degree in communications, and worked in public relations and development as a prelude to a writing career. Her books include By the Banks of Cottonwood Creek and Secrets of the Dark Closet. A member of American Christian Fiction Writers and local writing groups, Gayle can often be found at the Bismarck Public Library. She has led Bible studies for over thirty years, and enjoys reading, gardening and adventures with her family.

To learn more about Gayle, read her blog, or contact her at **www.GayleLarsonSchuck.com**